Skills Training for Children with Behavior Disorders:
A Parent and Therapist Guidebook

SKILLS TRAINING FOR CHILDREN WITH BEHAVIOR DISORDERS

A Parent and Therapist Guidebook

MICHAEL L. BLOOMQUIST

THE GUILFORD PRESS
New York London

Library of Congress Cataloging-in-Publication Data
Bloomquist, Michael L.
    Skills training for children with behavior disorders :
a parent and therapist guidebook / Michael L. Bloomquist.
        p. cm.
    Includes bibliographical references and index.
    ISBN 1-57230-080-9
    1. Behavior disorders in children—Treatment—Handbooks,
manuals, etc. I. Title.
RJ506.B4459 1996
618.92'89—dc20   96-27
                                                          CIP

To my sons, Andrew and Erik

Acknowledgments

Many people helped make this book possible. A great thanks to my wife, Rebecca Syverts, for her continued love, support, and encouragement. I am grateful to Lauren Braswell, Gerald August, Janette Concepcion, and Dennis Cantwell for ideas and suggestions that were incorporated into the text. Many thanks to Jay Sieler for doing a fine job on the illustrations. I am indebted to Jean Martin for assistance in editing. I greatly appreciate Lois Laitinen's excellent word processing. Sharon Panulla of The Guilford Press has been most helpful in producing this book, and to her I wish to express my gratitude.

The following charts are adapted from Braswell and Bloomquist (1991) by permission from The Guilford Press: Family Problem Solving, Family Anger and Conflict Management, Listen and Obey, Time-Out, Removal of Privileges for Noncompliance, Daily Child Behavior, Daily Behavior Contract, Reinforcement Ideas, and Problem-Solving Skills.

Foreword

It is a pleasure to write the foreword for this very valuable book. Michael Bloomquist has put together a document that should be of great use for parents whose children have behavior disorders, either alone or complicated by other conditions. In addition there is an updated section on information for therapists to use in conjunction with parents in dealing with their children's behavior disorders.

Children with behavior disorders as described by Bloomquist generally have a combination of attention-deficit disorder, oppositional defiant disorder, and conduct disorder. The overlap between these three conditions is extremely high. As pointed out in Chapter 1 in this book, it is extremely common for children with behavior disorders also to have other problems such as learning disorders, mood disorders, and anxiety disorders.

These problems are important to developing children for a variety of reasons. They are common in the general population. They tend to be relatively persistent over time and they tend to affect children's development in many areas, not just in academic achievement in school. Generally these children have impairments in areas such as behavior in school; the ability to keep and make friends; the ability to deal with siblings and parents in the home setting; the ability to deal with adults outside of the home settings, such as Scout masters or coaches; and difficulties in leisure time activities, that is, their behavior disorders interfere with their ability to do things that other children of their developmental age and stage do, such as play sports or be in after school clubs. It has been recognized, for at least the last 15 years, that any one treatment is not likely to be sufficient for taking care of all the problems of any one of these children. Moreover, any one particular child may need one package of treatments early on, and the need for treatment may change with development. Medication is not stressed in this volume, but it does play a role with certain symptoms of certain disorders, particularly attention-deficit disorder. Educational intervention of a variety of types, including special classes in special schools, may be necessary for children who have severe language and learning disorders.

What this document does is give parents and therapists the ability to deal with certain of the common core problems that these children have by using a skills training approach. One of the gratifying developments in the field of child behavior disorders has been the creation, out of need, of parent support groups, such as Children and Adults with Attention Deficit Disorders (CH.A.D.D.) and others. Parents have begun to recognize that they are not necessarily the cause of their child's problems, many of which have biological underpinnings. However, there are things that can be done by parents in the home setting to improve certain aspects of their child's behavior using the skill based program that Bloomquist outlines in this volume. Therapists likewise have come to recognize that traditional psychodynamic psychotherapy is not the treatment of choice for the great majority of children with these problems. Effective use of the material presented in this book should enable most parents of children with behavior disorders to improve their child's and their family's functioning. Moreover, if used in conjunction with therapeutic intervention and other modalities, these methods are likely to effect these children's longterm outcome in a positive fashion. The ideas and techniques described in this book deserve wide dissemination among parents, school personnel, and therapists of all persuasions and ideologies.

—Dennis P. Cantwell, M.D.
Professor of Child Psychiatry
Department of Psychiatry and Biobehavioral Sciences
University of California, Los Angeles

Introduction

This book has evolved over many years out of my applied and research experience working with children who have behavior disorders and with their families. Skills training for children with behavior problems is difficult and complex. It seemed helpful to provide instructions to aid children and parents to learn and use the skills. These instructions kept getting longer and longer until eventually it seemed a good idea to put them into a book.

The first edition of this book, *A Parents' Skills Training Guide for Children with Attention Deficits and Disruptive Behavior*, published by the Department of Professional Development at the University of Minnesota, was revised for the current volume. The book has been updated, expanded, reorganized, and now contains a section for therapists to enable them to use this text in their work with parents.

The book is for both parents and therapists to use either separately or together. The book is "parent driven" in that it is mainly for parents. Chapters 1–16 provide information and practical suggestions for parents. Chapters 17 and 18 provide information and practical suggestions for therapists as to how to use this book with parents. Parents and therapists are encouraged to read each other's sections.

A word about the pronouns "he" or "she" and "child" or "adolescent" as used in this book. To avoid the awkward "he or she" description, the words "he" and "she" will be alternated throughout the book, sometimes chapter by chapter, when describing children. **All ideas and skills discussed are equally applicable to males and females.** In a similar way, the terms "child" or "children" are used throughout. In most instances, the **ideas discussed are applicable to children and early teens.** Specific references to teens or adolescents are made in only a few sections of the book.

PARENTS

This book is intended to help parents with children exhibiting behavior disorders. **The term "parent," as used in this book, is defined as anyone who acts as a child's caregiver (e.g., biological parents, grandparents, guardians, foster parents, etc.).** Although information about children of all ages is discussed, **the book is most applicable for parents with elementary school age children and early adolescents** (roughly ages 6–16 years).

The purpose of this book is to provide practical knowledge and skills to parents. There are many helpful parent books already available about children with attentional and behavioral problems. Many of these books emphasize providing information and some techniques for managing problems. It is hoped that this book will help parents by emphasizing practical strategies for managing problems and developing coping skills. I wrote the book for parents who want "how to" instructions to help themselves and their children.

This book should be read in an exploratory fashion. It is not intended to be read from cover to cover. It would not be possible to do everything described in the book. Rather, parents should read through Chapters 1 and 2 in detail to get an idea about where to focus. Parents may then elect to focus on certain skill areas for a time, to be followed by other skill areas later. **The book could be used throughout a child's development.** At one point in time (e.g., child is 8 years old), certain skills may be applicable; then as the child gets older (e.g., child is 14 years old), other skills may be useful.

There are numerous charts at the end of each chapter to aid in implementing various skill procedures throughout the book. **Parents and mental health professionals have permission, and are encouraged, to make copies of the charts to use.**

The following assumption about parent–child relationships serves as the foundation for this book: Although children contribute to their own problems and account for much of the difficulty in the parent–child relationship, **it is the parent who is in the best position to help the child and change the nature of a parent–child relationship.** Parenting a child is similar to dancing, with the parent taking the lead and setting the stage for how the dance unfolds. All of the ideas and procedures described in this book involve either the parent changing his or her behavior, or the parent leading the child to make behavior changes. Indeed, research informs us that child-focused interventions with active parent involvement work better than child-focused interventions alone. Thus, the parent will need to work hard to make things better in a family with a behavior problem child.

It is also assumed that parents who intend to use this book successfully are "ready" to use it. Basically **parents who use ideas and strategies from this book will be doing a lot of work!** Interventionists and therapists have long ago recognized that not all people who want to make changes are "prepared for change." In other words, some people may have good intentions, but because of personal problems, stress, negative thinking, and/or other factors, they may not be able to do the work necessary to change. **Because this book is for parents, it is especially important that the parent deal with his or her own personal issues that could potentially be a roadblock to change.** In this regard, it is recommended that all parents read the information in Chapters 3 (Parent Stress) and 4 (Parent Thoughts) and take any necessary action before working on parenting and child behavior changes.

One caution about the methods discussed in this book needs to be mentioned. The **methods presented here have not been scientifically tested on the basis of parents implementing them through a self-help book format.** I adhered to the following criteria, however, to ensure the methods in this book are sound. First, I have included many scientifically tested methods that have been found effective for parents and children working with a therapist. Second, I have field-tested every method in the book in my work with parents and children over many years. This caution is discussed at the outset to make sure the parent is an informed consumer of this product.

The information contained herein may be useful to prevent family and child problems or to reduce mild to moderate levels of family and child difficulties. **The book should not be used by itself to help a family or child with more severe problems.** If you are unsure how severe your family's or child's problems are, it would be wise to consult a licensed mental health professional (e.g., psychologist, psychiatrist, therapist, social worker, etc.) for an evaluation to determine if other services (e.g., therapy, medications, school-based interventions, etc.) are necessary.

More often than not, it is best to work with a therapist. The therapist you choose should be a licensed mental health professional or should be supervised by a licensed mental health professional. The therapist should also have experience and expertise in working with children exhibiting behavior disorders. You and the therapist could collaborate using this book as a frame of reference. The therapist would be able to answer questions and provide more explicit, "hands on" training to you and your child.

Parents may benefit from reading Chapters 17 and 18. These chapters give therapists information to assist parents and children in skills training. By reading these chapters, parents may be informed of what to expect from a therapist, and thus may be better consumers of a therapist's services.

THERAPISTS

This book can be used by therapists to assist children with behavior disorders and their parents. **The term "therapist," as used in this book , is defined as a qualified mental health professional** (e.g., clinical/counseling/school psychologist, psychiatrist, social worker, counselor, etc.). It is assumed that the therapist using this book has had some training in developmental/clinical/counseling/school psychology methods of intervention, and behavioral/cognitive-behavioral therapy. The therapist should be a licensed mental health professional, or should at least be supervised by a licensed mental health professional.

This book could be used by parents and therapists to collaborate together as part of an intervention. The therapist can assist the parent by training the parent and/or child in skills training procedures, using the book as a basis for such training. The book can also serve as a bridge between the therapist's office and the family home. The book offers explicit instructions to parents in hope of enabling them to use at home the skills therapists help them learn.

It is recommended that therapists read Chapters 17 and 18 first. These chapters provide theory, research findings, and therapeutic suggestions regarding skills training for children with behavior disorders and their parents. The other chapters can be used as needed by therapists working with parents. Chapters 1–16 are written from the parents' perspective, but therapists can certainly understand the intent, and may find the instructions useful to guide application.

Therapists have permission to copy charts at the end of Chapters 3–14 for purposes of professional consultation and interventions with clients.

Contents

I

INFORMATION FOR PARENTS

1

What Are Behavior Disorders in Children?

Children with behavior disorders are quite challenging for parents. These children display behaviors that have a negative impact on individuals in their environment (e.g., parents, peers, teachers, etc.), and that often result in those individuals displaying negative behaviors back toward the children. The American Psychiatric Association's *Diagnostic and Statistical Manual of Mental Disorders,* fourth edition (DSM-IV; American Psychiatric Association, 1994), defines three types of disruptive behavior disorders including attention-deficit/hyperactivity disorder (ADHD), oppositional defiant disorder (ODD), and conduct disorder (CD). Although all three disruptive behavior disorders share some common features, there are some clear distinctions that make them unique. Nevertheless, many children have more than one of these disorders. This chapter will describe the different Disruptive Behavior Disorders, associated child and family problems, and common assessment and treatment procedures for these problems.

ATTENTION-DEFICIT/HYPERACTIVITY DISORDER

Symptoms

The basic problem of children with ADHD is their inability to regulate and maintain behavior. Because these children have problems controlling their behavior, they often do not display appropriate behaviors that match the environment they are in at a given moment. The cardinal symptoms of ADHD are limited attention span/distractibility, impulsivity, and hyperactivity.

The attention span problems of ADHD children can be seen in visual and/or auditory tasks and in situations that require mental **effort.** Children with ADHD may not look different than other children when watching TV, playing video games, or engaging in a variety of activities they enjoy or have mastered, because such tasks require little effort. Differences emerge between children exhibiting ADHD and other children, however, on tasks that require sustained effort and concentration, for example, many tasks at school. Children with ADHD also have difficulty screening out distractions because their brains seem to process too much sensory information.

The symptom of impulsivity is present when ADHD children do not think before they act. It is difficult for many children with ADHD to focus on one thing at a time. Impulsive children do not stop to evaluate/anticipate consequences or to think of alternative ways to handle situations and problems. Rather, these children simply act without thinking. The impulsive behavior may be seen when they blurt out answers in the classroom, engage in reckless behavior, throw things, or annoy other children.

Hyperactivity is seen in ADHD children who are "on the go" all the time. These children appear to be "driven by a motor," are restless and fidgety, and have difficulty sitting still.

The DSM-IV diagnostic system distinguishes between three types of ADHD: (1) **predominantly inattentive type,** (2) **predominantly hyperactive–impulsive type,** and (3) **combined type.** The child with ADHD, predominantly inattentive type, has problems with sustaining attention and completing tasks, and is disorganized and distractible. Researchers have found that these children have problems with academic tasks. The child with ADHD, predominantly hyperactive–impulsive type, has problems with disruptive behavior. Researchers have shown that these children, and children with ADHD, combined type (who show both attentional and hyperactive–impulsive symptoms), show symptoms in many settings and have problems with academics, peers, family members, school officials, and so forth. **To be diagnosed with ADHD, a child must have displayed the symptoms prior to age 7 years, the symptoms must be of a greater magnitude than in other children of the same age, and the symptoms must have been evident for at least 6 months.** Table 1 summarizes the symptoms of ADHD and the subtypes according to the DSM-IV classification.

Research suggests that approximately 3–5% of all children have ADHD. Statistics on the differences between boys and girls generally show that boys outnumber girls by approximately a four or six to one ratio. Many children who have ADHD eventually develop more significant disruptive behavior disorders such as ODD and CD (to be discussed later).

Developmental Course

There is a fairly typical developmental course that occurs over the lifespan of ADHD children, but there may be differences among children, depending on severity of problems. The following description is based mostly on ADHD children with hyperactive–impulsive symptoms, because less is known about the developmental course of ADHD children with primarily inattentive symptoms. Children with ADHD may be more active in the womb during the pregnancy. As infants, they are often characterized as active, restless, fussy, and difficult to soothe. They may have problems establishing regular sleeping and eating routines. As toddlers and pre-schoolers, they may have a difficult temperament. They are often described as being

TABLE 1. DSM-IV Diagnostic Criteria for Attention-Deficit/Hyperactivity Disorder

A. Either (1) or (2):

    (1) Six (or more) of the following symptoms of **inattention** have persisted for at least 6 months to a degree that is maladaptive and inconsistent with developmental level:

      Inattention
- (a) often fails to give close attention to details or makes careless mistakes in schoolwork, work, or other activities
- (b) often has difficulty sustaining attention in tasks or play activities
- (c) often does not seem to listen when spoken to directly
- (d) often does not follow through on instructions and fails to finish schoolwork, chores, or duties in the workplace (not due to oppositional behavior or failure to understand instructions)
- (e) often has difficulty organizing tasks and activities
- (f) often avoids, dislikes, or is reluctant to engage in tasks that require sustained mental effort (such as schoolwork or homework)
- (g) often loses things necessary for tasks or activities (e.g., toys, school assignments, pencils, books, or tools)
- (h) is often easily distracted by extraneous stimuli
- (i) is often forgetful in daily activities

    (2) Six (or more) of the following symptoms of hyeractivity–impulsivity have persisted for at least 6 months to a degree that is maladaptive and inconsistent with developmental level:

      Hyperactivity
- (a) often fidgits with hands or feet or squirms in seat
- (b) often leaves seat in classroom or in other situations in which remaining seated is expected
- (c) often runs about or climbs excessively in situations in which it is inappropriate (in adolescents or adults, may be limited to subjective feelings of restlessness)
- (d) often has difficulty playing or engaging in leisure activities quietly
- (e) is often "on the go" or often acts as if "driven by a motor"
- (f) often talks excessively

      Impulsivity
- (g) often blurts out answers before questions have been completed
- (h) often has difficulty awaiting turn
- (i) often interrupts or intrudes on others (e.g., butts into conversations or games)

B. Some hyperactive–impulsive or inattentive symptoms that caused impairment were present before age 7 years.

C. Some impairment from the symptoms is present in two or more settings (e.g., at school [or work] and at home).

D. There must be clear evidence of clinically significant impairment in social, academic, or occupational functioning.

E. The symptoms do not occur exclusively during the course of a Pervasive Developmental Diosorder, Schizophrenia, or other Psychotic Disorder and are not better accounted for by another mental disorder (e.g., Mood Disorder, Anxiety Disorder, Dissociative Disorder, or a Personality Disorder).

Code based on type:

    314.01 Attention-Deficit/Hyperactivity Disorder, Combined Type: if both Criteria A1 and A2 are met for the past 6 months

    314.00 Attention-Deficit/Hyperactivity Disorder, Predominantly Inattentive Type: if Criterion A1 is met but Criterion A2 is not met for the past 6 months

    314.01 Attention-Deficit/Hyperactivity Disorder, Predominantly Hyperactive–Impulsive Type: if Criterion A2 is met but Criterion A1 is not met for the past 6 months

Note. From American Psychiatric Association (1994, pp. 83–85) Copyright 1994 by the American Psychiatric Association. Reprinted by permission.

"into everything" and needing constant monitoring and supervision. Some ADHD children have a poor history of attachment or bond with their caretakers during infancy. As toddlers and preschoolers, ADHD children are often much more difficult to discipline than other same-age children. It is during the elementary school years when most of these children's symptoms are noticed and diagnosed. Their problems with attention span and concentration are more obvious in school. They find it difficult to complete work and stay on-task at school. During the elementary school years they may also start having problems getting along with family members and peers, and may develop low self-esteem. During the adolescent years, the hyperactivity often declines in these children, but the problems with attention span and impulsivity typically prevail. Unfortunately, many secondary problems also develop as a result of a history of dealing with the difficulties from ADHD. These adolescents are at greater risk for delinquent behavior, depression, peer relationship problems, school failure, and so forth. The problems of ADHD may persist into adulthood, and many of the secondary problems become more severe. Adults with a history of ADHD are at greater risk for a wide range of emotional, interpersonal, psychiatric, and functional problems (e.g., occupational difficulties, marital problems, etc.). It is thought that, without treatment, approximately 30–50% of ADHD children can learn to adapt to their disability in later life. The other 50–70% of these individuals are "at risk" for developing the problems described above. In particular, **children who have ADHD who also develop ODD and/or aggressive social behavior problems are more likely to experience the difficulties described above.**

Possible Causes

The cause of ADHD appears to be primarily a biological or neurodevelopmental one. These children may have subtle abnormalities in parts of the brain that are responsible for maintaining attention, screening out distraction, and regulating motor activity. Researchers using electrophysiological, cerebral blood flow, positron emission tomography, and magnetic resonance imaging measures have found differences in brain functioning when they compare ADHD individuals with other groups. Emerging evidence suggests the frontal lobe (especially on the right side), basal ganglia, and reticular activating systems of the brain are the areas implicated in ADHD children. It is possible that a neurochemical imbalance accounts for ADHD with lower levels of dopamine and norepinephrine neurotransmitters in the implicated areas of the brain. However, in some instances, researchers have found it difficult to replicate findings, which suggests the need to view findings about the cause of ADHD cautiously. There is no evidence to support a pure environmental cause such as poor parenting, poverty, diet, and so forth as a cause for ADHD.

Although there appear to be specific areas in the brain responsible for ADHD, there are multiple ways in which a child may end up with the subtle brain abnormalities. In most cases, heredity plays a dominant role in which predispositions to subtle brain differences are passed on from one generation to the other.

In some cases, there may be actual subtle structural brain damage that occurs as a result of problems with the pregnancy or birth, or by exposure to a trauma or toxin after birth. In any event, regardless of how it happens, it appears that the same areas of the brain are affected.

OPPOSITIONAL DEFIANT DISORDER

Symptoms

Children who have ODD are generally noncompliant and display irritable and negative mood. These problems are often reoccurring and chronic in nature. Developmental factors need to be considered when trying to figure out if a child has ODD. **Children with ODD display oppositional and defiant behavior at a level that is more severe and of a greater magnitude than same-age peers.** Specific behaviors that ODD children may display include violation of minor rules, tantrums, arguments with authority figures, annoying others, blaming others for their own problems, swearing, and so forth.

The DSM-IV diagnostic system describes only one general type of ODD. Although there is no specific age of onset, **DSM-IV suggests that most children develop ODD prior to age 8 years.** The child must have displayed the symptoms for at least 6 months. Table 2 summarizes the symptoms of ODD according to the DSM-IV classification.

Recent research suggests that approximately 2–16% of the general population have ODD. About 50–65% of children who have ADHD go on to develop ODD. Children with other neurological problems and/or developmental delays may eventually develop ODD too. Again, as with ADHD, boys are more likely than girls to develop ODD.

Development Course

Less is known about the specific developmental course of ODD. As stated above, most children develop ODD before age 8 years. Some of these children have difficult temperaments and/or other developmental delays prior to developing ODD. **Children who have persistent oppositional and defiant behavior early in their development that maintains itself into the later stages of development are at significant risk for developing antisocial and delinquent behavior.** (This will be expanded upon in the Conduct Disorder section.) Children with ODD are more likely to have functional problems related to home, school, and peer group relationships, as well as lower self-esteem and a greater number of emotional difficulties, than the general population.

Possible Causes

Researchers are not clear about the specific cause of ODD. Some speculate that there is a neurological or biological cause because there seems to be high overlap between ODD and ADHD. Many children who develop ODD are often described as irritable

TABLE 2. DSM-IV Diagnostic Criteria for Oppositional Defiant Disorder

A. A pattern of negativistic, hostile, and defiant behavior lasting at least 6 months, during which four (or more) of the following are present:

   (1) often loses temper
   (2) often argues with adults
   (3) often actively defies or refuses to comply with adults' requests or rules
   (4) often deliberately annoys people
   (5) often blames others for his or her mistakes or misbehavior
   (6) is often touchy or easily annoyed by others
   (7) is often angry and resentful
   (8) is often spiteful or vindictive

   Note: Consider a criterion met only if the behavior occurs more frequently than is typically observed in individuals of comparable age and developmental level.

B. The disturbance in behavior causes clinically significant impairment in social, academic, or occupational functioning.

C. The behaviors do not occur exclusively during the course of Psychotic or Mood Disorder.

D. Criteria are not met for Conduct Disorder, and, if the individual is age 18 years or older, criteria are not met for Antisocial Personality Disorder.

Note. From American Psychiatric Association (1994, pp. 93–94). Copyright 1994 by the American Psychiatric Association. Reprinted by permission.

and as having a difficult temperament during the infancy, toddler, and preschool years. This difficult temperament is characterized by having negative mood, problems adapting to new situations, and irregular eating and sleeping routines. When children exhibit these characteristics, parenting behavior is thought to be negatively influenced, and **ineffective parenting contributes to the development of ODD.** These children are much more challenging to parent than other children, so parents may not be adequately providing the consistent and effective discipline needed to deal with these difficult behaviors. Parents of ODD children are often described as inconsistent, harsh, and/or ineffective in their discipline practices. The child and the parents seem to affect each other back and forth over time; as a result, the child's problems increase and the parenting behavior problems become worse. The combination of a difficult child and ineffective parenting can result in an ODD child.

CONDUCT DISORDER

Symptoms

Children with CD display a persistent pattern of violating the rights of others and accepted social norms and rules. These children may display these behaviors at home, at school, or in the community. Generally, these children display a wide range of problem behaviors, from "confrontive overt" behaviors to "nonconfrontive covert" behaviors. Confrontive overt behaviors may include assaulting others, stealing with confrontation, aggressiveness, sexually violating others, and so forth—that is, behaviors that directly affect others. Nonconfrontive covert behaviors may include stealing without confrontation, truancy, running away, and substance abuse. Although these behaviors violate social rules and norms, they affect other individuals less directly. Some CD children may have a mixture of both confrontive overt and nonconfrontive covert behavior problems.

The DSM-IV diagnostic system distinguishes between two subtypes of CD: (1) **childhood-onset type (before 10 years),** and (2) **adolescent-onset type (after age 10 years).** The child with CD, childhood-onset type, is typically aggressive and displays confrontive overt, antisocial behavior. Research suggests that children with CD, childhood-onset type, are more likely to be boys than girls, typically have an early history of ADHD and/or ODD, and are more likely to have adjustment problems in adolescence and adulthood. The child with CD, adolescent-onset type, is less aggressive and more likely to display nonconfrontive covert behaviors. Children with CD, adolescent-onset type, are more likely to be girls than boys, and are less likely to have adjustment problems in adolescence and adulthood. DSM-IV also distinguishes between mild, moderate, and severe categories of CD. Mild CD children will show less confrontive overt behavior than moderate and severe children. Again, children must show the symptoms for at least 6 months to obtain a CD diagnosis. Table 3 summarizes the symptoms of CD and the subtypes according to the DSM-IV classification.

Research examining the prevalence rates of CD often does not take into account different rates for the CD subtypes but instead lumps all CD subtypes together. It is estimated that anywhere between 4 and 10% of the general population has the full syndrome of CD. About 60% of the general population of children display some antisocial behavior at some point in their development (e.g., isolated acts of stealing, vandalism, drug experimentation, etc.), but they would not be considered to have the full syndrome. Socioeconomic factors also seem to play a contributing role. CD is more likely to occur in the low socioeconomic class than in the middle and upper classes. **CD in children is highly related to ODD and ADHD.** It has been estimated that 82–95% of childhood-onset CD children had ODD, and 60% of childhood-onset CD children were earlier diagnosable with ADHD. Approximately 20–30% of ADHD elementary school age children have CD, and about 40–60% of ADHD adolescents also have CD. Obviously, CD children are at high risk of developing serious emotional, social, academic, and occupational problems as they get older.

Developmental Course

Some research has charted the typical developmental course and outcome of CD. Generally, **the earlier the onset of the CD problems, and the more pervasive and long-lasting the problems, the poorer the prognosis.** As with ODD, many CD children are thought to have a difficult temperament very early in life. Many CD children also have a history of a poor attachment or bond with caretakers during infancy. Between the preschool years and adulthood, a number of stages have been hypothesized to occur in the development of CD. In 1989, Craig Edelbrock proposed a four-stage theory regarding the development of childhood-onset CD (discussed

TABLE 3. DSM-IV Diagnostic Criteria for Conduct Disorder

A. A repetitive and persistent pattern of behavior in which the basic rights of others or major age-appropriate societal norms or rules are violated, as manifested by the presence of three (or more) of the following criteria in the past 12 months, with at least one criterion present in the past 6 months.

Aggression to people and animals
(1) often bullies, threatens, or intimidates others
(2) often initiates physical fights
(3) has used a weapon that can cause serious physical harm to others (e.g., a bat, brick, broken bottle, knife, gun)
(4) has been physically cruel to people
(5) has been physically cruel to animals
(6) has stolen while confronting a victim (e.g., mugging, purse snatching, extortion, armed robbery)
(7) has forced someone into sexual activity

Destruction of property
(8) has deliberately engaged in fire setting with the intention of causing serious damage
(9) has deliberately destroyed others' property (other than by fire setting)

Deceitfulness or theft
(10) has broken into someone else's house, building, or car
(11) often lies to obtain goods or favors or to avoid obligations (i.e., "cons" others)
(12) has stolen items of nontrivial value without confronting a victim (e.g., shoplifting, or stealing without breaking and entering; forgery)

Serious violations of rules
(13) often stays out at night despite parental prohibitions, beginning before age 13 years
(14) has run away from home overnight at least twice while living in parental or parental surrogate home (or once without returning home for a lengthy period)
(15) is often truant from school, beginning before age 13 years

B. The disturbance in behavior causes clinically significant impairment in social, academic, or occupational functioning

C. If the individual is age 18 years or older, criteria are not met for Antisocial Personality Disorder.

Specify type based on age at onset:
   Childhood-Onset Type: onset of at least one criterion characteristic of Conduct Disorder prior to 10 years
   Adolescent-Onset Type: absence of any criteria characteristic of Conduct Disorder prior to age 10 years

Specify severity:
   Mild: few if any conduct problems in excess of those required to make the diagnosis and conduct problems cause only minor harm to others
   Moderate: number of conduct problems and effect on others intermediate between "mild" and "severe"
   Severe: many conduct problems in excess of those required to make the diagnosis **or** conduct problems cause considerable harm to others

Note. From American Psychiatric Association (1994, pp. 90–91). Copyright 1994 by the American Psychiatric Association. Reprinted by permission.

in Barkley, 1990). Edelbrock speculates that during the preschool years to early elementary school years, these children are noncompliant and oppositional primarily at home. During the late elementary school years, these children are much more disruptive at school, start to have poor peer relationships, lie, cheat, swear, and engage in some aggressive behavior. During the late elementary school years to adolescence, all of the above problems continue to occur, but the children also start to show overt aggressive behavior of a higher magnitude. During the middle and later adolescent years, these children are more likely to run away, skip school, and abuse alcohol and/or drugs. As adults, these individuals continue to be highly at risk for antisocial behavior, criminal activity, interpersonal relationship problems, occupational difficulties, psychiatric difficulties, and physical health problems. Researchers are now providing evidence to support Edelbrock's developmental theory.

Possible Causes

There appear to be multiple potential causes for childhood-onset CD. Both child biological factors and environmental factors may contribute to the development of this problem. A variety of biological or neurodevelopmental causes have been speculated regarding childhood-onset CD. These children may show "soft signs" common to a variety of neurological difficulties, and may have lower levels of dopamine neurotransmitters in certain areas of the brain. Some highly aggressive CD children may have higher levels of the hormone testosterone. As with ADHD and ODD, there appears to be a strong genetic influence in childhood-onset CD. Research has shown that even when environmental factors can be controlled, these problems are passed from generation to generation. Parental psychopathology also contributes to the development of CD. Children with CD are more likely to have parents with psychiatric problems of their own. These children often have fathers with antisocial behavior problems, mothers who are depressed, and/or both parents with possible substance abuse problems. Other stresses, such as financial difficulties, divorce/marital problems, and low parental support have also been found to exist and may contribute to the development of CD. Poor parenting practices have been connected directly to CD. Parents of these children are often ineffective, coercive, and/or harsh in the way they discipline these children. As mentioned earlier, negative peers influences are also related to some CD behavior in children.

Family and/or peer influences may be related to the development of adolescent-onset CD. These children usually do not display problems until adolescence, but because of family problems and/or the influence of the peer group, they develop CD behavior problems. **Children with adolescent-onset CD usually have a better prognosis than children with childhood-onset CD.**

DEVELOPMENT OF AGGRESSION IN CHILDREN

Aggression in children was mentioned briefly above in the description of the three disruptive behavior disorders. Special consideration of childhood aggression is warranted, however, because it is a significant factor related to long-term adjustment in children.

Aggressive children think and behave differently from nonaggressive children. They often have a "world view" or general belief that the world is a hostile place and that others act hostile toward them. As a result, they often "look" for information in their environment that will confirm this general belief. They misinterpret the behavior of others and assume that these people are "out to get them." Aggressive children often prefer aggressive solutions to interpersonal problems.

An example of a 12-year-old boy will illustrate how aggressive children think and behave. Assume that this child views the world as a hostile place. He gets bumped by another boy while he walks down a school hall. The aggressive 12-year-old assumes that the other boy bumped him "on purpose" and that therefore it is "the other boy's fault." Because the aggressive boy thinks aggressive solutions work best, he then pushes the boy who bumped him.

For most children, developing aggressive behavior may involve temperamental or environmental factors. Some of them may be more difficult or irritable early in life, which could start an early pattern of aggressive behavior. For most severely aggressive children, with or without a difficult temperament, environment is an influential cause. Many aggressive children experience abuse and/or aggressive adult role models throughout their early years. Many of these children are neglected and/or don't have caretakers who consistently meet their emotional needs, which results in early emotional detachment from these caretakers. Because of these early experiences, these children develop a belief that the world is hostile and that aggressive behavior is the best way to deal with problems. Everyday life events are then "processed" through this world view. These children misinterpret others' behavior as hostile and believe aggressive solutions are best, which causes them to behave aggressively to solve the problems they encounter.

Many aggressive children do not have good social behavior skills. They do not know how to share, take turns, cooperate, play games fairly, express feelings, and so forth. When interpersonal problems develop, aggressive children are less able to use helpful social skills to solve the problems, which can lead them to respond aggressively.

COERCIVE FAMILY PROCESS

Researchers have shown that a "coercive family process" exists in many families of children with disruptive behavior problems. **The coercive family process is seen when parents and children learn to use negative behaviors to control one another and when parents are ineffective in "managing" their child.** When a coercive family process exists, it is not uncommon for parents to give frequent commands, yell, blame, criticize, and so forth in an effort to control the child. Likewise, the child often behaves in a stubborn manner, yells, blames, has tantrums, criticizes, and so forth in an effort to control the parent. Usually either the parent or the child "gives in" to the other, which is reinforcing to both. The following examples illustrate the coercive family process as it relates to a parent trying to get a child to comply:

Example 1. Parent gives a command, child acts negatively, parent withdraws command.

Example 2. Parent gives a command, child acts negatively, parent acts more negatively than child, child complies.

In these two examples, both "negative reinforcement" and "positive reinforcement" occurred. Negative reinforcement occurs when something negative is removed and it feels good. Positive reinforcement occurs when something positive is experienced and it feels good. In Example 1, the parent receives negative reinforcement when he or she gives in to the child and the child stops behaving negatively. The child is positively reinforced because he "gets his way" for acting negatively. In Example 2, the child receives negative reinforcement because he complied and was able to stop the negative parent behavior. The parent was positively reinforced for acting negatively because "it worked" to get the child to comply. When these behavior patterns are enacted over and over in a family, increases in child behavior and emotional problems may occur.

When a coercive family process exists, the parents are often ineffective in other areas of parenting. They may give their child more attention when the child is behaving negatively than when he is behaving positively. The parent may not supervise or monitor the child enough. Finally, the parent and child may not have a "bond" or close relationship. The parent may not be taking adequate care of the child or spending enough time with the child to enhance the parent–child bond.

Researchers are not entirely clear as to what causes the coercive family process. It could be that parents are not skilled in parenting. It could also be that the child is so difficult that the child's behavior "disrupts" normal parenting.

COMMON COEXISTING DISORDERS ASSOCIATED WITH BEHAVIOR DISORDERS

This section provides a brief review of some of the more common coexisting problems experienced by children with behavior disorders.

Learning Disabilities/Speech and Language Problems

There is a well-established link between behavioral and social difficulties and diagnosable learning disabilities in children. As many as 26% of ADHD children may also have a learning disability. Children with behavior problems typically do not have major problems with receptive language. However, as many as 54% of ADHD children may have minor problems with expressive language.

Mental Retardation

By definition, children with limited intellectual capabilities will struggle more with attention span, self-control, and social relationships as compared to same-age children of normal intelligence. Children with moderate to severe mental retardation are at risk for developing aggressive and oppositional behavior.

Tourette or Tic Disorder

Gilles de la Tourette syndrome and tic disorder are neurological disorders characterized by involuntary motor and/or vocal tics. Children with Tourette or tics are also at risk for displaying one or more of the disruptive behavior disorders. These children have neurologically based deficits in self-control that make behavior problems more likely to emerge. Children with ADHD do not necessarily "develop" Tourette or a tic disorder, but up to 70% of children with Tourette or a tic disorder have ADHD.

Anxiety and/or Mood Disorders

Children with "internalizing" problems such as anxiety and depression often exhibit behavior problems too. Anxious and depressed children may display problems with attention/concentration and are sometimes misdiagnosed as ADHD. Research suggests that few ADHD-only elementary school age children exhibit clinical depression, but some ADHD adolescents will. As many as 7–23% of adolescents diagnosed with CD are also diagnosed with a depressive disorder. Some children start out with an anxiety or mood disorder and eventually develop a behavior disorder. Other children start out with a behavior disorder and eventually develop an anxiety or mood disorder. Regardless of which starts first, we know that many children have both types of problems.

FUNCTIONAL PROBLEMS RELATED TO DISRUPTIVE BEHAVIOR DISORDERS

There are a variety of functional problems associated with disruptive behavior disorders in children. These functional problems seem to exist, in varying degrees, for children with any of the three disruptive behavior disorders. Not all children with disruptive behavior disorders will exhibit all of these functional problems.

Social Problems

Children with disruptive behavior disorders often have difficult social relationships. They may display poor social skills and don't "read" other people's social cues very well. They may have difficulty taking the perspective of other people (i.e., understanding others' thoughts and feelings) and are deficient in solving interpersonal problems. Aggressive children often mistakenly think other children are "out to get them," and they will behave aggressively in many social interactions. Eventually, many of these children are either rejected and/or neglected by their peers.

As a result of these difficulties, these children tend to "bug" other people and act in a disruptive manner in social situations, and they may be aggressive.

Emotional Problems

Over time, many children with disruptive behavior disorders receive more negative than positive feedback from their environment (e.g., peers, parents, teachers, neighbors, etc.). This negative feedback sometimes results in a child developing low self-esteem. The child may become demoralized and give up. Occasionally, low self-esteem and demoralization can turn into depression. These children are also more likely to worry and be negative thinkers.

Academic Problems

There seems to be a strong relationship between disruptive behavior disorders and academic difficulties. As mentioned earlier, many ADHD or disruptive children also have a diagnosable learning disability. Even if a child is not diagnosed with a learning disability, he may still struggle in school. Behavior disordered children often are off-task and don't get their work done. They may be unorganized, have poor study skills, and have difficulty managing their time effectively. Children with behavior problems may also have poor relationships with their teachers, which may affect their academic performance.

Family Relationship Problems

Most researchers do not think that family factors play a causative role in ADHD, but it is widely known that these children dramatically affect the family. Research shows that ADHD children seek more assistance, and parents give more directions, when the children are attempting to solve a problem. With ODD and CD, parenting may play a part in the cause of these problems, where coercive parent–child interactions and ineffective parenting seem to contribute to the disruptive behavior problems getting worse over time. Siblings can also be negatively affected by children with behavior problems. There may be more negative sibling interactions, and siblings often have trouble coping with a difficult brother or sister.

EVALUATION

This section will provide a very brief overview of how disruptive behavior disorders in children are evaluated and diagnosed. Typically, the parent is the one who makes the initial referral, as it is rare that a child with this type of behavior problem would refer him- or herself. The parent should start with a medical and/or a mental health professional who has some experience in working with children with these types of problems. **Eventually, most parents bring their child to both**

a medical and a mental health professional before the evaluation is completed.
One of these professionals should conduct a detailed parent and child interview.
The interviewer should obtain information on the extent and nature of the child's
behavior problems and information on how the child is functioning in terms of
emotional status, peer relationships, family relationships, and academic endeavors.
The interviewer should also obtain a clear developmental history of the child as
well as the history of the family over time. Finally, the interviewer should focus
on a detailed understanding of family psychiatric history. Parents and teachers
should complete rating scales that broadly assess child functioning and narrowly
focus on behavior problems. It is often helpful to have the child fill out some
self-report questionnaires. Other psychological testing that evaluates intellectual
functioning, neuropsychological status, achievement, and personality may also be
helpful in some instances. A medical evaluation should be conducted to rule out
any physical problems. Many children benefit from school-based assessments to
determine if special education services are needed at school. The professionals
conducting these evaluations should coordinate their findings to come up with a
diagnosis as well as recommendations.

COMMON TREATMENT APPROACHES

It is necessary to have a comprehensive treatment approach when working with
children who have disruptive behavior disorders. Often the intervention needs to
include the child, parent/family, school, peers, and occasionally the community.

Parent/Family Therapy

Even if the parents/family are not the cause of the particular disruptive behavior,
they certainly are likely to be a big part of the solution. The focus of parent/family
therapy is to help parents improve their discipline and management skills of their
difficult and challenging child. Parents also learn how to cope with their own stress
due to being a parent of a difficult child. Often family communication, problem-
solving, and conflict resolution skills are taught in this type of therapeutic setting.
Parents can also be trained to help their child develop skills (such as the ones in
this book) in a therapeutic setting. Parent and family therapy approaches have
been found by researchers to be effective in reducing behavior problem symptoms
in children and changing parent–child and family interactions.

Social and Problem-Solving Skills Groups

Many children with disruptive behavior disorders benefit from group therapy
where they learn social and problem-solving skills. Social skills training can be
useful for children of all ages. Problem-solving training is only of benefit to children who are at least over the mental age of 8 years old. Research has established
that this type of therapy is successful in reducing aggressive behavior in children,
but not too useful in improving the behavior of ADHD children. These groups

should not be the sole intervention for any child, but could be used in combination with other interventions.

Specialized School Interventions

At the very least, the school should be consulted and some sort of monitoring program should be in place so that school personnel are keeping track of the child with disruptive behavior disorders. Sometimes a more restricted intervention is necessary in which a child receives special education services for learning or emotional/behavioral difficulties. It is vital that parents and school personnel form a collaborative and respectful relationship with each other on the child's behalf.

Many children with disruptive behavior problems qualify for special education services. **Parents should also be aware that, in 1991, the United States Department of Education clarified the qualification guidelines so that ADHD children can obtain special education services and modifications in general education to help them succeed at school.**

Individual Therapy

In some instances, it may be helpful for the child to have his or her own individual therapy. This is especially helpful if a child with a disruptive behavior disorder has emotional problems or comes from a background and a history of having been abused, neglected, or in a situation of severe family disruption. The individual therapy in this case may help the child "work through" unresolved emotional issues and gain insight. Individual therapy should never be the primary or only treatment for these children, but can be useful as a component of an overall intervention.

Psychopharmacology

Psychopharmacology is usually helpful for children diagnosed as ADHD. Often psychostimulants, such as methylphenidate, dextroamphetamine, or pemoline, are prescribed to help children improve their attention span and reduce their impulsivity. **About 70–75% of ADHD children respond positively to psychostimulants.** These medications have been shown to be effective in improving on-task behavior, academic productivity, social interactions, and parent–child interactions. Methylphenidate is usually the first choice of the psychostimulants because it has been researched the most and has been used by physicians for many years with ADHD children. Recently, clonidine has been shown to reduce hyperactive and aggressive behaviors in ADHD children. The research evaluating clonidine is somewhat sparse at this point, so caution is advised when using this medication with children. Lithium and haloperidol (Haldol) has been suggested as one form of treatment for severely aggressive children. Very few studies have been conducted to examine the effectiveness of lithium and haloperidol with severely aggressive children, so these results are tentative. Tricyclic antidepressants are sometimes used with children exhibiting either ADHD or attentional problems with a mood disorder because these drugs may affect both attentional and mood symptoms. Antidepressants are often prescribed to ADHD children who don't respond to, or have side effects from, psychostimulant medication.

The combination of medications and other psychological/environmental interventions has been shown to be more effective than either alone. Parents should strongly consider medications as an important component of their child's treatment. It is wise to consult a physician regarding the medication option.

Multimodal Intervention

Most professionals agree that a multimodal approach is necessary in treating children with disruptive behavior disorders. This approach means that children would receive many or all of the interventions described above at some point or other in their lives. **Research has shown that children who receive multimodal intervention have the best outcome in later years.** Often interventions are started and stopped, depending on the child's progress, as he or she goes through different developmental stages. Parents are encouraged to consult mental health professionals for more information on different treatment approaches.

Institutional Intervention

Some children eventually show severe behavior problems, and they do not benefit from outpatient therapeutic, special education, and medication interventions. When all else has been tried, the residential treatment option can be used for these children. Most residential treatment centers offer child group skills training, academic/vocational services, parent/family therapy, medications, and milieu interventions around the clock in a controlled environment for an extended period (e.g., 6–18 months). Research shows that children who receive such treatment make significant progress while in the residential center and often show short-term follow-up improvements. Over the long term, many of the children relapse and again show behavior problems. A rigorous outpatient therapy program should be used after a child is discharged from a residential treatment center.

2

What Can I Do to Help My Child?

The fact that you are reading this book says you are very concerned about your child and family. The level of your concern needs to be considered at the outset. **If you are very concerned and feel as if your family is severely affected by your child's behavior problems, then you may well need to seek the help of a licensed mental health professional.** The ideas discussed in this book may be helpful, but they may not be enough. Getting an evaluation and following any treatment recommendations that may come as a result of the evaluation are good first steps. Don't use this book by itself if the problems are serious. The ideas in this book are most effective if your child and/or family are having relatively mild problems, or if you use the book in combination with the help of a mental health professional. It may be useful to review the common treatment approaches discussed in Chapter 1.

This book uses a skills training approach that focuses on enhancing the competence of children and families. Children can be taught skills to make them more competent. Important individuals in the child's life, however, also need to be involved. The parents are the most important individuals to involve, but others, including teachers, coaches, neighbors, peers, siblings, and so forth, could also assist the child. It is essential for parents not only to learn their own skills, but also to serve as teachers to help the children learn their skills.

The ideas and concepts discussed in this book have a developmental focus. It is helpful to think of a child's problems as developmental delays in certain areas and skills. A child can be trained to develop skills so that her development is enhanced to a level appropriate for her age. Further, it is extremely important to be familiar with developmental norms so as to target skills training in ways that will be effective. It would be unrealistic, for example, to train a toddler to develop problem-solving skills, which are more characteristic of elementary school age children.

This book emphasizes a "cognitive-behavioral" skills building approach. The skills building strategies described throughout this book focus on how parents and children think and behave. **Procedures described in this book are designed to enable parents and children to think and behave in ways that build strengths and enhance coping abilities.**

TEN AREAS OF FOCUS

The remainder of this book focuses on ten important areas that can help parents learn to help themselves and their children. Research and clinical experience suggest that these areas are critical to children and families struggling with disruptive behavior problems. The ten areas of focus are as follows:

1. Parents' stress
2. Parents' thoughts
3. Parental involvement and positive reinforcement
4. Family interactions
5. Discipline related to compliance and rule following in children
6. Children's social behavior skills
7. Children's social and general problem-solving skills
8. Children's ability to cope with anger
9. Children's ability to engage in self-directed academic behaviors
10. Children's emotional well-being and level of self-esteem

The idea is to learn skills to improve parent, family, and child functioning in these ten areas of focus. In so doing, the parent will be helping to reduce current problems and will also help improve the long-term outcome for their child.

RATING OF SELF, FAMILY, AND CHILD IN TEN AREAS OF FOCUS

Before proceeding any further, it will be helpful to engage in evaluation of yourself, your family, and your child. By doing this self-evaluation, you will be better able to know where to focus your efforts.

Listed below are a variety of descriptors, thoughts, and behaviors that may describe yourself, your family, and/or your child. Read each sentence or question, and indicate how well that sentence or question describes you and/or your child. Try to keep in mind what is developmentally appropriate for your child. For example, you shouldn't expect younger elementary school age children to be good at problem solving. See Table 4 in Chapter 4 for more information on development if you are unsure of normal developmental expectations. If more than one parent is reading this book, discuss each question and try to come to an agreement about each question. Keep in mind that there are no right or wrong answers to these questions. Rate each question using the 5-point scale below and add up your score for each section:

1	2	3	4	5
Strongly disagree	Disagree	Neutral	Agree	Strongly agree

Parents' Stress

_____ 1. I feel overwhelmed with responsibilities.

_____ 2. I feel depressed and unhappy.

_____ 3. I am physically unhealthy.

_____ 4. It seems like I am not taking care of myself.

_____ 5. I use drugs and/or alcohol too often.

_____ 6. I have recently experienced stressful life events (e.g., loss of job, death of significant person, divorce, etc.).

_____ 7. My spouse/partner and I don't communicate (if applicable).

_____ 8. My child is very difficult to discipline.

_____ 9. My spouse/partner and I don't agree on parenting issues (if applicable).

_____ 10. I feel like I have no support and I am all alone.

_____ Total score

Parents' Thoughts

_____ 11. I often have the thought, "My child is behaving like a brat."

_____ 12. I often have the thought, "My child does it on purpose."

_____ 13. I often have the thought, "My child is the cause of all our family problems."

_____ 14. I often have the thought, "If I wasn't such a poor parent, my child would be better off."

_____ 15. I often have the thought, "It is his/her fault (other parent/guardian) that my child is this way."

_____ 16. I often have the thought, "My child's future is bleak; he/she will probably be irresponsible, a criminal, a high school dropout (etc.) when grown up."

_____ 17. I often have the thought, "My child should behave like other children; I shouldn't have to teach my child how to behave."

_____ 18. I often have the thought, "Our family is a mess."

_____ 19. I often have the thought, "I give up; there is nothing more I can do for my child."

_____ 20. I often have the thought, "I have no control over my child, I've tried everything, nothing seems to work."

_____ Total score

Parental Involvement and Positive Reinforcement

_____ 21. I don't pay much attention to my child's good behavior.

_____ 22. I don't praise my child as much as I could.

_____ 23. I have more negative interactions than positive interactions with my child.

_____ 24. I probably give my child more attention when he/she acts negatively than when he/she acts positively.

_____ 25. I'm too busy and spend little time with my child.

_____ 26. When I'm with my child, I'm usually doing things (e.g., cleaning, running errands, shopping, etc.) and not really paying attention to him/her.

_____ 27. I'm not involved in my child's activities (e.g., school, athletics, scouts, etc.).

_____ 28. My child and I are not very close to each other.

_____ 29. My child and I are emotionally disconnected.

_____ 30. I'm too stressed out and tired to spend "quality" time with my child.

_____ Total score

Family Interactions

_____ 31. We are seldom aware of when we are having communication problems.

_____ 32. We express ourselves in "unhelpful" ways (e.g., put-downs, blaming, interrupting, talking on and on, etc.).

_____ 33. We are not good at listening to each other (e.g., making poor eye contact, daydreaming, thinking about what one is going to say without listening to the other person, etc.).

_____ 34. We often communicate different messages on verbal and nonverbal levels (e.g., saying, "I love you," in a loud, screaming voice while pounding one's fist on a table).

_____ 35. We have difficulty recognizing and defining family problems.

_____ 36. Our family uses the same solutions over and over, and we don't think of new ways to solve our problems.

_____ 37. We don't think ahead about whether a solution to a problem might work.

_____ 38. We may figure out a good solution to a family problem, but we usually don't follow through and use it.

_____ 39. We usually don't recognize when anger and conflict are becoming destructive.

_____ 40. We rarely know how to control anger and conflict, and it gets out of hand in our family.

_____ Total score

Discipline Related to Compliance and Rule Following in Children

_____ 41. I give in and allow my child to "get his/her way" because he/she is so difficult and belligerent.

_____ 42. It's easier to do things myself rather than ask my child to do them.

_____ 43. I have to yell, threaten, and so forth to get my child to do anything.

_____ 44. My child and I have power struggles.

_____ 45. I am inconsistent in disciplining approaches.

_____ 46. My spouse/partner and I don't agree on discipline approaches (if applicable).

_____ 47. I seem to "tune into" my child the most when he/she is acting negatively.
_____ 48. I often don't know where my child is or what he/she is doing.
_____ 49. I have no clear rules established at my home.
_____ 50. There is no set time for curfew, bedtime, homework, and so forth.
_____ Total score

Children's Social Behavior Skills

_____ 51. My child doesn't have good eye contact with other children.
_____ 52. My child has difficulty expressing feelings appropriately to other children.
_____ 53. My child doesn't share with other children.
_____ 54. My child doesn't know how to cooperate very well with other children.
_____ 55. My child doesn't know how to start conversations with other children.
_____ 56. My child is passive with other children.
_____ 57. My child is aggressive with other children.
_____ 58. My child doesn't ask questions of other children.
_____ 59. My child doesn't listen to other children.
_____ 60. My child doesn't ignore other children when he/she should.
_____ Total score

Children's Social and General Problem-Solving Skills

_____ 61. My child doesn't think about what he/she is doing.
_____ 62. My child gets into trouble because of not thinking ahead about consequences of behavior.
_____ 63. My child doesn't work toward a goal.
_____ 64. My child seems unaware when he/she is having a problem.
_____ 65. My child does the same thing over and over, even though it doesn't work to solve problems.
_____ 66. My child doesn't use good strategies to solve problems.
_____ 67. My child doesn't know when he/she is having a social problem.
_____ 68. My child is unaware of his/her effect on others.
_____ 69. My child doesn't use good strategies to solve interpersonal difficulties.
_____ 70. My child uses primarily aggressive solutions to solve disagreements with others.
_____ Total score

Children's Ability to Cope with Anger

_____ 71. My child has an anger problem.
_____ 72. My child gets upset very easily.
_____ 73. My child is unaware when he/she is getting angry or frustrated.
_____ 74. My child destroys or damages personal or others' belongings/property.
_____ 75. My child is violent toward others.
_____ 76. My child blows up and has anger outbursts.

_____ 77. My child is easily frustrated.
_____ 78. My child tends to be irritable and cranky.
_____ 79. I get angry at my child too much.
_____ 80. I have an anger problem.
_____ Total score

Children's Ability to Engage in Self-Directed Academic Behaviors

_____ 81. My child is unable to organize school materials.
_____ 82. My child doesn't effectively budget his/her time.
_____ 83. My child often doesn't know what homework is supposed to be done.
_____ 84. My child is usually off-task and doesn't get work done at school.
_____ 85. My child is usually off-task and doesn't get homework done at home.
_____ 86. My child has poor study skills and habits.
_____ 87. My child doesn't have a routine time and place set up for homework in our home.
_____ 88. I don't really know why my child is having problems at school.
_____ 89. I am uninvolved in my child's schooling.
_____ 90. I don't work closely with my child's teacher.
_____ Total score

Children's Emotional Well-Being and Level of Self-Esteem

_____ 91. My child doesn't understand his/her own emotional experience.
_____ 92. My child tends to deny his/her feelings.
_____ 93. My child doesn't express feelings very well.
_____ 94. My child doesn't tell anyone about his/her troubles.
_____ 95. My child tends to think negative thoughts.
_____ 96. My child doesn't like him/herself.
_____ 97. My child tends to think things are awful.
_____ 98. My child focuses on the negative and loses sight of the positive.
_____ 99. My child tends to blame him/herself for too many problems.
_____ 100. My child puts him/herself down a lot (e.g., says negative things about him/herself).
_____ Total score

Review your answers to the above questions carefully. Total up the score within each of the ten areas of focus and indicate the total score where designated above. Those areas of focus with higher scores may indicate problem areas for yourself, your family, and/or your child. Those questions that were rated as a 3, 4, or 5 may indicate specific problems.

DECIDING ON A FOCUS

In the space below, rank the ten areas of focus, putting the area with the highest score at the top, going down to the second highest score, and so forth until you've ranked all ten areas of focus.

1. _____
2. _____
3. _____
4. _____
5. _____
6. _____
7. _____
8. _____
9. _____
10. _____

By ranking the ten areas of focus by their scores, you are making use of "scientific method." Now examine the list again, and use your "gut reaction" to rank the areas according to those you think are the most important to focus on. **Keep in mind that it is usually less effective to focus on child skills if the parent or family is having problems. Instead, focus on parent and/or family skills before going on to child skills.** List below the final selection and order of the problems according to what you perceive to be the most important area down to the least important.

1. _____
2. _____
3. _____
4. _____
5. _____
6. _____
7. _____
8. _____
9. _____
10. _____

HOW TO USE THIS BOOK

Listed below are chapters in this book that are related to the ten areas of focus:

Area	Chapter
Parents' Stress	3
Parents' Thoughts	4
Parental Involvement and Positive Reinforcement	5
Family Interactions	6
Discipline Related to Compliance and Rule Following in Children	7, 8
Children's Social Behavior Skills	9
Children's Social and General Problem-Solving Skills	10
Children's Ability to Cope with Anger	11
Children's Self-Directed Academic Behavior	12
Children's Emotional Well-Being and Self-Esteem	13, 14, 15

You can turn to specific chapters to learn skills to improve those areas you have identified as problems. As you're looking through each chapter, be sure to follow each and every step. Don't skip any steps, because each one builds on the other. Keep in mind that utilizing the strategies described in each chapter will require a lot of effort on your part. The old saying, "No pain, no gain," applies here. **You need to put in the effort if you really want to make changes for yourself and/or your family.** It is helpful to think of long-term benefits rather than short-term gains. If you put in the effort now, it could potentially pay off in the long run. It is also necessary to keep in mind that, sometimes, when trying new strategies, problems become worse before they get better. **You will see positive results if you stay with it long enough to make it work.**

HELPING YOUR CHILD/FAMILY IN OTHER AREAS BEYOND THE SCOPE OF THIS BOOK

Think of an iceberg. An iceberg has a very small visible part that pokes out of the water. There is a very large part of an iceberg submerged and not visible. Icebergs are dangerous because one cannot really see all the ice underneath when coming toward it in a ship. Think of your child as an iceberg (see Figure 1). **The behavior problems you see are only a small part of what's really going on with a child.** Often, underneath, there may be other child, family, or social problems that contribute to the child's behavior problem. If you do not take into account all of the potential problems that may influence your child's observable behavior, you may miss important areas to focus on that could help your child/family. On the next page is a picture of a child on an iceberg. The observable part is the child's behavior problem. The submerged part includes other child, family, or social problems that may influence the child's problem.

If your child is trying to cope with some of the child, family, or social problems depicted above, these factors may be related to your child's behavior problems. You may need to address these problems by involving your child or family in a variety of interventions. See Chapter 1 for ideas about common treatment approaches for children with behavior problems to get additional ideas about what else you can do to help your child and family.

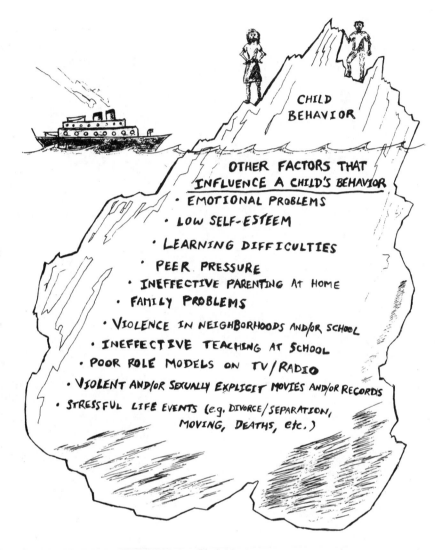

FIGURE 1. Child behavior iceberg.

II

INSTRUCTIONS FOR PARENTS TO ENHANCE PARENT AND FAMILY SKILLS

3

Parent Stress Management

The importance of the parent as a direct influence on the child's behavior must not be understated. Indeed, if the parent is having personal problems, there is the risk that the child's behavior problems will increase. This chapter will address how parent stress relates to child behavior disorders and how parents can better manage their stress.

Parents under Stress

John and Judy have been married 17 years and have two children, 10-year-old Sarah and 8-year-old Jacob. Sarah is a "handful" who has significant behavior problems at home, at school, and in interacting with her friends in the neighborhood. She is especially noncompliant and oppositional at home. She seems to refuse even the smallest requests by her parents. Her parents have also observed that Sarah starts many fights with her brother. They have resolved that they are going to try to be more consistent and "not let her get her way anymore."

John and Judy lead a very busy and hurried lifestyle. John works one full-time job and a part-time job. Judy also works full-time. The parents need to work a lot of hours to make ends meet and to pay the bills. Judy is responsible for most of the household chores. John often seems depressed. He is frequently irritable and he complains a lot. When John is at home, he watches a lot of TV and he doesn't spend much time with the family. Judy complains that John is "lazy" and that she "feels like a single parent" because he is so uninvolved in family matters. John and Judy find themselves arguing frequently. Judy has even thought of leaving John, but has never done so because of the children.

Last Tuesday an incident occurred at the family home. After dinner, Judy asked Sarah to clean the dishes off the table and bring them to the sink. By the time Judy made the request, Sarah, Jacob, and John were already watching television. Judy nagged Sarah several times. She asked John for assistance, but he didn't move. Finally, after several attempts to get Sarah to clean off the table without any assistance from John, Judy cleaned the table off herself.

WHAT IS PARENT STRESS?

Parents are under increasing stress in modern society. Financial concerns and the ever-changing nature of society and the family contribute to these difficulties. We know that individuals can't function well if they are under too much stress, and this also affects their ability to parent. Stress is defined broadly here as personal stress, marital/relationship stress, parenting stress, and low social support.

Personal Stress

If a parent is under too much stress, he or she may feel very overwhelmed. High personal stress may also be an indication of depression and/or anxiety in a parent. The parent may be abusing alcohol or drugs to cope with personal problems. There is much evidence in research studies that links high personal stress in parents with children exhibiting emotional and behavioral problems.

Marital/Relationship Stress

When a parent experiences marital problems or finds it hard to get along with a partner, it will be difficult for him or her to meet the needs of a child. These problems might range from frequent arguments to violence between partners. Marital/relationship problems with the parents are often seen in the families of children experiencing a variety of adjustment problems.

Parenting Stress

A child may be so difficult to manage that being with him causes the parent to experience stress. Occasionally, parents become so stressed or "burned out" from their children's behavior that they don't discipline when needed. If the parent gives up in this way, the child's problems may increase.

Low Social Support

If a parent is isolated and/or feels "alone," he or she will experience more stress than parents who feel they have social support (e.g., friends, family, etc.). Studies have found a relationship between parents with low social support and children with emotional and behavior problems.

HOW IS PARENT STRESS RELATED TO CHILD BEHAVIOR DISORDERS?

Chapter 1 described how ineffective parenting may be related to the development of ODD, CD, and aggressive behavior in children. Children at risk for behavior problems need nurturant, involved parents who provide effective, consistent discipline. **If a parent has too much stress, he or she will be less able to be a good**

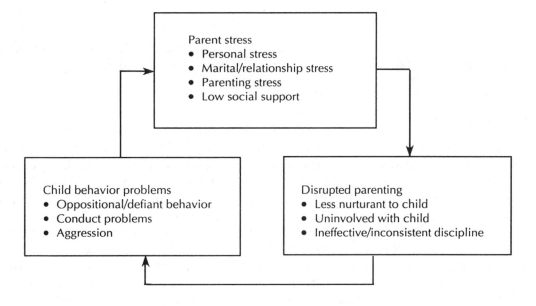

FIGURE 2. Parent stress and child behavior problems.

parent. Unfortunately, as children develop more behavior problems, it "stresses out" parents, which leads to further **disruption of parenting,** which can lead to more behavior problems for the child. Thus parent stress, disrupted parenting, and child behavior problems can affect each other in a circular fashion as depicted in Figure 2. The main lesson from this is that parents must take steps to reduce parent stress to deal effectively with a child's behavior problems.

PARENTAL STRESS MANAGEMENT

The point has already been made that you cannot provide what your child needs unless you manage your own stress and personal problems. Clearly, you need to take care of yourself in order to be available to meet the needs of your child. Below is a discussion of possible ways in which a parent might enhance his or her ability to cope with stress. These suggestions are presented briefly, as they are not a major emphasis of the book. It is necessary to raise these issues, however, because your family and child will not be able to benefit from the strategies discussed in the remainder of the book unless you address these stress issues.

Seek Professional Help

If you have determined that you are under too much stress, consider seeking professional help. **It may be helpful for you to consult a mental health and/or**

chemical health professional. This individual could conduct a thorough assessment of your level of stress and determine whether you may have problems that need to be addressed through counseling or other psychiatric services. You could seek out a consultation and see if the professional offers an explanation for your stress and a reasonable treatment plan. If the professional recommends a specific course of treatment, then it would be wise to pursue it. In many instances, individual therapy, chemical dependency treatment, couple or family therapy, and/or medications may be indicated.

Modify Your Values and Lifestyle Regarding Your Children

Many philosophers and mental health professionals have described three basic tasks of life: work, play, and love. Parents often find themselves too involved in work or other activities and, therefore, neglect play and love. Sometimes parents are too involved in work out of necessity, but often excessive working is an indicator of certain values and priorities. An individual may emphasize work because he or she has high career aspirations or because he or she values financial and material things. If people do not live balanced lives in which they also play (e.g., recreation, relaxation, etc.) and have opportunity for love (e.g., family relationships, friendships, etc.), they often find themselves under stress and dissatisfied. Also, to be effective as a parent, it is necessary to emphasize play and love, especially within the family. There is a gradually accumulating consensus in the field of child development that **parents need to provide quality time and quantity of time for their children**. In other words, parents need to make time and spend that time wisely with their children.

It may be helpful to clarify one's values and to determine which activities are most important and deserve the most time. The following exercise is offered to aid in value clarification. First, make a list of the activities you value and think are worthy of your time and effort. The list may include activities such as work, cleaning the house, projects around the house, time with children, time with spouse/partner, time for yourself, exercise, playing musical instruments, taking classes, gardening, and so forth. Next, on a second piece of paper, arrange the original list in order of which activities you value most, followed in descending order by less valued activities. Then, on a third piece of paper, rearrange the original list in order of how you actually spend time in the activities during an average week. The activity you spend the most time on should be on the top of the list, followed by the activity you spend the second most time on and so forth. **If you find time with your children toward the top of your list of valued activities and far down on the list of actual activities you do, you have a dilemma.** You may need to examine this and perhaps plan how you can spend more time with your child. Consult Chapter 5 for ideas on how to increase involvement with your child. In some instances, you may have little choice but to work a lot of hours for financial reasons. In this case, you may want to think about how you could eventually take care of financial needs and still make time for your children in the long term.

Specific Stress Coping Strategies

Parents with mild to moderate levels of stress can use a variety of coping strategies. These strategies are common sense approaches, but they may also require the assistance of a mental health professional to help the individual develop the necessary skills. The coping strategies are as follows:

1. **Relax.** Learn to relax your body through various relaxation procedures. It may be helpful to consult professional publications and/or a mental health professional to learn specific relaxation strategies.

2. **Take time away from children and family.** It can be rejuvenating to schedule time for yourself to pursue an activity or interest. You may need to arrange for a babysitter, or, if there are two parents, you might take turns caring for your children so that each parent can get out occasionally.

3. **Take time to be with your spouse/partner (if applicable).** If parents spend time with each other without their children around, they may improve their relationship.

4. **Seek out social support.** Parents who are feeling overwhelmed and isolated could benefit from seeking out active support from other family members, neighbors, or mental health professionals. This support could involve getting babysitters, talking and sharing feelings with friends or family members, asking for help from friends or family members, getting individual therapy, and so forth.

5. **Schedule pleasant events.** Stress can be relieved by scheduling specific pleasant events that you will participate in. For example, it may be pleasant to schedule going to a concert, going out to dinner with a friend, going to the park with your children, going to a baseball game with your son or daughter, and so forth.

6. **Develop good health habits.** It is universally accepted that increasing one's exercise level, eating a healthy diet, getting enough rest, and relaxing periodically can improve one's ability to cope with stress. Consult professional publications and/or a physician regarding a health promotion program for you.

7. **Utilize effective problem solving.** If you find yourself continually dealing with the same problems, then utilizing problem-solving strategies could be helpful. In later chapters (Chapters 6 and 10), we will review family problem solving and how to train children to utilize problem solving. Parents may benefit from these skills. A parent may want to consult a mental health professional for more information on improving problem-solving skills.

8. **Learn to think more accurately and rationally.** Often our stress is caused by the way we think about ourselves, others, and the events of life. You can learn how to reevaluate and change thoughts. We will be focusing on changing thoughts related to one's child and parenting abilities in Chapter 4. However, it can also be beneficial to learn how to think more rationally about oneself. Chapter 14 discusses how to help children think more accurately and rationally. You may find it helpful to review Chapter 14 and determine if similar ideas may be helpful for you. Again, you might consider consulting professional publications and/or a mental health professional to learn about how to think more accurately and rationally.

9. **Learn to control anger.** Parents often get very angry at their child or spouse (partner) when dealing with behavior problem children. A parent learning to control anger can be helpful. Chapter 11 describes anger management for children. Some of these ideas may be applicable to a parent. However, if you have a big anger problem, you should consult a mental health professional.

10. **Spend special time with your child.** Spend time with your child to build a quality relationship. You will have fewer problems getting along if you schedule special time. See Chapter 5 for ideas to promote involvement with your child.

11. **Join a parent support group.** I have been conducting parent groups for many years. These groups focus on skills training, but also allow parents to share "war stories" and obtain support from each other. Many parents comment that the support and opportunity to share experiences/ideas are very beneficial (sometimes more beneficial than the skills training!). If you have a child with serious, chronic behavior problems, you may benefit from joining a parent support group. Consult with a local mental health professional or social service agency about such groups in your community. A list of parent support organizations is also provided in the appendix of this book.

12. **Plan lifestyle changes.** The above examples of stress management really involve changing one's lifestyle. Changing a lifestyle involves much effort and planning to make it work. One helpful strategy might be for the parents to sit down together each Sunday and plan the following week by scheduling in stress management activities and priorities. For example, both parents may schedule going out, a mother may schedule visiting her sister on Thursday evening, a parent schedules which weekday mornings he or she will exercise, and so forth.

13. **Take parent stress management seriously.** If you are reading this book to help your child, then you have good intentions. **But you cannot really help your child unless you are healthy yourself.** Take time to take care of yourself, and you will be better able to take care of your child.

STAYING CALM WITH STRESSFUL CHILDREN

Because the major focus of this book is about parenting difficult children, it is important to address the stress involved in being a parent of a child with behavior problems. Parents often find themselves angry at or overwhelmed by these children. Learning techniques for staying calm when dealing with these children on a day-to-day basis may be helpful. **Staying calm while interacting with your stressful child involves being aware of and controlling how you react to stressful events with your child.**

Try to be more aware of your body, thoughts, and actions while interacting with your child. For example, imagine you are getting ready to go to an appointment and you need to get out of the house soon, but your child is taking her time. Your body might feel tense (e.g., muscles tense, heart rate goes up, breathing rate increases, etc.). Your thoughts might be unhelpful (e.g., "That brat!", "Why do we have to go through this same old stuff everyday?", "I'm going to ground her for a year this time!", etc.). Your actions might be unhelpful (e.g., yelling, threatening, hitting, etc.). Make a list of typical stressful events that often occur for you and your child and how you typically react as far as your body, thought, and actions are concerned.

The essential tasks for staying calm involve learning to control your body, thoughts, and actions in the face of parenting stress. This means learning to relax your body, to think helpful "coping" thoughts, and to take effective action when under stress from your child. The Staying Calm chart found at the end of this chapter summarizes techniques you can use to control your body, thoughts, and actions when dealing with stressful situations with your child. You could post this chart in your house to remind you what to do. It's also a good idea to let your child know you are working on staying calm, because then you are modeling behavior that most children with behavior problems need to acquire.

SUMMARY POINTS

1. Parental stress can take the form of personal stress, marital/relationship stress, parenting stress, and/or low social support.
2. Seek professional help if personal stress is too high or if there is evidence of significant marital/relationship/family problems.
3. Reset your priorities by examining what you value in life and what you actually do in life. Try to make your behavior match your values.
4. Develop skills and make lifestyle changes to cope with stress better.
5. Learn techniques to control your body, thought, and action responses when your child is causing you to experience parenting stress.

Let's Take Care of Ourselves

Back to John and Judy: John and Judy have become familiarized with parent stress management ideas through a parent support group they attend. One day they sit down to discuss how they might be able to manage their stress better. They decide that at least twice a month they are going to try to go out for dinner, a movie, or some other pleasant activity. John will schedule and arrange babysitters for these two monthly rendezvous. John also has decided that he will consult a mental health professional for an evaluation because he realizes he is not as happy as he would like to be. Both parents decide that they will take turns every other morning exercising while the other takes charge of the responsibilities of breakfast, getting the children ready for school, and so forth. Judy has decided that she will try to go out with her sister once a month because she finds her sister to be very supportive and a lot of fun to be with. The parents are also trying to use techniques to stay calm when dealing with Sarah and the parenting challenges she presents. In the future, they hope that their stress management techniques will help them to be more consistent with disciplining and helping Sarah learn to be more compliant.

CHART FOR CHAPTER 3

STAYING CALM

1. **Recognize Stress**—Be aware of stress "signals."

Body signals	Thought signals	Action signals
• Breathing/heart rate increased	• "That brat!"	• Punch/hit
• Tense muscles	• "I'm not going to take any more!"	• Yell/threaten
• Increased sweating	• "I'm a worthless parent."	• Cry
• Face turns red	• "I can't handle this!"	• Tremble
• Body feels hot	• "I hate him/her."	• Withdraw
	• "I give up."	

2. **Relax Your Body**—Do deep breathing, tense and release muscles, count to 10, and so forth.

3. **Use "Coping Self-Talk"**—Examples of coping self-talk include the following:
   - "Take it easy."
   - "Don't let it bug you."
   - "I can handle this."
   - "I'm going to be OK."
   - "Stay cool."
   - "Relax."
   - "I'll try my best."

4. **Taking Effective Action**—Walk away, ignore it, take a walk, try to discuss it, express feelings, use problem solving, and so forth.

From *Skills Training for Children with Behavior Disorders: A Parent and Therapist Guidebook* by Michael L. Bloomquist. © 1996 The Guilford Press.

4

Examining and Changing Parents' Thoughts

The way a parent thinks about his or her child or self affects that parent's behavior toward the child, which ultimately is likely to affect the child's behavior. Helpful thoughts are more likely to result in more positive parent–child interactions and positive child behavior. A habitual pattern of negative or inaccurate thoughts could result in the opposite outcome. This chapter will help the parent understand how thoughts can influence parent–child relationships and the child, as well as provide several ideas about how to change unhelpful thoughts.

There's No Hope

James and Shayla are the parents of 14-year-old Tanya. Tanya has "always been a problem." Her parents recall that since kindergarten they have been getting notes and calls from teachers about her disruptive behavior in the classroom. At home, she has been a significant challenge since her birth. She has seen psychologists and psychiatrists and has been involved in special education services at school. Recently, she has been "running around" and is hardly ever at home. She doesn't tell her parents where she is going, what she will be doing, or who she is with. She has been truant from school and has repeatedly broken the house curfew. Her parents wonder if she's starting to experiment with alcohol.

One Saturday night, after Tanya missed yet another midnight curfew, James and Shayla were having a conversation. They were both very frustrated. James said, "I give up! There's nothing more I can do. It seems like we have no control over Tanya anymore." Shayla responds, "I feel like I have failed as a parent. Our family is such a mess. Tanya is heading for trouble." (These thoughts are very typical of James and Shayla.)

WHAT ARE UNHELPFUL PARENT THOUGHTS?

Many mental health professionals have studied the relationship between parents' thoughts and parent–child interaction problems. Research and clinical experience shows that **parents' thoughts about their children and themselves affect parent–child relationships and the child's development of emotional/behavioral prob-**

lems. Parents who are prone to using harsh, punitive discipline often think their child is solely the cause of that child's misbehavior. They may not realize that their own parenting behavior or other factors may also contribute to the child's behavior problems. These parents may also expect their child to do things that the child is developmentally unable to do. Expecting such behavior, when the child can't do it, sets up negative parent–child interactions. Parents who believe their child's behavior is out of the parents' control have also been found to have children with behavior problems. Parents who blame themselves, their spouse/partner, or school personnel may not be able to take effective action for the child. For these reasons, it is very important that parents examine and, if needed, change their own thoughts.

CHANGING UNHELPFUL PARENT THOUGHTS

A parent can change the way he or she thinks about something. **There are three stages involved in changing unhelpful parent thoughts: (1) Identify the unhelpful thoughts, (2) understand the unhelpful nature of these thoughts, and (3) counter these unhelpful thoughts with more helpful thoughts.**

The first step is identifying one's own unhelpful thoughts. Do a self-evaluation of your thoughts by completing the Unhelpful Parent Thoughts chart found at the end of this chapter. The next step is to understand the unhelpful nature of these thoughts. This can be accomplished by asking yourself the questions found at the bottom of the chart.

As an example, let's examine the thought, "My child acts up on purpose," using the questions from the bottom of the chart. **What is unhelpful about this thought?** There may be times when your child misbehaves without even being aware of it. Your own parenting behavior may also be contributing to the child's misbehavior. If you have this thought, you may not be examining your own contribution to the problem. Even if it is true, is it helpful to keep thinking the thought? **How would this thought influence my behavior toward my child?** If you assume your child misbehaves on purpose, you are more likely to blame her, get angry with her, or punish her. **How would my behavior, which relates to my thought, affect my child?** If you think of your child as misbehaving on purpose, it could lead you to blame, punish, and so forth, and it sends a negative "message" to her. She is more likely to blame herself, and your behavior may tell the child that she is "not good enough." Over time, your behavior might lower your child's self-esteem. Ask yourself similar questions for other unhelpful thoughts that you have checked off for yourself.

Once you understand the unhelpful nature of these thoughts, then you can change them to be more helpful. A technique known as "countering" is often useful in this regard. **Countering involves rethinking your thoughts in a more helpful manner.** To accomplish this, you can use the Helpful "Counter" Thoughts for Parents chart found at the end of this chapter. The counter thoughts listed on the

Helpful chart correspond directly to the unhelpful thoughts on the Unhelpful chart. For example, the previously listed Unhelpful Thought 1 can be countered with Helpful Thought 1.

Carefully examine the helpful counter thoughts. Ask yourself the questions at the bottom of the Helpful "Counter" Thoughts for Parents chart. Chances are your answers to the questions pertaining to helpful thoughts are more favorable than your answers regarding the unhelpful thoughts.

UNDERSTANDING NORMAL CHILD DEVELOPMENT

It is important to examine your expectations for your child and determine whether or not they are developmentally appropriate. The developmental norms in Table 4 provide a guideline. **Look through the four major areas of child development, and ask yourself whether or not you may be expecting your child to behave in ways that are developmentally beyond her capabilities.** For example, with social development, it would be unhelpful to expect a preschooler to understand other people's thoughts and feelings (i.e., perspective taking), which is more developmentally characteristic of a child in the elementary school years. Becoming familiar with what is developmentally normal can help you adjust your expectations to be more in line with what is realistic for your child's capabilities.

Even if your child "should" be able to achieve a certain behavior, she still may not. For example, it may be typical of an elementary school age child to understand others' thoughts and feelings (i.e., perspective taking). But if you have an elementary school age child who doesn't exhibit this skill, it can be harmful simply to expect it. Perhaps your child needs to have this skill taught to her first. Later chapters will give ideas on how parents can teach a child these and other skills.

Understanding normal child development and thinking of a child's problems as "developmental delays" can also have a positive effect on a parent. In Chapter 1, we discussed various disorders. It is helpful to understand whether or not a child has one of the disruptive behavior disorders, but only thinking of the problem can be demoralizing and doesn't really inform a parent of what to do. **If you think of your child as developmentally delayed, it suggests the child can "catch up," and it also may suggest what to do to help the child.** For example, instead of only thinking that your child has ADHD and ODD, you may benefit from also thinking that she is delayed in self-control development. If she is delayed, then perhaps she can be taught skills to enhance her self-control development.

Look at the four areas of child development displayed in Table 4 to think about where your child might be delayed. For example, you may look at the self-control development column in Table 4 and determine that your elementary school age daughter is still having problems complying with adults' requests (a developmental task usually accomplished in the toddler years). If this were true for your child, it would be wise to concentrate on that developmental task before attempting more advanced developmental skills. In this example, it would be unhelpful to expect

TABLE 4. Developmental Tasks in Four Areas of Child Development

Age	Self-control development	Social development	Academic development	Affective development
Infancy (0–1 yr)	Explores environment using caregiver as a secure base	Attaches with primary caretaker Displays social smile and cry	Explores environment using caregiver as a secure base	Displays basic emotions
Toddler (1–3 yr)	Responds to external control of adults Complies with adults' requests	Separates from caregiver to interact with others Plays with others in a parallel fashion	Is curious about world	Displays more complex emotions Expresses emotions through behavior and play
Preschool (3–6 yr)	Follows rules Talks out loud when playing or as a means to control own behavior	Plays with others in an interactive fashion Cooperates with others Shares with others Helps others Competes with others	Adjusts to being away from parents Develops an attitude of excitement about learning	Expresses emotions verbally Sympathizes with others
Elementary school (6–12 yr)	Uses thoughts to direct own behavior Develops beginning problem-solving skills Manages impulses Develops awareness of own behavior	Understands others' perspectives Conforms to peer group norms and standards Solves social problems Plays fair Has primarily same gender friends	Concentrates and stays on-task Organizes school materials and tasks Begins to develop special skills and interests	Overcomes fears Regulates strong emotions such as anger, frustration, anxiety, sadness
Adolescence (12–20 yr)	Develops more sophisticated problem-solving skills and is more aware of own behavior	Interacts primarily in cliques Has same gender and opposite gender friends "Launches" from family	Consolidates special skills and interests Engages in career planning and preparation	Understands relationship between thoughts, behavior, and emotions Thinks accurately and rationally about self and world

Note. It is assumed that early developmental tasks are mastered and remain operational throughout later development. These are "typical" stages of development. Not all children, however, meet all of these tasks at the same age.

your child to display more advanced self-control development skills (e.g., problem-solving skills) until she masters the earlier skills (e.g., compliance with adults' requests).

SUMMARY POINTS

1. Unhelpful parent thoughts can interfere with being an effective parent.
2. To change unhelpful parent thoughts, you need to identify common unhelpful thoughts, understand the unhelpful nature of these thoughts, and counter the unhelpful thoughts with more helpful thoughts.
3. Try to keep your expectations for your child in line with normal development. Determine where your child is in terms of self-control, social, academic, and affective development to understand your child better.

Let's Give It Our Best Shot

Back to James, Shayla, and Tanya: At one point, James remembers that he had read about parent thoughts with challenging children. He realizes that his thoughts are not very helpful and states, "You know, honey, we just can't give up. This is our daughter we're talking about. We need to keep trying." During a long discussion, James and Shayla realize that they can't predict the future, but that, if they don't try something, their future fears may come true. They realize that it doesn't help to blame themselves; rather, they need to take some action. At that point, James and Shayla start thinking about different ways in which they might approach the challenge of parenting Tanya.

CHARTS FOR CHAPTER 4

UNHELPFUL PARENT THOUGHTS

Listed below are a variety of common thoughts that parents of children with behavior problems may have. Read each thought and indicate how frequently that thought (or a similar thought) typically occurs for you over an average week. There are no right or wrong answers to these questions. Use the 5-point rating scale to help you answer these questions.

1	2	3	4	5
Not at all	Sometimes	Moderately often	All the time	Often

Unhelpful Thoughts about the Child

1.____ My child is behaving like a brat.
2.____ My child acts up on purpose.
3.____ My child is the cause of most of our family problems.
4.____ My child is just trying to get attention.
5.____ My child's future is bleak. When he/she grows up, he/she will probably be irresponsible, a criminal, a high school dropout, and so forth.
6.____ My child should behave like other children. I shouldn't have to make allowances for my child.
7.____ My child must do well in school, sports, scouts, and so forth. It is unacceptable if my child does not do well in these activities.
8.____ My child has many problems. My child does not fit in with other children, and so forth.

Unhelpful Thoughts about Self/Others

9.____ It is my fault that my child has a problem.
10.____ If I wasn't such a poor parent, my child would be better off.
11.____ It is his/her fault (other parent) that my child is this way.
12.____ If he/she (other parent) wasn't such a poor parent, may child would be better off.
13.____ Our family is a mess.
14.____ I can't make mistakes in parenting my child.
15.____ I give up. There is nothing more I can do for my child.
16.____ I have no control over my child. I have tried everything, and so forth.
17.____ The teacher is more of a problem than my child.
18.____ The teacher complains too much about my child.

Unhelpful Thoughts about Who Needs to Change

19.____ My child is the one who needs to change. All of us would be better off if my child would change.
20.____ I am the one who needs to change. My family would be better off if I would change.
21.____ My spouse/partner needs to change. We would all be better off if he/she would change.
22.____ The teacher needs to change. We would be better off if he/she would change.
23.____ Medications are the answer. Medications will change my child.

For each thought you rated a 3, 4, or 5, ask yourself the following questions:

1.____ What is unhelpful about this thought?
2.____ How would this thought influence my behavior toward my child?
3.____ How would my behavior, which relates to my thoughts, affect my child?

HELPFUL "COUNTER" THOUGHTS FOR PARENTS

Listed below are "counter" thoughts that parents can think instead of unhelpful thoughts. Unhelpful Thought #1 corresponds to Helpful Thought #1 and so on. Compare the unhelpful thoughts to the helpful thoughts.

Helpful Thoughts about the Child

1. My child behaves positively too.
2. It doesn't matter whose fault it is. What matters are solutions to the problems.
3. It is not just my child. I also play a role in the problem.
4. My child may be trying to get attention.
5. I'm being irrational. I have no proof that my child will continue to have problems. I need to wait for the future.
6. I can't just expect my child to behave. My child needs to be taught how to behave.
7. I need to accept my child. It's OK if my child is not great at school, sports, scouts, and so forth. I need to focus on my child's strengths.
8. It will be more helpful to focus on my child's strengths and not on weaknesses or "failures."

Helpful Thoughts about Self/Others

9. It is not just my fault; my child also plays a role in the problem.
10. It doesn't help to blame myself. I will focus on solutions to the problem.
11. It doesn't help to blame him/her (other parent). We need to work together.
12. It doesn't matter whose fault it is. I will focus on solutions to the problems.
13. It doesn't help to think about the family as being all messed up. Instead we need to take action.
14. My child is perhaps more challenging to parent than others, and therefore I will make mistakes. I need to accept the fact that I am going to make mistakes.
15. I have to parent my child. I have no choice. I need to think of new ways to parent my child.
16. My belief that I have no control over my child might be contributing to the problem. Many things are in my control. I need to figure out what I can do to parent my child.
17. It doesn't matter whose fault it is. We need to collaborate and work with the teacher.
18. It doesn't help to blame the teacher. My child can be a handful who would challenge any teacher. We need to work together with the teacher.

Helpful Thoughts about Who Needs to Change

19. It's unhelpful to think of my child as the only one needing to change. We all need to change.
20. It's unhelpful to think only of myself as needing to chang.e We all need to change.
21. It's unhelpful to think of my spouse/partner as being the only one who needs to change. We all need to change.
22. It's unhelpful to think only the teacher needs to change. We all need to work together.
23. Medications may help, but will not solve all the problems. We will also need to work hard to cope with the problems.

Ask yourself the following questions about these helpful thoughts:

1. What is helpful about this thought?
2. How would this thought influence my behavior toward my child?
3. How would my behavior, which relates to my thought, affect my child?

From *Skills Training for Children with Behavior Disorders: A Parent and Therapist Guidebook* by Michael L. Bloomquist. © 1996 The Guilford Press

5

Increasing Parental Involvement and Positive Reinforcement

Parents need to have a close emotional bond with their children and provide them with much positive reinforcement. It is also critical that the parents be involved—spend time and feel "connected"—with their children. Parents who do these things are more likely to have better adjusted children. This chapter provides information on how to increase involvement and positive reinforcement with children.

Sometimes the Best Things Go Unnoticed

Marcia is a busy, working, single mother. She has an 8-year-old ADHD son, Carlos. Marcia's life is hectic. There seems to be too much to do—work, housekeeping, errands, and so on. Occasionally Marcia needs a break and relaxes by reading or going out with friends.

There doesn't seem to be enough time for Carlos. He does a lot of independent things around the house such as playing, drawing, and reading. Marcia often doesn't pay much attention to him because she has so much work to do. Sometimes she'll ask Carlos to do household chores such as clean his room or clear the dishes. Carlos seems to "drag his feet" and rarely gets tasks done. Marcia nags him to get these things done. She and Carlos get into many power struggles and conflicts about him completing these household chores. Marcia thinks that they are arguing and yelling at each other too much. She finds herself not wanting to spend much time with Carlos.

WHAT IS INVOLVEMENT AND POSITIVE REINFORCEMENT?

Child and family experts universally agree that being involved—spending time together and fostering an emotional bond between parent and child—is extremely important for every child's psychological development. Yet parents often find themselves uninvolved and emotionally distant from their child. This can be especially true if one is parenting a child with behavior problems who may not always be enjoyable to spend time with. It is important to know, however, that

uninvolvement and emotional distance between parent and child can make child and family problems grow and intensify.

Positive reinforcement involves giving a child attention, or something extra, for "good" behavior. In some studies, researchers have observed families of children known for behavior problems, and families of children without behavior problems. These studies show that in families of children with behavior problems, the parents do not pay as much attention to their child's neutral or positive behavior as they do to their negative behavior. The opposite is true in families of children without behavior problems. **Apparently positive reinforcement of good behavior is related to well-behaved children.** It's difficult to know what causes what (i.e., does parental positive reinforcement cause well-behaved children, or do well-behaved children elicit more positive parent reinforcement?), but there is a definite connection. Many therapists have stressed the importance of building a good parent–child relationship and helping the parent to provide more positive reinforcement as part of parent–child therapy.

POSITIVE ACTIVITY SCHEDULING

Positive activity scheduling can be used to increase involvement and to improve positive parent–child interactions. Positive activity scheduling involves a parent spending time with a child in **child-directed activities** while doing **parent relationship building behaviors** during these special times. The goal is to incorporate involvement activities into the average week and to change parent behaviors during these activities in order to build a relationship with a child. This typically is accomplished through a four-step procedure. It works best to sit down with your child and accomplish these steps together. Try to work together with each having input.

Step 1: List Activities

List as many activities as possible that you and your child enjoy doing together that can be accomplished in 30 minutes or less. Let your child select the activity.

Examples of activities that work well are as follows:

- Go for a walk
- Ride bikes
- Play a game
- Play with cars/dolls
- Play catch
- Play one-on-one basketball
- Talk
- Go for a drive
- Bowl
- Do a spontaneous activity
- Build something
- Bake/cook something

Step 2: Schedule "Appointments" with Child

Schedule two or more 30-minute appointments per week when you and your child will engage in one or more of the above activities together (indicate day, date, and time). Make sure that you and your child have agreed on this time and have marked it on a calendar. If something comes up and you can't keep the appointment, be sure to reschedule it.

Step 3: Modify Parent Behavior during Activity

During the activity, **allow the child to "direct" the play or activity while you try to behave in a responsive way.** While your child is leading the play or activity, **try to increase praising, describing, and touching.**

Examples of these behaviors are as follows:

    I. **Praising**—verbally reinforcing the child during the activity.
- "That looks good."
- "You did a nice job."
- "Good boy."
- "Good girl."
- "That's great!"
- "It looks nice."

    II. **Describing**—comments that describe what the child is doing, how the child might be feeling, what the child is experiencing, where the child is, and so forth during the activity.
- "You're looking at the toys."
- "You caught the ball!"
- "You look happy!"
- "You're hiding."
- "You seem to be mad."
- "It looks like you're thinking."

    III. **Touching**—any positive physical contact with the child during the activity.
- Hugs
- Kisses
- Touching on the shoulder
- Patting the head

While interacting with your child, **try to avoid or reduce questions, commands, and criticisms.**

Examples of these behaviors are as follows:

    I. **Questions**—when the parent asks the child what he is doing, why he is doing that, and so forth during the activity.
- "Why did you throw the ball?"
- "How about if we play a game?"
- "Why are you looking so mad?"

    II. **Commands**—when a parent tells a child what to do during the activity.
- "Put the dolls in the house."
- "Shake the dice."

- "You bat and I'll pitch."
- "Take a walk with me."

III. **Criticisms**—when the parent criticizes the child's behavior during the activity.

- "That doesn't look right."
- "I'll show you how to do it right."
- "Try harder next time."
- "You're supposed to do it this way."

Try interacting with your child in this manner. You'll notice that he appreciates and responds to the three positive parenting behaviors and may become upset, or at least somewhat tense, when you are engaging in the three negative parenting behaviors. This is not to say that parents would never ask questions, give commands, or criticize their child. These parent behaviors, however, are not necessary or helpful during positive activity times with the child.

Step 4: Evaluate Effects of Activity

After the activity has been completed, it can be helpful for you and your child to talk to each other and discuss your observations and feelings about the time together. Try to listen actively to what your child has to say, and try to offer as much positive feedback to your child as possible.

Try this for several weeks to "get things going." After that, it may be more natural and automatic for you and your child to interact in this positive way during play and special time activities.

SPECIAL TALK TIME

Every child can benefit from having a parent who "really listens" to him. The purpose of Special Talk Time is to talk with the child about what he is experiencing and going through. During these special conversation times, **the goal is to focus completely on your child and strive to understand how your child is feeling.** It is okay to ask your child some questions, but primarily strive to create an atmosphere in which your child feels free to talk to you about whatever is on his mind. Try to get your child to talk about what he is doing, what his interests are, how he feels, about problems that he may be experiencing, and about successes he may have had recently.

It may be helpful to schedule Special Talk Time with your child to make sure that these conversation times actually happen. One good idea is to get into a routine of asking your child these things each day at dinner or at the end of the day just before bed.

BE AVAILABLE AND DO SPECIAL ACTIVITIES

To be truly involved, you must demonstrate that you are there for your child. If you are involved, your child will seek you out when really needed. **It's important to make a great effort to be involved in your child's activities and interests.** Try to attend teacher conferences, watch little league games, attend dance recitals, and so forth. By doing so, your behavior demonstrates that you are involved with your child.

It can also be helpful occasionally to embark on special relationship building activities. Spending a large block of time one-on-one with your child can sometimes accomplish this objective. Examples of these activities are going out to dinner, on a weekend camping trip, or on a brief vacation. These activities provide opportunities to build and strengthen parent–child relationships.

NOTICING POSITIVE CHILD BEHAVIOR

It is surprising that parents often do not notice when their child is behaving positively. It is also surprising that simply noticing positive child behavior can not only increase the child's positive behavior, but can also improve the parent–child relationship. A fairly simple procedure can be used by a parent to notice the child's positive behavior and to make sure the child knows that he is being noticed.

A "Good Behavior Box" can be a helpful way to acknowledge a child's positive behavior. Keep a box on a counter, refrigerator, table, or other convieniant place in your home and label it the Good Behavior Box. When you notice your child behaving positively (e.g., sharing, sitting quietly, helping with a household chore, and so forth), take out a piece of paper, write down what you saw, and put it in the box. You may want to tell your child that you are putting a note in the box. At the end of the day, spend time with your child reviewing all the notes in the box. Make sure your child understands that you have noticed his positive behavior, and, in so doing, he will also become more aware of that behavior.

PARENTAL SELF-MONITORING AND GOAL SETTING TO INCREASE REINFORCEMENT

As was stated earlier, parents often find themselves paying more attention to negative behavior than positive behavior, and having more negative interactions than positive interactions with their child. Parents often realize they are doing this but find the habit hard to break. It requires a conscious effort on the parents' part to notice and reinforce positive child behavior more, while also downplaying mild negative child behavior. Parents can become more aware of themselves through a self-monitoring and goal-setting procedure. **Parental self-monitoring and goal** setting involves learning to observe one's own behavior and setting goals to change behavior.

Step 1: List Positive Target Behaviors to Reinforce

Make a list of your child's positive behaviors that you would like to reinforce more. Make sure your child is capable of doing the behaviors. Target positive behaviors that are the opposite of the usual problem behaviors for your child.

Examples of positive behaviors to reinforce might include the following:

- Listening to and obeying parental commands
- Sharing with sibling
- Engaging in quiet activities
- Cleaning up toys without being told
- Expressing feelings
- Solving problems
- Doing homework

Step 2: Determine How You Will Reinforce Positive Target Behaviors

Make a list of behaviors you will use to respond to your child's positive behavior. Think about behaviors you could do that you think will be positive and reinforcing to your child. Ask yourself if the child would like your response.

Examples of positive and reinforcing parent behaviors might include the following:

- Praising
- Touching
- Smiling
- Talking to the child
- Playing a game with the child
- Describing what the child is doing

Step 3: List Negative Child Behaviors to Ignore

Make a list of mild negative child behaviors that you would like to ignore.

Examples of mild negative child behaviors might include the following:

- Pouting
- Whining
- Throwing mild tantrums
- Slamming the door when mad

- Belching
- Throwing a toy when mad

Step 4: Determine How You Will Ignore Mild Negative Child Behaviors

Your response will be automatically to ignore these mild negative behaviors. Ignoring means you will stop all attention to the child. You will turn your head, walk away, and so on.

Step 5a: Implement a Formal Parental Self-Monitoring and Goal-Setting Procedure

You can use the Parent Self-Monitoring and Goal Setting chart found at the end of this chapter to encourage positive child behavior and ignore mild negative child behavior. Two tasks are accomplished by utilizing this chart and procedure. First, you learn to recognize positive child behavior and reinforce this behavior. For example, you may try to monitor your child when sharing with a sibling and respond by praising that behavior. Second, you learn to recognize mild negative child behavior and to ignore it. For example, you may monitor when your child is whining and respond by ignoring that behavior. These two goals are accomplished through subtle behavior modification of natural ongoing interactions between you and your child.

You can use the information from Steps 1–4 as discussed above with the Parent Self-Monitoring and Goal Setting chart. You should also follow the directions on the chart. Set a designated time you will use this chart (e.g., Saturday 8 A.M.–noon). You can change the targeted behaviors on the chart on different days, if you like. Use the chart as often as you like until you are better at self-monitoring and have reached your goals.

Some parents also allow their child to see the Parent Self-Monitoring and Goal Setting chart as the parent completes it. You could hang the chart on the refrigerator (or similar place) to remind you. Then you let your child observe you filling it out. It helps some children to observe that you are making the effort to change.

Step 5b: Implement an Informal Parental Self-Monitoring and Goal-Setting Procedure

If you think the formal parental self-monitoring is too difficult, you could do it more informally. Before doing this informally, it would still be helpful to read the previous section on the formal procedure to understand the rationale and method better.

The basic idea with informal parental self-monitoring and goal setting is still to increase parental positive reinforcement of positive behavior and ignoring of mild negative behavior. You should still do Steps 1–4 as stated in the above section. Step 5b is accomplished with marbles! Put three marbles (or more if you prefer) in one of your pockets. Each time you reach into your pocket, the marbles will remind you to notice and praise your child. Each time you praise your child, take one marble from your pocket and put it with the other one. Once you have transferred all the marbles, you have reached the goal. As for ignoring, just try to be more aware of it, and don't respond to mild behavior problems.

VALUES CLARIFICATION REGARDING CHILDREN

You are encouraged to reread the section on values clarification regarding children in Chapter 3. Parents must value their child over most other aspects of life to be able to get truly involved with that child.

REINFORCEMENT

In many ways, this chapter is about reinforcing a child in order to improve parent–child relationships and child behavior. Reinforcement is also important in disciplining children and in teaching them new skills. Indeed, to do many of the discipline and skills building procedures discussed in the remainder of this book, it is necessary to be able to use reinforcement effectively to help children develop new behaviors. Thus far, reinforcement has been discussed in general terms. This section will present specific ideas on how to select reinforcers for children to be used in discipline and skills training with children.

The first step in selecting a reinforcer is to **ask your child what is reinforcing.** The Reinforcement Ideas chart found at the end of this chapter will give you some ideas. It may be helpful to review this chart with your child. In any event, you and he should discuss the reinforcer. Make sure it will really motivate and catch his interest. Next, and equally as important, **make sure the reinforcer is realistic for you to give.**

It is important to vary the reinforcer. Children can become used to, and bored by, the same old reinforcer. A powerful way to vary the reinforcer is to use a reinforcement menu. This involves creating a variety of reinforcers (10–15 reinforcers are preferable) and writing them down on a menu. A mystery reinforcer, where the child earns something without knowing what it is, is also very motivating for most children. When your child meets his behavior expectation, he would then be able to select one reinforcer from the reinforcement menu. If a child wants to earn a big reward (e.g., tape player, concert, etc.), you could use a token system. Each day he could earn tokens to be exchanged later for a bigger reward. See the Examples: Reinforcement Menu chart found at the end of this chapter for more ideas.

Reinforcers don't always have to be "extras." It's OK to take away privileges your child may take for granted and then allow him to "earn them back." For example, a child may find a video game reinforcing. A parent could take this privilege away and make the child adhere to a behavior expectation to earn video game time. Earning a privilege that may be taken for granted can be reinforcing to a child.

Try to emphasize social and privilege reinforcers over material reinforcers. Material reinforcers (e.g., toys, cars, money, etc.) often lose their reinforcing value and are very expensive. As was mentioned earlier, many children benefit from more involvement with their parents. Reinforcement involving time and activities with caregivers can be reinforcing and promote involvement at the same time.

After the reinforcer is selected, make sure the child knows what he has to do to earn it. Many of the procedures discussed in Chapters 7–14 state explicitly what a child must do to earn reinforcement. The link between the child's behavior and the reinforcement needs to be clear to the child.

SUMMARY POINTS

1. Parents who are highly involved with their children and provide them with frequent positive reinforcement are more likely to have well-behaved children.
2. Positive activity scheduling increases parental involvement with children. Try to engage in child-directed special activities with your child. During these special activities, attempt to increase describing, praising, and touching behaviors, and decrease commands, questions, and criticism.
3. Use parental self-monitoring and goal setting to become more aware of your child's and your own behavior. This awareness can help you learn to reinforce positive behavior and ignore mild negative behavior more often.
4. Ask your child for input and use a menu when coming up with formal reinforcers to be used with discipline and skills training procedures with your child.

Getting Involved

Back to Marcia and Carlos: Marcia decides to take some action to turn things around. She decides to set aside several times each week for "special time" with Carlos. She also decides to try informal self-monitoring and goal setting. She targets Carlos's independent play activity as something she should praise and notice. She is also going to try to get more involved in his school and sports activities. After Marcia and Carlos are feeling better about one another, she intends to implement some different discipline techniques as well.

CHARTS FOR CHAPTER 5

PARENT SELF-MONITORING AND GOAL SETTING

Parent name:_____

Child name: _____

Date and time: _____

Directions: Write down positive childs behaviors you will try to notice/reinforce and how you will respond. Also write down which mild negative behavior you will try to ignore. Set a time interval for using the chart. Rate yourself using the 5-point scale each time you use the chart to evaluate how it went.

Positive Child Behaviors I Will Notice and Reinforce

1. **When my child (positive behavior)** _____
   I will (positive response) _____
   _____

2. **How well did I accomplish my goal?** (circle one)

1	2	3	4	5
Not at all	A little	OK	Pretty good	Great

Mild Negative Child Behaviors I Will Ignore

3. **When my child (mild negative child behavior)** _____
   I will ignore it.

4. **How well did I accomplish my goal?** (circle one)

1	2	3	4	5
Not at all	A little	OK	Pretty good	Great

From *Skills Training for Children with Behavior Disorders: A Parent and Therapist Guidebook* by Michael L. Bloomquist. © 1996 The Guilford Press.

EXAMPLE:
PARENT SELF-MONITORING AND GOAL SETTING

Parent name: *Marcia*

Child name: *Carlos*

Date and time: *Tuesday after school to bedtime*

Directions: Write down positive childs behaviors you will try to notice/reinforce and how you will respond. Also write down which mild negative behavior you will try to ignore. Set a time interval for using the chart. Rate yourself using the 5-point scale each time you use the chart to evaluate how it went.

Positive Child Behaviors I Will Notice and Reinforce

1. **When my child (positive behavior)** *shares with sister*
   I will (positive response) *praise*

2. **How well did I accomplish my goal?** (circle one)

1	2	3	④	5
Not at all	A little	OK	Pretty good	Great

Mild Negative Child Behaviors I Will Ignore

3. **When my child (mild negative child behavior)** *whines*
   I will ignore it.

4. **How well did I accomplish my goal?** (circle one)

1	2	③	4	5
Not at all	A little	OK	Pretty good	Great

From *Skills Training for Children with Behavior Disorders: A Parent and Therapist Guidebook* by Michael L. Bloomquist. © 1996 The Guilford Press.

REINFORCEMENT IDEAS

1. Favorite dessert
2. Favorite meal
3. Special snack
4. Small toy
5. Sports equipment
6. Records/tapes
7. Rent special videos
8. Furnishing for room
9. Attention
10. Praise
11. Post work
12. Special privileges
13. Private time in room
14. Special TV privileges
15. Stay up late
16. Have a friend over for dinner or for overnight
17. Special time with one parent
18. Go to a movie
19. Go to a concert
20. Go on a special trip
21. Attend a sporting event
22. Camping
23. Traveling
24. Have a party
25. Tokens for general exchange

Note. Make sure the reward is motivating for the child and is realistic for the parent to give to the child.

From *Skills Training for Children with Behavior Disorders: A Parent and Therapist Guidebook* by Michael L. Bloomquist. © 1996 The Guilford Press.

EXAMPLES: REINFORCEMENT MENU

For an 8-year-old

____ Use of TV for 2 hours during 1 day

____ Use of computer video game for 2 hours during 1 day

____ Take a 30-minute walk with Mom

____ Play one-on-one basketball with Dad for 30 minutes

____ Special snack at bedtime

____ Bike riding with both parents for 30 minutes

____ Dad cooks a favorite meal

____ Get to have a friend over for supper

____ Earn one token per day until collects five tokens to exchange for a movie

____ Earn one token per day until collects seven tokens to exchange for a 1-day fishing outing with a parent

____ Mystery reinforcer

For a 16-year-old

____ Many of above might work

____ Extra driving privileges for a day

____ Stay out 30 minutes late

____ Get to stay on phone extra 30 minutes past phone curfew

____ Earn a token per day until collects five tokens to exchange for a concert

From *Skills Training for Children with Behavior Disorders: A Parent and Therapist Guidebook* by Michael L. Bloomquist. © 1996 The Guilford Press.

6

Enhancing Positive Family Interaction Skills

Many families find their members interacting with each other mostly in a negative manner. This chapter deals with family interaction skills such as communication, problem solving, and anger/conflict management. All concepts in this chapter are also applicable to couples. Children under the age of 8 years may not benefit from the exercises described.

Why Do You Always Do That?

Steve and Martha are the parents of 14-year-old Mike. It's 10 P.M. on a school night and Mike is out past his 9 P.M. curfew. He finally comes in, and the following discussion takes place:

STEVE *(angry and yelling):* Do you see what time it is? How many times have we told you to be in by 9 o'clock?

MIKE *(annoyed and voice raised):* Everyone else gets to stay out later than me. Why can't I? You guys aren't fair.

MARTHA *(angry and firm tone):* We've told you time and time again that you need to be in by 9 o'clock. If you don't get in by 9 o'clock, then you're not going to get to bed on time, you'll stay up too late, and you won't get enough sleep. Besides that, we're not sure where you are, we'd like to know what you're up to, and we don't think it's right for a child your age to be out past 9 P.M. When I was your age, I had to be in much earlier than you do. You have a lot more privileges than I had when I was your age. If my father set a curfew, I obeyed it. You're starting a pattern here that's going to turn into a much bigger problem in the future.

STEVE *(to Mike, voice raised):* I'm sick of you causing so many problems in this house.

MIKE *(angry):* I'm sick of you too. You guys are so damn unfair.

MARTHA: This is just another example of you thinking you can run the show. You'd better shape up, young man!

WHAT ARE FAMILY INTERACTION PROBLEMS?

It is no surprise that families that do not interact together very positively or effectively experience problems. Families with poor communication skills often find themselves blaming, putting each other down, not listening, and so forth. Families that are poor problem solvers find themselves repeatedly trying to solve the same problems over and over using ineffective means. These families also find it difficult to resolve anger and conflict between each other. They tend to escalate each other's angry behavior and sometimes find themselves yelling, and/or even getting into physical fights. Families characterized by these types of interactions are more likely to have children with emotional and/or behavioral problems.

FAMILY COMMUNICATION SKILLS

Family communication is an essential family interaction skill. Many families in distress tend to be vague, blame each other, talk on and on, not listen, interrupt each other, put each other down, yell, get off the topic, and so forth. **Good communication skills are necessary to be able to solve family problems and resolve family conflicts.**

Step 1: Introduce Family Communication Skills to the Family

To introduce communication skills to the family, it is necessary to arrange and conduct a meeting with all family members. This meeting should be at a convenient time for everyone. It is absolutely necessary that there be no particular problem discussed, and that everyone is feeling good about being with each other. Don't introduce these skills and try to resolve a big problem.

Give each member of the family a copy of the Family Communication Skills chart found at the end of this chapter. Everyone should look over the chart carefully. First, discuss the "DON'Ts." Ask each member to do self-evaluation to determine which DON'Ts apply to themselves. As long as the tone of the meeting remains positive, family members can give each other feedback about specific DON'Ts they see in the other family members. Then, it is necessary for each family member to declare one or two "DOs" that they will work on while trying to improve communication within the family. Usually, the DOs selected to work on are the opposite of the DON'Ts each member views as a problem for him- or herself. (The chart is designed with the DON'Ts opposite the corresponding DOs.)

Step 2: Practice Family Communication Skills

It would be helpful if family members took turns demonstrating and role playing examples of the DON'Ts and the DOs. For example, you may role play a "lecture" or "sermon" such as the following: "It is important for you to clean up your room when I tell you. If you don't start learning how to clean up now, you will probably be a slob the rest of your life. You will never be able to get a good job, get married, or have a family if you don't know how to clean up after yourself. When I was your age, my parents always made me clean up, and I did not give them any trouble. . . ." Next, try to model a brief and direct approach to the same problem by saying, "I want you to clean up your room right now." A brother may perhaps model poor listening such as sitting back in the chair, crossing arms, staring away, and so forth. The brother could then model better listening such as leaning forward, giving feedback, making good eye contact. Ideally the family members would take turns practicing the DON'Ts and the DOs in a similar manner. Encourage family members to coach one another as they practice specific skills.

At first, practice should be somewhat formal and done with neutral or easy problems and situations. The family could conduct another meeting, or use the communication skills spontaneously, to solve an easy problem. It would be helpful if all family members had the Family Communication Skills chart in their hands as they try to discuss something. Examples of neutral or easy problems to discuss would be what to watch on TV that night, planning how each family member will get to a sibling's baseball game after school/work, or the mother stating her intentions for her activities that evening. Each family member would practice the communication skills and would give each other feedback about DON'Ts and DOs. Family members would try to practice the skills until they feel they have learned them.

One exercise a family could try is to audio- or videotape a family discussion. While taping, practice using the communication skills discussing an easy topic. Play back the recording to review and learn how to improve family communication further.

Step 3: Use Family Communication Skills in Real Life

After the family has practiced and learned the communication skills, the family could try to use them to solve more difficult and "real" problems. It would be helpful, again, if the family members had the Family Communication Skills chart in their hands while carrying on the discussion. Examples of more difficult and real problems to discuss would be homework, rules of the house, when individuals should come in from outside, parents' concerns regarding a child's grades, child's concerns regarding parents' rules, and so forth.

Here are several other tips that may help the family learn communication skills. One idea is to post copies of the Family Communication Skills chart in conveniently accessible places within the home. For example, posting the chart on a refrigerator or a bulletin board might be helpful. Another hint is to review and discuss the communication skills periodically to maintain the improvements, because many family members utilize communication skills for a while but later forget them. (See the "Using All Family Interaction Skills Together" section at the end of this chapter.)

The Working on Family Communication Goals chart found at the end of this chapter can also be used to help get things going to use communication skills in real life. Each family member writes one or two communication DOs they will try to increase. Set a time period that family members agree to use the chart (e.g., Tuesday evening from 5 P.M. to 8 P.M.). At the end of the designated time period, family members could rate themselves as to how well they accomplished the goals. Family members could also give each other feedback about how they observed the each other working on the goals. Different goals could be set on different days. Use the procedure as many times as you feel necessary to improve family communication.

FAMILY PROBLEM SOLVING

A sure sign a family is having problems is when members can't solve day-to-day problems. Families who are having difficulties seem to hash over the same problems repeatedly. They find it difficult to identify the problem. They keep doing the same things over and over. Occasionally, they think of solutions, but don't really use them. The goal of family problem solving is to help families define problems, generate alternatives, think of consequences of possible solutions, pick a solution, and then actually use the solution effectively. **It will be helpful for the family to have developed good family communication skills before trying family problem solving.**

Step 1: Introduce Family Problem-Solving Skills to the Family

As with family communication skills training, the first step is to conduct a meeting that is convenient for everyone and where everyone is feeling good and is not bothered by any particular issue. You may need to act as a moderator for the meeting.

Next give everyone a copy of the Family Problem Solving chart found at the end of this chapter. The family members should discuss how good they think their family is currently at family problem solving. Family members should determine whether or not they want to work toward a goal of their family improving family problem solving. Family members should then review all the steps. They should talk through each of the steps and make sure that everyone understands the purpose of each step.

Step 2: Practice Family Problem-Solving Skills

After the family problem-solving skills have been introduced, the family members need to practice using them to solve relatively neutral or easy problems. At first, try to solve a contrived problem such as how to spend $10,000 that your family just won in the lottery. Next try to solve real-life, easy problems such as deciding what to have for dinner, where to go for an evening out, what show to watch on TV, and so forth.

It is highly recommended that you and your family practice family problem solving in a formal way using the Family Problem-Solving Worksheet found at the end of this chapter. This worksheet requires the family to write down each step of the family problem-solving process. For example, use the Family Problem-Solving Worksheet to solve the problem of how to spend the mythical $10,000 your family just won in the lottery. Then use this worksheet later to solve other family problems.

As with family communication skills, it may be helpful to make an audio- or videotape of the family using family problem solving. The family could review the recording to give each other constructive feedback and to learn.

Step 3: Use Family Problem Solving in Real Life

The final step is to use family problem solving with real-life, difficult problems. It may be helpful to have the Family Problem Solving chart available to family members while discussing these difficult issues. It is critical that family members go through each step very carefully, one at a time. It is also essential that family members use good communication skills while trying to solve these problems. (See the "Using All Family Interaction Skills Together" section at the end of this chapter.)

One note of caution about family problem solving: **Make sure your child understands that all disputes are not open to negotiation and family problem solving.** The parent is still in charge and with some issues the parent holds "veto" power because he or she knows what's best for the child.

FAMILY ANGER/CONFLICT MANAGEMENT

Family communication and problem-solving skills are essential to family life. There are times, however, when there is so much conflict in a family, that it is impossible to use these valuable skills. However, this makes it even more important to solve the problems that keep creating the conflict! In these cases, it is necessary for the family to work on family communication and problem-solving skills first with neutral and easy situations only. **It may be a good idea to use the communication and problem-solving skills along with family anger/conflict management skills.**

Step 1: Introduce Family Anger/Conflict Management Skills to the Family

Again, to accomplish many of these goals, it may be necessary to have a family meeting. You may need to act as a moderator.

The first task for the family is to recognize the "signals" that tell the members of the family that they are angry and that they are having too much conflict. Make sure everyone understands the importance of first recognizing family conflict signals. If you don't recognize anger or conflict, you can't do anything about them. In this regard, it would be helpful to review three different types of anger/conflict signals: (1) body reactions, (2) thoughts, and (3) actions of self/other. All family members should participate in a discussion in which the family tries to generate examples of these types of signals. It is very helpful to have someone write down the family-generated signal examples.

Some signals that could be discussed include the following:

Body signals	Thought signals	Action signals
• Breathing rate increased	• "He's making me mad."	• Raised voices
• Heart rate increased	• "I hate him!"	• Angry facial expressions
• Sweating increased	• "I wish he were dead!"	• Angry body postures
• Face color flushed	• "I'm going to hit her."	• Put-down verbalizations
• Muscle tension increased	• "I wish she would move	• Interrupting
• Voice tone raised	out of the house."	

After the family members learn how to recognize anger/conflict, they need to learn how to cope with it. There are a variety of strategies that can be used to cope with anger/conflict. The most helpful strategy is to separate and take a "time-out." Time-out is used here in a different sense than with trying to teach children to be more compliant (see Chapter 7). Time-out here involves family members separating from each other for a period of time to "cool off." Family members should agree ahead of time that any one of them can call a time-out when someone recognizes that there is too much anger/conflict. The time-out involves separating for some agreed-upon time (e.g., 5 or 10 minutes). While the family members are separated, they practice coping with their own anger and frustration. This might involve deep breathing, tensing and relaxing muscles, and reciting "coping self-statements" to themselves (e.g., saying statements to themselves such as, "I'm not going to let him get to me," "I'm going to try and stay cool," "I'll try to say it a different way to get my point across to him," etc.).

After the family members have settled down and the time-out has elapsed, they come back together and use family communication and problem-solving skills. It is essential that they solve the original issue that caused the conflict.

The Family Anger/Conflict Management and the Family Cool-Down charts found at the end of this chapter summarize all the procedures just discussed. The family members could have one or both of these charts in their hands as they try to solve problems and cope with family anger/conflict.

Step 2: Practice Family Anger/Conflict Management Skills

As before, it is helpful to practice these skills with neutral and easy problems before implementing them with difficult problems. To accomplish this, do some role-play exercises with the family, acting out "pretend" conflict situations. All family members should work together to practice all the skills.

Step 3: Use Family Anger/Conflict Management Skills in Real Life

After all members of the family have learned the skills in practice, they can use them when real-life anger/conflict emerges. When anger/conflict happens, try to use the anger/conflict management skills. It may be difficult, but try to go through each step one by one. After the family has cooled off, try to use family communication and problem-solving skills to solve the original problem that caused the anger/conflict. It may be helpful to post the Family Cool-Down chart for family members to refer to when conflict arises.

USING ALL FAMILY INTERACTION SKILLS TOGETHER

Although we have discussed all of the family interaction skills separately, in actuality, they are usually used together. It might be helpful to post or give family members copies of the charts at the end of this chapter to look at as everyone tries to solve the problems at hand.

Moderator

Another tip to using family interaction skills successfully is to have a moderator. If, for example, a mother and child are having a dispute, the father could ask them to sit down and use the family interaction skills to work out the problem. The father could give the others feedback as they try to solve the problem. Before trying the moderator idea, make sure everyone agrees to this procedure.

Family Meetings

Family meetings involve assembling family members together to work on and/or resolve family issues/problems. It may be a good idea to schedule ongoing family meetings (e.g., meet on Sunday evenings) to discuss family issues. Another strategy is to call on-the-spot family meetings when problems and/or conflicts emerge.

Apologize and Analyze

This stuff is hard to do. Old habits are difficult to break. Your family will not be good at this initially. It may be helpful to review family interaction skills even after a big blow-up. If a problem occurs, someone could apologize and then family members could analyze what just happened and learn from it. Just because it didn't go well is no reason to give up on family interaction skills. Plan how your family could make family interaction skills work better in the future.

SUMMARY POINTS

1. Families who have difficulty communicating, solving ongoing problems, and managing conflict are more likely to have children with behavioral and emotional problems.
2. Learn to identify and understand destructive ways of communicating in your family and to replace them with constructive communication procedures.
3. Learn to identify problem(s), generate alternative solutions, evaluate alternative solutions to determine which solution is best for all (or most) family members, and implement the best solution to solve family problems.
4. Learn to recognize when conflict exists, cool off, and then apply family communication and problem-solving skills to reduce family conflict.
5. Try to use all three family interaction skills together.

Let's Work It Out

Let's retell the original story of Steve, Martha, and Mike: Steve and Martha are the parents of 14-year-old Mike. It is 10 P.M. on a school night and Mike is out past his 9 P.M. curfew. Mike finally comes in and the following discussion takes place:

STEVE *(firm):* You're late. You know the curfew is 9 o'clock and you are one hour late.

MIKE: Everyone else gets to stay out later. Why can't I? You guys are unfair.

MARTHA *(firm):* Mike, you know you are supposed to be in by 9 o'clock.

STEVE: OK, things are getting too hot here. Let's take a time-out for 10 minutes and then discuss this.

MIKE *(sarcastically):* Oh, come on! You have got to be kidding.

MARTHA: Mike, we agreed that we would try to solve our problems a little bit better. Let's take a time-out like your father said, then come back and try to discuss it.

MIKE *(reluctantly):* OK.

During a 10-minute break, Steve steps outside and takes some deep breaths, Martha thinks about how she can constructively state her thoughts to Mike, and Mike watches TV.

STEVE: Let's practice communicating while we try to solve this problem. Let's look at the Family Communications Skills chart.

MIKE: Do we have to?

MARTHA: Come on. Let's try it. Let's try to use the DOs as we discuss this.

The family goes on to discuss the problem using family communication skills.

CHARTS FOR CHAPTER 6

FAMILY COMMUNICATION SKILLS

DON'Ts	DOs
• Long lectures or "sermons"	• Use brief statements of 10 words or less
• Blaming (e.g., "You need to stop ____." "It's your fault," etc.)	• Use I statements (e.g., "I feel ____ when ____") or take responsibility for your own actions
• Vague statements (e.g., "Shape up," "Knock it off," "I don't like that," etc.)	• Use direct and specific statements (e.g., "Stop teasing your sister")
• Asking negative questions (e.g., "Why do you always do that?", "How many times must I tell you?")	• Use direct and specific statements (e.g., "Stop teasing your brother")
• Poor listening with looking away, silent treatment, crossing arms, and so forth	• Actively listen with good eye contact, leaning forward, nodding, and so forth
• Interrupting others	• Let each person completely state his/her thoughts before stating yours
• Not checking to see if you really understand others	• Give feedback/paraphrase (e.g., restate what another said to you)
• Put-downs (e.g., "You're worthless," "I'm sick of you," etc.), threats, and so forth	• Be constructive (e.g., "I'm concerned about your grades," "Something is bothering me; can we discuss it?", etc.)
• Yelling, screaming, and so forth	• Use a neutral/natural tone of voice
• Sarcasm	• Say what you mean, be specific and straightforward
• Going from topic to topic	• Stay on one topic
• Bringing up old issues, past behavior	• Focus on here and now
• Not matching verbal and nonverbal communications (e.g., saying, "I love you," while pounding one's fist angrily on the table)	• Match verbal and nonverbal communication (e.g., saying, "I love you," while smiling)
• Keeping feelings inside	• Express feelings to others appropriately
• Scowling, directing antagonistic facial expressions toward others	• Use appropriate facial expressions toward others
• "Mind reading" or assuming you know what other people think	• Really listen to others' point of view, ask questions to make sure you understand

From *Skills Training for Children with Behavior Disorders: A Parent and Therapist Guidebook* by Michael L. Bloomquist. © 1996 The Guilford Press.

WORKING ON FAMILY COMMUNICATION GOALS

Name: _____

Date and time: _____

Directions: Indicate which family communication DOs you will be working on below. Designate a time period for using this chart. At the end of the designated time period, rate how well you accomplished your goals. It may be helpful to get feedback from others (family members, etc.) as to how well they think you are accomplishing your goal.

Family Communication DOs

1. **I am working on increasing:**

2. **How well did I accomplish my goal?** (circle one)

1	2	3	4	5
Not at all	A little	OK	Pretty good	Great

Family Members' Feedback (optional)

3. **How well did family members think I accomplished my goal?** (circle one)

1	2	3	4	5
Not at all	A little	OK	Pretty good	Great

From *Skills Training for Children with Behavior Disorders: A Parent and Therapist Guidebook* by Michael L. Bloomquist. © 1996 The Guilford Press.

EXAMPLE:
WORKING ON FAMILY COMMUNICATION GOALS

Name: *Steve*

Date and time: *Wednesday, 4–9 P.M.*

Directions: Indicate which family communication DOs you will be working on below. Designate a time period for using this chart. At the end of the designated time period, rate how well you accomplished your goals. It may be helpful to get feedback from others (family members, etc.) as to how well they think you are accomplishing your goal.

Family Communication DOs

1. **I am working on increasing:**

    Using brief statements
    Neutral/natural tone of voice

2. **How well did I accomplish my goal?** (circle one)

1	2	3	(4)	5
Not at all	A little	OK	Pretty good	Great

Family Members' Feedback (optional)

3. **How well did family members think I accomplished my goal?** (circle one)

1	2	(3)	4	5
Not at all	A little	OK	Pretty good	Great

From *Skills Training for Children with Behavior Disorders: A Parent and Therapist Guidebook* by Michael L. Bloomquist. © 1996 The Guilford Press.

FAMILY PROBLEM SOLVING

1. **Stop!! What is the problem we are having?**
   - Try to avoid blaming individuals.
   - Focus on how family members are interacting and causing problems together.
   - State specifically what the problem is so that everyone agrees.

2. **What are some plans we can use?**
   - Think of as many alternative plans as possible.
   - Don't evaluate or criticize any family member's ideas.
   - Don't discuss any one solution until you have generated many alternatives.

3. **What is the best plan we could use?**
   - Think of what would happen if the family used each of the alternatives.
   - Think about how each alternative would make each family member feel.
   - Decide which alternative is most likely to succeed and make most family members feel OK.
   - Reach an agreement by most or all family members if possible.

4. **Do the plan.**
   - Try the plan as best the family can.
   - Don't criticize or say, "I told you so."

5. **Did our plan work?**
   - Evaluate the plan.
   - Determine if everyone is satisfied with the way the problem was solved.
   - If the solution didn't work, repeat the entire family problem-solving process again.

Note. **Try to stay focused on the here and now.** Do not bring up old issues when trying to do family problem solving.

From *Skills Training for Children with Behavior Disorders: A Parent and Therapist Guidebook* by Michael L. Bloomquist. © 1996 The Guilford Press.

FAMILY PROBLEM-SOLVING WORKSHEET

Directions: The family completes this form together as they attempt to solve a problem. Answer each question as it pertains to the problem being solved.

1. **What is the problem we are having?** Decide as a family what the problem is and write it down.

2. **What are some plans we could use?** Write down as many plans as you can think of. Let each family member have input.

3. **What is the best plan we could use?** Select the plan that is most likely to work and make most or all family members feel OK. Write down the plan the family decided to use.

4. **Do the plan.** Write down exactly what the family will do when using the plan. Be specific.

5. **Did our plan work?** Write down if the plan worked or not. Also, write how you know whether it worked or not.

Family Problem-Solving Rating (circle one)

1. We didn't use family problem solving at all.
2. We tried to use family problem solving, but it didn't really work.
3. We tried hard, went through the family problem-solving steps, but didn't really use the plan.
4. We tried hard, went through the family problem-solving steps, and used the plan.

From *Skills Training for Children with Behavior Disorders: A Parent and Therapist Guidebook* by Michael L. Bloomquist. © 1996 The Guilford Press.

EXAMPLE:
FAMILY PROBLEM-SOLVING WORKSHEET

Directions: The family completes this form together as they attempt to solve a problem. Answer each question as it pertains to the problem being solved.

1. **What is the problem we are having?** Decide as a family what the problem is and write it down.

   Which video should we rent? Mike wants to rent an "R" movie, but Steve and Martha don't want anyone in the house to rent "R" movies.

2. **What are some plans we could use?** Write down as many plans as you can think of. Let each family member have input.

   (1) Rent the "R" movie anyway. (2) Don't rent any movies. (3) Rent movie we can all agree on.

3. **What is the best plan we could use?** Select the plan that is most likely to work and make most or all family members feel OK. Write down the plan the family decided to use.

   We will rent a movie we all agree on.

4. **Do the plan.** Write down exactly what the family will do when using the plan. Be specific.

   We will create a list of movie possibilities and discuss each one until we find one we all agree on. We will try not to criticize each other's selections.

5. **Did our plan work?** Write down if the plan worked or not. Also, write how you know whether it worked or not.

   We selected a movie we all liked.

Family Problem-Solving Rating (circle one)

1. We didn't use family problem solving at all.
2. We tried to use family problem solving, but it didn't really work.
3. We tried hard, went through the family problem-solving steps, but didn't really use the plan.
4. We tried hard, went through the family problem-solving steps, and used the plan.

From *Skills Training for Children with Behavior Disorders: A Parent and Therapist Guidebook* by Michael L. Bloomquist. © 1996 The Guilford Press.

82

FAMILY ANGER/CONFLICT MANAGEMENT

1. **Recognizing Anger/Conflict**—Each family member learns to recognize when they or others are so angry that effective problem solving and communication are impossible. Family members become aware of destructive anger "signals" such as loud voices, angry facial expressions, destructive communication, angry thoughts, increased heart and/or breathing rate, increased sweating and/or muscle tension, and so forth.

2. **Coping with Anger/Conflict**—The family agrees ahead of time that when they recognize destructive anger/conflict, they will take a previously agreed-upon break (e.g., separate for 10 minutes). Each family member will then try to cope with anger through relaxation, through deep breathing, and by utilizing "coping self-statements" (e.g., "I'm going to try to stay calm," "I'm going to try to think of a better way to get my point across to him," etc.).

3. **Constructive Problem Solving and Communication**—The family reunites and tries to resolve conflicts using family problem-solving and communication skills. Family members try to be assertive, not agressive, in getting their points across to others.

From *Skills Training for Children with Behavior Disorders: A Parent and Therapist Guidebook* by Michael L. Bloomquist. © 1996 The Guilford Press.

FAMILY COOL-DOWN

1. Are we too angry?

2. Briefly separate to cool down.

3. Come back together to solve the problem.

From *Skills Training for Children with Behavior Disorders: A Parent and Therapist Guidebook* by Michael L. Bloomquist. © 1996 The Guilford Press.

III

INSTRUCTIONS FOR PARENTS TO ENHANCE CHILD SKILLS

7

Helping Children Learn to Comply

Getting children to listen and obey adults' directives is very important. In an effort to make children comply, parents often use the methods they learned from their own parents and/or learned by trial and error. They often use methods that don't work and may make parent–child relationship problems worse. This chapter describes problems related to children's noncompliance and what parents can do to improve this state of affairs.

Can't You Do What I Tell You?

Dan is a single parent who is trying to raise his 10-year-old daughter, Shelby. He complains that he can't get Shelby to do anything. He has to tell her over and over to do basic things that "kids her age should be able to do." Dan wonders if it is too much to expect a 10-year-old girl to make her bed each day and complete her homework. He finds himself interacting very negatively with Shelby. He always has to nag her and "get on her case." She is frequently argumentative, talks back, and generally tries to blame him for her problems. They often get into big power struggles and start yelling at each other.

WHAT IS NONCOMPLIANCE IN CHILDREN?

Children who are told to do something by a parent and do not do it are noncompliant. Note that there are two parts to the definition of noncompliance. One part is a child being told to do something (parent's part) and another part is the child not doing what she is told (child's part). **Both the parent and child must change behavior to increase a child's compliance.**

Noncompliance is probably the most common complaint that parents have about their children. Research has shown that significant noncompliant behavior in children, starting early in development and persisting into middle childhood age, is strongly related to delinquent and antisocial behavior in adolescence and adulthood. This is not to say that developmentally appropriate noncompliance in a toddler or a preschooler will predict later problems. If noncompliance is not dealt with sufficiently, however, and if it persists, it may lead to further troubles.

Noncompliance is also often related to conflict in families. The parent tries to get the child to comply, they get involved in a power struggle, and before long an all-out fight has emerged. One way to deal with conflict in families is to resolve the problems related to a child's noncompliance.

Noncompliant children are very challenging, and parents may lack skills to discipline them effectively to help them learn to comply. These parents often yell, are inconsistent, use ineffective commands, give in to their child's stubborn behavior, are over controlling, and sometimes use physical punishment. All of these approaches may accidentally reinforce problem behavior. The parent and child often get into power struggles, each trying to "win." If the child wins too often, the behavior problem escalates.

COMPLIANCE TRAINING

Parents are keenly aware of how difficult it can be to obtain their child's compliance with even simple requests. Research on parenting practices has established that **there are several behaviors that parents can modify to increase a child's compliance.**

Step 1: Give Effective Commands

As stated earlier, the definition of noncompliance is that a child was told to do something and did not do it. It may be helpful to think about whether the way you tell your child to do things may be contributing to the problem.

Read the list of types of commands below and consider which of these commands are typical of you:

Vague command. Telling the child in vague terms what she is expected to do (e.g., "Shape up," "Knock it off," etc.).

Question command. Asking a question in an attempt to gain a child's compliance (e.g., "Would you please pick up your toys?").

Rationale command. Explaining to the child why she needs to comply (e.g., "You need to get dressed now, because if you don't, we will be late for our appointment").

Multiple command. Telling the child to do too many things at once (e.g., "Pick up your toys, make your bed, wash your hands, and then come to dinner").

Frequent command. Repeating the same command over and over to the child.

Specific, one-step command. Stating a specific, one-step command in 10 words or less (e.g., "Put all your toys on the shelf").

Vague, question, rationale, multiple, and frequent commands are associated with noncompliance in children. Try to avoid using these commands. A vague command does not tell the child exactly what she is expected to do. A question command doesn't work because a child is given the option to comply or not to comply, given the fact that the command was stated in a question. A rationale command is problematic because the child may choose to dispute the rationale rather than comply with the command (e.g., "We have plenty of time, we won't be late"). The multiple command is difficult for the child because she may become overwhelmed and/or confused by the many steps in the command process. The frequent command is ineffective because the child learns that the parent does not necessarily mean it when he or she says the command the first time.

The specific, one-step command stated in 10 words or less is associated with compliance in children. The specific command tells the child exactly what is expected of her. For the specific command to be most effective, it should be stated only once. Strive to give specific, one-step commands when you want your child to comply with a request.

Step 2: Use Effective Warnings

Just stating specific commands and reinforcing compliance may not be enough to gain a noncompliant child's cooperation. Using effective warnings and mild punishment is also important. **The best way to state a warning is in the form of an "if . . . then" statement.** For example, if a child refuses to pick up her toys and put them on the shelf, the parent could say, "**If** you don't pick up your toys and put them on the shelf, **then** you will (have a mild punishment)." "If . . . then" statements clearly tell the child what will happen if she doesn't comply. It's also very important to **state the warning only once**. Eventually, your child will learn to comply with your warning without having a mild punishment, if you are consistent in giving only one warning. It may be helpful to state the warning and count out loud to 5 before administering a mild punishment.

Step 3: Give Positive or Negative Consequences to Child for Compliant or Noncompliant Behavior

Give your child reinforcement if she complies with your command or warning. This might take the form of praise or a tangible reinforcement such as extra privileges or tokens and so forth. If your child is reinforced for complying, she is more likely to comply again in the future. (See the "Reinforcement" section of Chapter 5 for more ideas on reinforcement with children.)

Give your child a mild punishment if she doesn't comply with your command or warning. Effective mild punishments should be a negative consequence designed to teach and inform the child. Typically, mild punishments are quite effective if they are enforced consistently. Examples of good mild punishments include sitting in a chair or in a stairway for several minutes, losing selected privileges, and so forth.

Step 4: Deescalate and Stay Cool

It is extremely important to **stay cool and deescalate potential power struggles** that may result from your attempts to increase your child's compliance. Try to maintain a matter-of-fact, unemotional style when enforcing compliance. Try to avoid becoming overly angry or frustrated. If you can maintain a calm style, you will reduce power struggles and you will have more success in shaping compliant behavior in your child. (See the "Staying Calm with Stressful Children" section in Chapter 3 for more ideas on how to stay cool.) If it's getting too hot between you and your child, walk away, collect yourself, and wait until your child is calmer. Then go back and try again.

Step 5a: Implement Specific Compliance Training Procedures for Early Elementary School Age Children

The reinforcement procedure for early elementary school age children involves using the Listen and Obey for Rewards chart found at the end of this chapter. To use this chart, keep a tally of the number of times that your child complies and does not comply with your command or warning by assigning smiling and frowning faces. Rewards are administered depending on whether your child was more compliant or more noncompliant (see directions on the Listen and Obey for Rewards chart). The child receives immediate reinforcement from the smiling face, but also receives tangible reinforcement at the end of the day or week if she receives more smiling than frowning faces during the designated time period (see the "Reinforcement" section in Chapter 5).

The Time-Out chart found at the end of this chapter describes a mild punishment procedure for noncompliance with early elementary school age children. The procedure involves giving a command, followed by a warning, followed by a consequence (mild punishment), and then followed by restating the original command (see the Time-Out chart for details).

It is best to use the Listen and Obey for Rewards (for reinforcing compliance) and the time-out (for mild punishment of noncompliance) procedures together. This way your child has an opportunity to earn reinforcement for complying, but will receive a mild punishment for not complying. If your child does not comply with your command and warning, mark a frowning face on the Listen and Obey for Rewards chart and give a time-out. Keep using these procedures until your child is more compliant. **Sometimes it can take days, weeks, or even months to help your child become compliant. Don't give up.** Keep working at it, and it will come.

The Listen and Obey chart found at the end of this chapter can be used to remind your child of your expectation that she comply and what will happen if she doesn't. The Listen and Obey chart could be posted for your child to refer to when you remind her to listen and obey.

This section describes how to use several charts, which may be confusing. Keep in mind that the Listen and Obey for Rewards and the Listen and Obey charts are for your child. You may want to use one or both of them. The Time-Out chart is for you to refer to as a reminder of the basic steps to follow with the time-out procedure.

Review the charts carefully with your child before implementing the procedures. Explain them to your child and inform her about what will be occurring. It may be helpful to role play with her about what will happen if she is noncompliant.

Step 5b: Implement Specific Compliance Training Procedures for Late Elementary School Age Children and Teens

The reinforcement procedure for late elementary school age children and teens involves using the Parental Requests chart found at the end of this chapter. It is similar to the Listen and Obey for Rewards chart, in that you give a specific, one-step command to your child/teen, and, if she complies, she receives a tally in the "Yes" column for that day. If she doesn't comply, she gets a tally in the "No" column for that day (see the "Reinforcement" section in Chapter 5).

The mild punishment for a child this age involves using the steps described in the Removal of Privileges for Noncompliance chart found at the end of this chapter. As with time-out, this involves stating a command and giving a warning, but, instead of time-out, a privilege is removed as the mild punishment for noncompliance (see the Removal of Privileges for Noncompliance chart for details). Finally, the command is restated.

The procedures discussed in the Parental Requests and Removal of Privileges for Noncompliance charts can be used together. If your child/teen doesn't comply with your command or warning, mark the "No" column on the Parental Requests chart and remove a privilege. Keep using these procedures until your child/teen is more compliant. As with early elementary age children, **it may take a long time to increase the older child's level of compliance, so be persistent.**

STAY WITH IT

The procedures discussed in this chapter are highly effective ways to improve children's compliance if they are done properly. **Success will come if you are consistent and persistent.** Often, when these procedures fail, it is because the parent uses them only occasionally and/or gives up too easily. Be prepared, because it may take several weeks or months to improve a child's behavior. **Sometimes a child's difficult behavior gets worse before it gets better when these procedures are utilized.** Don't get demoralized if this occurs. One key point is to try to avoid power struggles with your child and to let your actions do the talking for you. Stay with it, and it will work.

SUMMARY POINTS

1. A high level of noncompliance in children is strongly related to delinquent and antisocial behavior in adolescence and adulthood.

2. To gain your child's compliance, state a specific, brief, one-step command. Follow this with one warning, and follow that with either reinforcement if your child is compliant or a mild punishment if your child is noncompliant.

Actions Speak Louder than Words

Back to Dan and Shelby: Dan decides to try some new and different approaches to working with Shelby. He realizes that "actions speak louder than words," and he decides to use some behavioral management techniques. He employs the Listen and Obey for Rewards and Time-out procedures together to improve Shelby's compliance. He and Shelby have developed a reinforcement menu for the Listen and Obey for Rewards chart that both are in agreement with. Dan is resolved to keep these procedures going for as long as it takes to improve Shelby's behavior.

CHARTS FOR CHAPTER 7

LISTEN AND OBEY FOR REWARDS

Name: _____

Date: _____

Directions: When your child is noncompliant, ask him/her to "listen and obey." If he/she does listen and obey, put a smiling face in the "Yes" column; if not, put a frowning face in the "No" column. At the end of the day, add up the smiling faces and the frowning faces. If there are more smiling faces, put a smiling face in the box below; likewise with the frowning faces. At the end of the week, add up the smiling faces and the frowning faces in the big boxes.

Monday		Tuesday		Wednesday		Thursday		Friday		Saturday		Sunday	
Yes	No	Yes	No	Yes	No	Yes	No	Yes	No	Yes	No	Yes	No

Are there more smiling faces or frowning faces today?

If using a daily reward, give the child a reward if a smiling face appears in one of the big boxes.

The reward is _____ .

If using a weekly reward, add up total smiling faces at the end of the week. Give the child a reward if there are more smiling faces than frowning faces in the big boxes.

The reward is _____ .

EXAMPLE:
LISTEN AND OBEY FOR REWARDS

Name: *Shelby*

Date: *Friday*

Directions: When your child is noncompliant, ask him/her to "listen and obey." If he/she does listen and obey, put a smiling face in the "Yes" column; if not, put a frowning face in the "No" column. At the end of the day, add up the smiling faces and the frowning faces. If there are more smiling faces, put a smiling face in the box below; likewise with the frowning faces. At the end of the week, add up the smiling faces and the frowning faces in the big boxes.

Monday		Tuesday		Wednesday		Thursday		Friday		Saturday		Sunday	
Yes	No	Yes	No	Yes	No	Yes	No	Yes	No	Yes	No	Yes	No
☺	☹	☺	☹	☺			☹	☺		☺		☺	☹
☺			☹					☺		☺		☺	
☺								☺					

Are there more smiling faces or frowning faces today?

☺	☹	☺	☹	☺	☺	☺

If using a daily reward, give the child a reward if a smiling face appears in one of the big boxes.

The reward is *select from reinforcement menu* .

If using a weekly reward, add up total smiling faces at the end of the week. Give the child a reward if there are more smiling faces than frowning faces in the big boxes.

The reward is *select from reinforcement menu* .

From *Skills Training for Children with Behavior Disorders: A Parent and Therapist Guidebook* by Michael L. Bloomquist. © 1996 The Guilford Press.

TIME-OUT

1. **Make a request of the child.** Be sure that the **request is short and clear** as to exactly what is expected of the child. Do not ask a question, make a suggestion or plead when something is requested.

2. **Give a warning.** If the child does not follow through with the request, then the child should be given a warning. A warning is an **"if . . . then"** statement. The warning should be stated clearly and concisely. For example, "If you don't (request), then you will have to sit in the chair for time-out." It may be helpful to count out loud to 5 before going to the next step.

3. **Time-out.** If, after 5 to 10 seconds, the child does not comply, then immediately put the child in the designated time-out place. The child is required to sit quietly in his/her chair. It may be helpful to set a timer for 2 to 5 minutes (the parent should judge what is an adequate time length and utilize the same time length for every time-out). **If the child leaves the chair or acts in any disruptive manner, the parent should warn him/her that the timer will be set back until he/she can sit in the chair quietly.** If this does not work, the parent may have to use a consequence such as taking away a future privilege. For example, if the child doesn't sit in the chair, he/she has to go to bed 30 minutes earlier. If the child is able to sit again quietly, then set the timer again for the designated time period.

4. **After time-out.** Ask the child to comply with the request. If he/she is still noncompliant or resistant, repeat the above steps.

Note. **Discontinue time-out if there is too much yelling or physical conflict.** Try another idea or technique in the book, or consult a mental health professional.

From *Skills Training for Children with Behavior Disorders: A Parent and Therapist Guidebook* by Michael L. Bloomquist. © 1996 The Guilford Press.

LISTEN AND OBEY

1.

Command—specific, one step:
"I want you to . . ."

2.

Warning—if . . ., then:
If you don't (command), *then* (time-out).

3.

Time-Out—sit in chair
and set timer.

From *Skills Training for Children with Behavior Disorders: A Parent and Therapist Guidebook* by
Michael L. Bloomquist. © 1996 The Guilford Press.

LISTEN AND OBEY

1.

Command—specific, one step:
"I want you to . . ."

2.

Warning—if . . ., then:
If you don't (command), *then* (time-out).

3.

Time-Out—sit in chair
and set timer.

From *Skills Training for Children with Behavior Disorders: A Parent and Therapist Guidebook* by
Michael L. Bloomquist. © 1996 The Guilford Press.

LISTEN AND OBEY

1.

Command—specific, one step:
"I want you to . . ."

2.

Warning—if . . ., then:
If you don't (command), *then* (time-out).

3.

Time-Out—sit in chair
and set timer.

From *Skills Training for Children with Behavior Disorders: A Parent and Therapist Guidebook* by
Michael L. Bloomquist. © 1996 The Guilford Press.

LISTEN AND OBEY

1.

Command—specific, one step:
"I want you to . . ."

2.

Warning—if . . ., then:
If you don't (command), *then* (time-out).

3.

Time-Out—sit in chair
and set timer.

PARENTAL REQUESTS

Name: _____

Date: _____

Directions: Give your child/teen a clear, specific, brief command. If he/she obeys your command, put a tally in the "Yes" box for that day. If he/she does not obey, put a tally in the "No" box for that day. Follow the reward directions at the bottom of this chart.

	Monday	Tuesday	Wednesday	Thursday	Friday	Saturday	Sunday
Yes							
No							

Daily tally:
Is there
more Yes
or No?

___   ___   ___   ___   ___   ___   ___

If using daily reward, give child/teen a reward if more Yes than No for a specific day.

Reward is: _____

If using weekly reward, give child/teen a reward if more Yes than No on daily tallies for the week.

Reward is: _____

EXAMPLE:
PARENTAL REQUESTS

Name: *Shelby*

Date: *Friday*

Directions: Give your child/teen a clear, specific, brief command. If he/she obeys your command, put a tally in the "Yes" box for that day. If he/she does not obey, put a tally in the "No" box for that day. Follow the reward directions at the bottom of this chart.

	Monday	Tuesday	Wednesday	Thursday	Friday	Saturday	Sunday
Yes	I I I	I I	I I I	I I I	I I I I	I I I	I I
No	I I	I I I	I I	I	I I	0	0

Daily tally:
Is there
more Yes
or No?

Yes	*No*	*Yes*	*Yes*	*Yes*	*Yes*	*Yes*

If using daily reward, give child/teen a reward if more Yes than No for a specific day.

Reward is: *select from reinforcement menu*

If using weekly reward, give child/teen a reward if more Yes than No on daily tallies for the week.

Reward is: *select from reinforcement menu*

From *Skills Training for Children with Behavior Disorders: A Parent and Therapist Guidebook* by Michael L. Bloomquist. © 1996 The Guilford Press.

REMOVING PRIVILEGES FOR NONCOMPLIANCE

1. **Make a request of the child/teen.** Be sure that the **request is short and clear** as to exactly what is expected of the child/teen. Do not ask a question, make a suggestion, or plead when something is requested.

2. **Give a warning.** If the child/teen does not follow through with the request, then the child/teen should be given a warning. A warning is an **"if . . . then"** statement. The warning should be stated clearly and concisely. For example, "If you don't (request), then you will (lose a privilege)." Privileges to remove may include TV time, access to the telephone, going outside, driving privileges, and so forth. It may be helpful to count to 5 before going to the next step.

3. **Loss of privilege.**

   Option 1: The child/teen is told that the privilege is lost until he/she is compliant with the original command.

   Option 2: The child/teen is told the privilege is lost for a specified period of time (e.g., 24 hours).

   The parent should try to avoid power struggles if the child/teen becomes upset or belligerent at the loss of the privilege. **If the child/teen does not comply with the loss of privilege, then the child/teen should be told that eventually he/she will have to comply with the loss of privilege whether it be at the current time or later.** Further, the child/teen should be told that further privileges can be revoked if he/she is noncompliant with the original loss of privilege.

4. **After compliance.** Once the child has complied with the original command, then the lost privilege is returned to the child/teen.

Note. **Discontinue removing privileges for noncompliance if there is too much yelling or physical conflict.** Try another idea or technique in the book, or consult a mental health professional.

From *Skills Training for Children with Behavior Disorders: A Parent and Therapist Guidebook* by Michael L. Bloomquist. © 1996 The Guilford Press.

8

Helping Children Learn
to Follow Rules

Most children learn the rules of home, school, peer groups, and community gradually during early childhood. They both observe and are taught what is right and wrong. Children with behavior problems often have not learned these rules, or they ignore them. Parents find it quite challenging to help a child learn to follow rules. This chapter focuses on specific methods parents can use to help teach children to follow rules.

When Will You Ever Learn?

Harold and Opal have tried many things to get 12-year-old Latoya to follow the household rules. Latoya repeatedly doesn't do her homework, breaks her curfew, and goes to the mall when she has been told not to go there. The parents are frustrated. They end up yelling at Latoya a lot, which hasn't made much difference because she still breaks the rules.

WHAT IS POOR RULE FOLLOWING IN CHILDREN?

Rules are everywhere and children who don't learn to follow them are going to get into trouble. Most children "forget" or otherwise don't follow the rules from time to time, however children with behavior problems frequently break the rules. Parents can have a big impact on how their children learn the important lesson of following rules.

Not following the rules can range from minor problems such as not doing homework to major problems such as not obeying curfew. When children don't follow the rules, they get in trouble more frequently, and family conflict often emerges. Another issue related to rule following is the notion of "monitoring." Children who engage in delinquent and antisocial behavior are often not monitored sufficiently by their parents to make sure they follow the rules. These parents are not sure where their child is, what their child is doing, when their child will be home, who their child is with, and so forth. The parents often have not established clear rules (e.g., curfew, bedtime, etc.) and boundaries (e.g., specified areas where the child can and cannot go).

DISCUSS AND WRITE DOWN THE RULES

Many parents assume their child understands the rules, when in fact he may not. Sometimes parents have not stated what the rules are, but they expect their child to follow the rules anyway. It's helpful to focus on the most important rules and communicate them clearly to your child.

Take some time by yourself to think of all the rules your child seems to violate. This might include not doing homework or chores, staying out too late, getting up too late in the morning, and so forth. Write all of the rules on a list. Next, arrange the list of rules in order of importance. The most important rule would be on top and so forth. Initially, it's wise just to focus on two or three of the most important rules. You can address other rules with your child at a later time.

Conduct a meeting with your child and inform him what the rules are and write the rules down on a piece of paper. Be very clear and specific about the rules. For example, don't just say, "Do your homework;" instead, say, "Do your homework each day before 7 P.M." Make sure your child clearly understands your rules. It may be helpful for each of you to have a copy of the rules.

Be very careful about rules that restrict friendships. Often, if a parent restricts a child from a certain friend, the children sneak to see each other anyway. Although a parent can restrict friendships should they desire, it may be more successful to have rules about friendships instead. These rules might include stating where the child can go when with the friend, stating a time to come home, and so forth. It may also be useful to get to know the other child's parents.

DAILY BEHAVIORAL CONTRACTING

Daily behavioral contracting involves establishing behavioral expectations (or rules of conduct) and contingencies (e.g., rewards and punishments) for your child's behavior. Your child is reinforced for positive behavior and mildly punished for negative behavior each day.

Step 1: Designate Behavior Expectations

Sit down with your child and discuss rules that are violated regularly. The rule violations will vary from child to child. Often they are behaviors for which a parent frequently has to reprimand or remind a child to follow.

Examples of rules derived from problem behaviors might include:

- Complete chores or homework by a certain time.
- Get up on time on school days.
- Go to school each day.
- Feed the dog.
- Do not go to restricted areas (e.g., local mall or park) without an adult.
- Do not go into a friend's home unless a parent is home.
- Tell parent where you are going.

Step 2: Designate Privileges to Be Earned or Lost Contingent on Child's Behavior

Discuss and specify extra privileges your child would like to earn and specify which privileges your child could lose for a day.

Examples of privileges might include the following:

- Using the phone
- Watching TV
- Using the car
- Being able to go outside
- Playing computerized games

Step 3: Implement a Contract

Write down the behavior expectations and privileges to be earned or lost on a contract (examples are discussed below). Thereafter, do not nag your child or remind him of behavior expectations. Simply inform your child that he has earned or lost privileges when he has or has not met behavior expectations as set up in the contract.

Privileges are earned or lost for only 1 day, provided your child fulfills the behavior expectation the following day. A day consists of a 24-hour period designated by you. Try to review the contract with your child daily.

Step 4a: Implement a Specific Behavioral Contract for Early Elementary School Age Children

The Daily Child Behavior Chart found at the end of this chapter can be used for contracting with early elementary school age children (up to approximately age 9 or 10). You'll note that this chart provides some visual feedback (e.g., smiling and frowning faces) for younger children regarding their behavior each day. If you desire, your child can participate in drawing the smiling and frowning faces on the chart. Your child receives a small reinforcement for doing one or two positive behaviors per day, and a larger reinforcement for doing three or four positive behaviors each day. (See the "Reinforcement" section in Chapter 5.) A negative consequence is only given if a child breaks all the rules for an entire day and receives all frowning faces. The terms of the contract are reviewed on a daily basis. This means that your child's behavior is monitored over 1 day, and he receives a reinforcement or consequence within 24 hours after the chart is used that day.

Step 4b: Implement Daily Behavioral Contracting for Late Elementary School Age Children and Teens

The Daily Behavior Contract found at the end of this chapter is used for behavioral contracting with late elementary school age children (over age 9 or 10) and teens. It is somewhat different than the contract used with the early elementary school age children in that each behavior has its own reinforcement or consequence. Often late elementary school age children and teen behaviors are more challenging for parents to modify. By linking each behavior with its own reward or consequence, you have more leverage to modify your child's behavior. (See the "Reinforcement" section in Chapter 5.) Again, the terms of the contract are reviewed each day.

Step 4c: Modify a Daily Behavior Contract

It is a lot of work to use a Daily Behavior Contract. A parent could elect to designate the behavior expectations for a child and administer only the reinforcement or consequence part of the contract. It is better to use a modified and easier contract than to use the labor intensive contract that may be unrealistic to accomplish. Use your judgment to determine what works best for you and your family.

SUMMARY POINTS

1. Children who don't learn to follow rules are at greater risk for developing serious adjustment problems later in life.
2. To use daily behavioral contracts, state your daily behavioral expectations, and then administer a reinforcement or mild punishment contingent on whether or not your child meets the daily behavioral expectation. Use one of the behavioral contracts in this chapter.

Teaching a Lesson

Back to Harold, Opal, and Latoya: Harold and Opal figure out that they could yell "until they turn blue" and it wouldn't help Latoya follow their rules. They decided to try a Daily Behavioral Contract with her. Latoya is not happy about the contract, but after losing some privileges for a few days for violating the contract, she begins to follow the rules better. Harold and Opal notice that Latoya's behavior is improving and that they are arguing less with her.

CHARTS FOR CHAPTER 8

DAILY CHILD BEHAVIOR CHART

Name: _____

Week of: _____

Directions: Identify four (or fewer) target behaviors for your child to work on each day. Put a smiling face in the box if the behavior was completed. Put a frowning face in the box if the behavior was not completed. Always praise your child each time he/she gets a smiling face. At the end of the day, tally up smiling and frowning faces. Administer the reward or mild punishment sometime within 24 hours. There are two levels of rewards and one level of mild punishment.

Behavior	Mon.	Tues.	Wed.	Thurs.	Fri.	Sat.	Sun.

	Mon.	Tues.	Wed.	Thurs.	Fri.	Sat.	Sun.
Total smiling faces							
Total frowning faces							

Daily reward:

1–2 Smiling faces =

3–4 Smiling faces =

Mild punishment:

4 Frowning faces =

From *Skills Training for Children with Behavior Disorders: A Parent and Therapist Guidebook* by Michael L. Bloomquist. © 1996 The Guilford Press.

EXAMPLE:
DAILY CHILD BEHAVIOR CHART

Name: *Latoya*

Week of: *November 6–12*

Directions: Identify four (or fewer) target behaviors for your child to work on each day. Put a smiling face in the box if the behavior was completed. Put a frowning face in the box if the behavior was not completed. Always praise your child each time he/she gets a smiling face. At the end of the day, tally up smiling and frowning faces. Administer the reward or mild punishment sometime within 24 hours. There are two levels of rewards and one level of mild punishment.

Behavior	Mon.	Tues.	Wed.	Thurs.	Fri.	Sat.	Sun.
Up and dressed by 7:00 A.M.	☹	☺	☹	☺	☺		
Homework done before supper	☹	☺	☹	☺	☺		
Take dog out for walk	☹	☹	☺	☺	☺		
In bed by 7:30 P.M. with lights out	☹	☺	☺	☺	☺		
Total smiling faces	*0*	*3*	*2*	*4*	*4*		
Total frowning faces	*4*	*1*	*2*	*0*	*0*		

Daily reward:
1–2 Smiling faces = *Special bedtime snack*
3–4 Smiling faces = *Special activity with parent*

Mild punishment:
4 Frowning faces = *No TV for a day*

From *Skills Training for Children with Behavior Disorders: A Parent and Therapist Guidebook* by Michael L. Bloomquist. © 1996 The Guilford Press.

DAILY BEHAVIOR CONTRACT

Name: _____

Week of: _____

Behavior expectations	Privileges earned sometime over the next day	Privileges lost for the next day
1.	1.	1.
2.	2.	2.
3.	3.	3.
4.	4.	4.

Terms: For every expectation that is met, one privilege is earned over the next day. For every expectation that is not met, one privilege is lost for the next day.

Signatures: 1.

2.

3.

4.

EXAMPLE:
DAILY BEHAVIOR CONTRACT

Name: *Latoya*

Week of: *November 6–12*

Behavior expectations	Privileges earned sometime over the next day	Privileges lost for the next day
1. *Be home before 7:30 P.M.*	1. *Select from reinforcement menu*	1. *TV*
2. *Do homework before 8 P.M.*	2. *Select from reinforcement menu*	2. *Computer games*
3. *Brush teeth*	3. *Select from reinforcement menu*	3. *Outside privileges*
4. *Feed the dog*	4. *Select from reinforcement menu*	4. *Phone*

Terms: For every expectation that is met, one privilege is earned over the next day. For every expectation that is not met, one privilege is lost for the next day.

Signatures: 1. *Latoya*

2. *Harold*

3. *Opal*

4.

From *Skills Training for Children with Behavior Disorders: A Parent and Therapist Guidebook* by Michael L. Bloomquist. © 1996 The Guilford Press.

9

Enhancing Children's Social Behavior Skills

The ability to make and keep new friends is absolutely critical for all children. Children with chronic social difficulties are at high risk for social and emotional difficulties that continue into adolescence and adulthood. Your child's ability to form friendships depends in large part on how skilled he is at using social behavior skills. **Promoting social behavior skill development may be a good place to start with younger and/or very socially delayed older children.** This chapter will give you a few suggestions to improve your child's social skills.

Nobody Likes Me

Tony is a 10-year-old boy who has few friends. His parents, Debbie and Bruce, have received much feedback from school officials about Tony's social behavior. Apparently, he bugs other children and is sometimes aggressive towards them at school. In turn, he seems to be picked on and teased.

At home, Debbie and Bruce notice similar kinds of social interactions with Tony in the neighborhood and with his 8-year-old sister, Kathy. They observe that Tony is frequently bugging other children and Kathy and, again, is rejected, picked on, and teased. Although Tony goes out and plays with children frequently and does OK at first, after a little while it's not uncommon for Tony to come home crying, "Nobody likes me."

WHAT ARE SOCIAL BEHAVIOR PROBLEMS?

Many children who have difficulties in the social arena simply do not know how to behave in social situations. These children often exhibit many negative social behaviors, such as hitting, interrupting, bugging, and so forth, and few positive social behaviors, such as making eye contact, expressing feelings, sharing, or cooperating. In order for children to develop friendships, they need to reduce negative social behaviors and increase positive social behaviors. Children typically learn social behavior skills in the toddler, preschool, and early elementary school age years of development. If your child does not possess these skills, he will need to have the skills taught to him.

TEACHING CHILDREN SOCIAL BEHAVIOR SKILLS

The following section describes how parents can help children develop social behavior skills. Social behavior skills training is a good first step toward promoting friendships for younger elementary school age children or for older children who are socially delayed. **These procedures can be used to improve children's relationships with parents, siblings, or peers.**

Step 1: Identify Social Behaviors to Target with Your Child

There are a variety of social behavior skills you could try to focus on to help your child learn. The first task is to figure out which negative social behaviors your child uses too often and which positive social behaviors your child does not use often enough.

Examples of negative social behaviors include the following:

- Physical aggression (hitting, kicking, etc.)
- Playing unfair
- Arguing
- Interrupting
- Name calling
- Bossing others
- Whining, complaining, and so forth
- Taking others' possessions
- Dominating the activity
- Making poor eye contact
- Being a poor sport
- Being too loud
- Showing off
- Teasing
- Butting in
- Bugging others
- Getting into others' space
- Withdrawing and isolating self
- Being passive
- Listening poorly
- Hoarding food, toys, and so forth
- Keeping feelings inside
- Talking too much
- Disobeying rules of play
- Being too rough in play
- Not handling peer pressure well (i.e., peers influence child to do things he shouldn't)

Examples of positive social behaviors include the following:

- Taking turns
- Sharing
- Expressing feelings
- Cooperating
- Making eye contact
- Starting conversations
- Being assertive
- Apologizing to others
- Asking questions
- Telling others about self
- Playing fair
- Ignoring when appropriate
- Inquiring about others' interests or desires

- Listening to others
- Complimenting others
- Accepting compliments
- Following rules of play
- Refusing to cooperate with peers' negative behavior
- Talking in a brief manner
- Asking for what one wants/needs
- Helping others
- Refusing to do negative things asked by peers

To figure out which behaviors to work on with your child you will need to take some time to observe him in social situations with peers and/or siblings. To get the information you need, it may be necessary to watch your child for several days or weeks in various social situations. You should observe your child in situations in which there is high structure (e.g., boy/girl scouting, sports, church activity, etc.) and low structure (e.g., playing with peers/siblings in the front yard or at the park, etc.). Try to notice how your child is accepted by his peers/siblings. Note whether your child seems to be rejected, neglected, or aggressive with other children. Furthermore, try to note which negative social behaviors your child uses too often and which positive social behaviors your child doesn't use enough (see previous examples of negative and positive social behaviors).

The Parent Observation of Child Social Behavior chart found at the end of this chapter may assist in identifying social behavior targets. This chart simply structures your observations to help you pinpoint negative and positive social behaviors in your child.

Step 2: Collaborate to Help Your Child Understand Social Behavior Problems and Select Target Social Behavior

It is very important to **work with your child** in selecting and working on specific positive social behaviors. It is often a very delicate situation because many children are nervous or defensive about working on social behaviors. At first, you should try to discuss the problem with your child in a supportive manner. Begin by pointing out that he seems to have some difficulty getting along with other children. Don't judge your child, but communicate to him that you would like to help. Explain that you have a plan on how he might be able to get along better with other children and that you would like to work with him to put the plan into action. **Don't bother trying to work with your child regarding social behavior skills until this collaborative relationship has been achieved.**

It's absolutely critical that your child understand his social behavior difficulties and have input about what to work on. The next step is to pinpoint which specific positive social behaviors your child would like to target. It can be helpful to review a list of possible behaviors (such as in the previous section). Ask for your child's input about which negative social behaviors he thinks he should do less and which positive social behaviors he thinks he should do more. If you think it helpful, share your observations regarding his interactions with other children. Together, select several target positive social behaviors to work on. Ideally the positive behavior selected is the opposite of the negative behavior (e.g., sharing vs. hoarding).

Step 3: Teach Your Child Social Behavior Skills

The next step is to teach your child specific positive social behavior skills. First, explain the targeted positive social behaviors and describe the behaviors in a way he will understand. The next step is to model or demonstrate what the positive social behaviors look like. This involves actual demonstration of the behaviors with your child observing. The next step is to role play the targeted positive behaviors. Take turns "acting" until your child can demonstrate what the behaviors look like. Usually, after explaining, modeling, and role playing, most children will have a good understanding of the targeted behaviors.

The following example pertains to teaching a child the positive social behavior of sharing toys. First the parent verbally explains the behavior by saying, for example, "Sharing toys means you let others play with you or you allow others to have some of the toys you have." Modeling in this case would be actual parent demonstrations of sharing behaviors. Finally, the parent would engage the child in role playing whereby the child demonstrates to the parent what sharing behaviors look like.

Similar explaining, modeling, and role-playing procedures would be used for other social behaviors. **Make sure your child understands completely and is able to perform the targeted social behavior before going on to the next step.**

Step 4: Coach and Reinforce Desirable Social Behaviors in Real Social Situations

Coaching is critical in actually helping children use their newly acquired social behavior skills in real-life situations. Ideally, you would coach your child when he is in real-life situations. **Coaching involves prompting or reminding your child to be aware of, and to perform, more positive social behaviors.** The goal is to notice when your child might be having social interaction difficulties and encourage him to utilize the skills he has just learned. **You could coach your child to practice the social skills in ongoing parent–child, sibling–child, or peer–child interactions.** All of these social interactions provide good opportunities to practice the skills.

It might also be helpful to plan ahead about how your child could work on social behavior skills in future social situations. For example, if a parent knows that a child will be going to a boy or girl scout meeting, the parent and child might plan ways for the child to work on social behavior skills during the meeting.

Reinforcing social behavior can be done in a formal or informal manner. The formal reinforcement could be to give your child a tangible reinforcer for practicing the desired social behavior. The informal reinforcement procedure would involve simply praising your child when he engages in the desired social behaviors.

Step 5a: Implement a Formal Social Behavior Skills Practice Program

The Practicing Social Behavior Skills chart found at the end of this chapter can be used to **help your child practice social behavior skills at a specified time during a specified event**. This chart has five steps. The first one is to designate which social behavior your child will try to improve during a particular social event. The second step is to note when and where your child will try to engage in this specific social behavior. The third step is for the child to evaluate himself on the 5-point rating scale after the event has occurred. Note that the scale ranges from 1 (Not at all) to 5 (Great). The fourth step requires your child to reflect back and write down what he did to support the rating. The fifth step involves you rating your child and reinforcing him if he did well in practicing the specific social behavior during the event.

The Daily Social Behavior Goals chart at the end of this chapter can be used to **help your child practice social skills on an ongoing basis.** The chart requires your child to specify one or more social behaviors he will work on each day. At the end of the day, your child rates himself using the 5-point rating system found on the chart to evaluate how well he met his goals. You also rate your child on how he met the social goal and provide reinforcement if he did well.

The Practicing Social Behavior Skills and Daily Social Behavior Goals charts can be used to improve social behaviors in parent–child, sibling–child, and peer–child interactions. You can use either chart depending on what you think will work best for your child. If your child receives ratings of 3 or more on either of the charts, he could earn reinforcement. (See the "Reinforcement" section in Chapter 5.)

Step 5b: Implement an Informal Social Behavior Skills Practice Program

If you prefer, you could use more informal procedures to promote social skill development. Steps 1–4 should still be utilized. You could then informally prompt your child to use certain social behaviors. This could be followed by praise as a reinforcement if your child does the desired social behavior.

TEACHING PEER PRESSURE "REFUSAL" SKILLS

Many children are negatively influenced by peers. To fit in or be accepted by peers, children will do things such as violate rules or exhibit other problem behaviors. These behaviors could range from showing off to using drugs in response to peer pressure. Indeed, peer influences have much to do with children using drugs, engaging in sex, skipping school, vandalizing, committing crimes, and so forth. Consequently, it is very important for children to learn to refuse peer pressure.

Refusal skills involve a child behaving assertively when pressured by peers to do something he doesn't really want to do. To assist a child in refusal skills, it is important to collaborate with, educate, and train your child how to respond assertively to peers.

Collaborating means you and your child **discuss peer pressure and agree to work together** to deal with the problem. Identify the areas where your child feels pressure. With younger children, the pressure might be to throw rocks on the playground, goof off in class, tease other children, and so forth. With teens, the pressure might be to use drugs, skip school, break curfew, and so forth. If your child wants to work with you on these pressures, proceed further with education and assertiveness training. **If your child does not cooperate, but has problems with peer pressure, then forget refusal skills, and try another procedure in this book or consult with a mental health professional.** You may need to set up special rules and/or monitor your child more closely (see Chapter 8 for ideas to help children learn to follow rules).

Educating involves discussing the potential consequences of submitting to peer pressure with your child. With a younger child, this may involve talking about how certain actions will get him in trouble and maybe could lead to physical harm of others. With an older child or teen, you may be able to take it further, and discuss how certain actions might make someone else feel.

Assertiveness training entails helping the child develop social behaviors to cope with peer pressure. This is best accomplished by planning, rehearsing and doing refusal behaviors. It will help to **plan** how the child will respond when peer pressure situations come up. Ask your child to "think ahead" and plan what to do next time. This may involve thinking what to say to peers and what to do. For example, a child may plan to say, "No, thanks, I have to go home," and to walk home when peers pressure him to go into a convenience store to steal candy. Role playing is a good way to **rehearse** the refusal skills. You and your child act out various peer pressure scenarios and the plan your child came up with to deal with the pressure. The role playing offers a chance to modify the plan if the plan doesn't seem to work. The final, and hardest, step is to **do** the refusing. Your child is alone on this one. But, you can check in with your child and discuss how it's going after each episode. This may present opportunities to modify plans and rehearse new plans.

You may want to use the Daily Social Behavior Goals chart found at the end of this chapter to promote refusal skills in your child. You could list "refusing peer pressure" as the target social behavior on the chart. See the previous section for instructions on how to use the Daily Social Behavior Goals chart.

OTHER HELPFUL SOCIAL BEHAVIOR SKILLS TRAINING IDEAS

Teach Siblings Similar Social Behavior Skills

Although siblings may not display social behavior difficulties with most children, they may do so with their behavior problem sibling. Therefore, it might be beneficial to train siblings to use social behavior skills too. It may also have more of an impact on your child if his siblings are involved.

Orchestrate Situations to Practice Social Behavior Skills

It may be helpful for you to arrange and plan specific activities in which your child can practice social behavior skills. For example, you could plan situations in which your child will be interacting with only one other child (e.g., sleep-over, dinner, trip to the fair, etc.). Once your child has achieved some success in one-to-one situations, you might arrange structured small group activities (e.g., invite several children for a sleep-over, invite a small group of children for a birthday party, etc.). Finally, once your child has achieved success in structured small group activities, you might want to orchestrate larger social situations for your child to practice the social skills behaviors (e.g., larger parties, larger group outings to events, etc.). During all of these activities, you should be involved in coaching and reinforcing your child according to the procedures discussed above.

Enroll Your Child in Specialized Groups

There are certain structured group activities that can help your child develop social behavior skills. Usually group activities without an intensive competitive atmosphere work best, for example, scouting, 4-H, church youth groups, arts and craft groups, and so forth. Emphasize cooperation and typically have structure, rules, and adult supervision. Look for opportunities to enroll your child in such groups. It may help for you to be actively involved as well.

Some children have a very difficult time with social behavior skills and may not really improve solely from the ideas in this chapter. **It may be helpful to enroll some children in a social behavior skills therapy group.** These therapy groups provide children with an opportunity to learn and practice these difficult skills in a controlled setting. Consult a mental health professional about social behavior skills groups in your child's school and/or community.

Find Peer Helpers

Many schools have peer helper programs where older children are paired up with younger children so the older one can tutor the younger one in academic areas. This experience also provides a good opportunity to learn and practice social behavior skills. You might inquire at your child's school to see if your child could participate in a peer helper program.

Collaborate with School Officials

Many of the procedures described in this chapter could be used by school personnel who work with your child. If possible, set up a meeting and discuss ways in which you and school officials can work together using a similar system at home and school. (See the "Home–School Note System" and "Intensive Home–School Collaboration" sections in Chapter 12 for more details.)

Work with Other Parents

Children who have social behavior problems are often teased and picked on by others. Sometimes a child with a behavior problem is the one doing the teasing. Occasionally, this teasing can get so out of hand that a child or group of children continue to have prolonged and chronic problems interacting with each other.

In these instances, it **may** be helpful to work with other children's parents. To accomplish this, it is obviously necessary that the other parent be willing to do so. One strategy is for only the parents to meet on their own and discuss ways to help their children get along better. Another strategy is for all parents to meet with all the involved children and work something out. The ultimate solution may be that your children agree to try harder to get along, that parents actively monitor social interactions, and that parents communicate periodically with each other.

HANG IN THERE

Social problems in children are often extremely difficult to change. It can take weeks, months, or even years for a child to use a new skill regularly. Even if your child changes his behavior, others still may not change their opinion of your child due to previous "labeling." For these reasons, you need to work very hard and long. It's going to take time to help your child develop social behavior skills and to be accepted by other children.

SUMMARY POINTS

1. Poor social relationships are related to children's behavioral and emotional problems.
2. It is critical to collaborate and work with your child in selecting target social behaviors.
3. Teach your child specific social behaviors by explaining, modeling, and role playing.
4. Coach and reinforce social behavior skills in real-life social situations with your child.
5. Utilize formal practice procedures to help your child really learn social behavior skills.

Somebody Likes Me

Back to Tony and his parents, Debbie and Bruce: The parents decide that drastic measures need to be taken to help Tony develop some social behavior skills. At first, they simply observe Tony at play in the neighborhood, at his little league baseball practice, and with his sister, Kathy. They observe that Tony seems isolated and by himself at first, and then he starts interacting negatively with other children. He does a lot of interrupting, bossing others, and bugging others, and very little taking turns and sharing. Later, they enlist Tony's cooperation through several discussions, and he agrees to work on social behavior skills. They explain, model, and role play the targeted behaviors with Tony until he really understands them. Then they utilize the Practicing Social Behavior Skills chart as a formal method of implementing and reinforcing the social behavior skills training. At first they focus on sibling–child interactions, and then on peer–child interactions, using these methods. Tony earns rewards for his efforts. Finally, Debbie and Bruce also talk to the parents of the next-door neighbor's child. All of the parents and their children have a meeting and make some agreements about acceptable and unacceptable social interactions. The parents agree to work together cooperatively to monitor and help the children get along better.

Note. See the "Teaching Children Problem Solving" section in Chapter 10 for more information related to children's social functioning.

CHARTS FOR CHAPTER 9

PARENT OBSERVATION OF CHILD SOCIAL BEHAVIOR

Name: _____

Date: _____

Directions: Set aside some time to observe your child interacting with peers and/or siblings. Answer each question below.

1. **What is the social setting of this observation?**

2. **What kinds of social problems did my child have?**

3. **What negative social behaviors did my child do too much?**

4. **What positive social behaviors did my child not do enough?**

From *Skills Training for Children with Behavior Disorders: A Parent and Therapist Guidebook* by Michael L. Bloomquist. © 1996 The Guilford Press.

EXAMPLE:
PARENT OBSERVATION OF CHILD SOCIAL BEHAVIOR

Name: *Tony*

Date: *Friday*

Directions: Set aside some time to observe your child interacting with peers and/or siblings. Answer each question below.

1. **What is the social setting of this observation?**

   Playing with children in the park

2. **What kinds of social problems did my child have?**

   At first, he was ignored by other children. Later he interfered in some children's game of baseball.

3. **What negative social behaviors did my child do too much?**

   Physical aggression, butting in, bugging others.

4. **What positive social behaviors did my child not do enough?**

   Taking turns, cooperating, asking questions, inquiring about others' interests and desires.

From *Skills Training for Children with Behavior Disorders: A Parent and Therapist Guidebook* by Michael L. Bloomquist. © 1996 The Guilford Press.

PRACTICING SOCIAL BEHAVIOR SKILLS

Name: _____

Date: _____

Directions: The parent and/or child can complete the form, but all involved should discuss it. Complete Steps 1 and 2 before the social event and Steps 3, 4, and 5 after the social event.

Before Social Event

1. **I will work on these social behavior goals:**

2. **When and where I will work on the social behavior goals** (designate time and place):

After Social Event

3. **How well did I accomplish my social behavior goal?** (circle one)

1	2	3	4	5
Not at all	A little	OK	Pretty good	Great
☹		☺		☺

4. **What did I do that tells me how to rate myself?** (Write down how you know you deserve the above rating.)

5. **If my parent agrees with my rating and it is a 3, 4, or 5, I get this reward:**

From *Skills Training for Children with Behavior Disorders: A Parent and Therapist Guidebook* by Michael L. Bloomquist. © 1996 The Guilford Press.

EXAMPLE:
PRACTICING SOCIAL BEHAVIOR SKILLS

Name: *Tony*

Date: *Saturday*

Directions: The parent and/or child can complete the form, but all involved should discuss it. Complete Steps 1 and 2 before the social event and Steps 3, 4, and 5 after the social event.

Before Social Event

1. **I will work on these social behavior goals:**

   Speaking to other children and making eye contact.

2. **When and where I will work on the social behavior goals** (designate time and place):

   Saturday morning at baseball practice.

After Social Event

3. **How well did I accomplish my social behavior goal?** (circle one)

1	2	3	④	5
Not at all	A little	OK	Pretty good	Great

4. **What did I do that tells me how to rate myself?** (Write down how you know you deserve the above rating.)

   I talked to Chris and Steve about the next game. I looked into their eyes when I talked to them. I asked Mr. Jackson to throw some balls to me. I looked into his eyes, too.

5. **If my parent agrees with my rating and it is a 3, 4, or 5, I get this reward:**

   Pizza for supper.

From *Skills Training for Children with Behavior Disorders: A Parent and Therapist Guidebook* by Michael L. Bloomquist. © 1996 The Guilford Press.

DAILY SOCIAL BEHAVIOR GOALS

Name: _____

Date: _____

Directions: Indicate below which negative and positive social behavior goals you will be working on. At the end of the day, rate how well you accomplished your goals. It may be helpful to get feedback from parents as to how well they think you are accomplishing your goals.

Child Evaluation

1. **I am working on these social behavior goals:**

2. **How well did I accomplish my goal?** (circle one)

1	2	3	4	5
Not at all	A little	OK	Pretty good	Great
☹		☺		☺

Parent Evaluation

3. **How well parent thinks child accomplished social behavior goals:** (circle one)

1	2	3	4	5
Not at all	A little	OK	Pretty good	Great
☹		☺		☺

Reward

4. **If my parent rates me as a 3, 4, or 5, I get this reward:**

EXAMPLE:
DAILY SOCIAL BEHAVIOR GOALS

Name: _Tony_

Date: _Saturday_

Directions: Indicate below which negative and positive social behavior goals you will be working on. At the end of the day, rate how well you accomplished your goals. It may be helpful to get feedback from parents as to how well they think you are accomplishing your goals.

Child Evaluation

1. **I am working on these social behavior goals:**

   Sharing and expressing feelings.

2. **How well did I accomplish my goal?** (circle one)

1	2	3	④	5
Not at all	A little	OK	Pretty good	Great

Parent Evaluation

3. **How well parent thinks child accomplished social behavior goal:** (circle one)

1	2	3	④	5
Not at all	A little	OK	Pretty good	Great

Reward

4. **If my parent rates me as a 3, 4, or 5, I get this reward:**

   Select from reinforcement menu.

10

Enhancing Children's Social and General Problem-Solving Skills

Being able to solve problems and think about what you are doing is essential in life. One part of problem solving involves being able to stop and think before acting. Another part is to think about what you are doing in a step-by-step manner while trying to solve a particular problem. Problem solving is also important in social relationships. People must be able to handle interpersonal problems in order to have good relationships. This chapter will present some ways to help children develop problem-solving abilities.

Why Don't You Think about What You're Doing?

Sally is an 11-year-old child who seems to get into lots of trouble. Her mother, Brenda, frequently has to discipline her for her misbehavior. Brenda can cite numerous times when Sally just doesn't seem to think about what she's doing. For example, she recently instructed Sally to rake up some leaves in the front yard. A friend came by on her bicycle and asked Sally to go to the park. Sally just put down her rake and went off to the park. Another more serious example is when a friend asked Sally to participate in stealing some candy from a local store. Sally did it and got caught. Similar difficulties also occur at home. Recently Sally's younger brother, Michael, went into Sally's room and messed it up. Sally went into her room, noticed the mess, and then immediately went out and punched Michael. Brenda is getting tired of constantly having to give Sally negative consequences for her behavior. She frequently asks Sally, "Why don't you think about what you're doing?"

WHAT ARE PROBLEM-SOLVING DEFICITS?

Children who are effective at problem solving are able to recognize when a problem exists and to plan a course of action to solve the problem. Many children with behavior problems are impulsive and are poor problem solvers. They may not recognize when a problem exists, they don't think ahead about the consequences of their behavior, they don't think of alternative ways to solve a problem, or, even if they think of a plan, they may not always follow that plan.

Children with social problems, especially aggressive children, do not solve interpersonal problems effectively. These children are prone to make "mistakes" in how they "see" (perceive) the problem, which causes them to solve the problem in an unhelpful way. Aggressive children, for example, often misinterpret others' behavior and intent, thinking that social problems are "the other person's "fault" and that the other person did it "on purpose." These children often fail to recognize their own role in causing problems. Aggressive children are also often poor at "perspective taking" or thinking of the problem from another's point of view. Often, only aggressive (not prosocial) solutions to handling social problems occur to these children, and they often think aggressive solutions are better than nonaggressive solutions anyway.

TEACHING CHILDREN PROBLEM SOLVING

Problem-solving training involves teaching a child to think before acting and to think in a goal-directed manner. Through problem-solving training, children learn how to handle their immediate problems better. They learn to recognize problems, produce alternative strategies, think of consequences, anticipate obstacles to problem solving, and implement effective strategies to solve social and general problems.

The problem-solving procedure includes the following steps:

1. Stop! What is the problem?
2. Who or what caused the problem?
3. What does each person think and feel?
4. What are some plans?
5. What is the best plan?
6. Do the plan.
7. Did the plan work?

Steps 2 and 3 can be skipped if the problem is not a social problem.

Step 1: Determine If Your Child Can Benefit
from Problem-Solving Training

Children of all ages can benefit to varying degrees from training in problem-solving. Typically, however, **parents should not expect children under the age of 8 to apply problem-solving strategies to real-life situations very well.** Children over age 8 can benefit to a greater extent from problem-solving training and are also more likely to apply these strategies to their own problems. Also, parents should not expect children to be able to do problem solving if they do not know how to comply and/or follow the rules. You need to ask yourself if your child is ready. If you think she is ready, then proceed to the next steps.

If your child is significantly noncompliant, or routinely breaks the rules, don't try to teach her problem solving. You will have more success with compliance training and other discipline techniques discussed in Chapters 7 and 8. Perhaps after your child is more compliant and better at following rules, you could teach her problem solving.

Step 2: Instruct Your Child in Basic Problem Solving

Instruct your child directly about the steps involved in problem solving. This could be accomplished by reviewing the steps on the Problem Solving chart found at the end of this chapter. You will likely need to discuss, demonstrate, and model how to use the problem-solving steps for your child. **It would be helpful at first to teach your child problem-solving skills with easy problems, and then later apply the skills to more difficult problems.** While discussing the problem-solving steps, it may be helpful to present a hypothetical problem and ask your child questions to lead her to solve the hypothetical problem verbally. For example, you might ask your child to solve the problem that comes up when she wants to watch a TV show, but you want her to complete chores. Guide your child through all the steps to help her solve this hypothetical problem. Continue instructing your child until it seems she is beginning to understand what problem solving is all about. **If your child is resistant to your instruction, don't push it too hard.**

An important point to keep in mind is that many children have a very difficult time with Step 6—Do the plan—of the problem-solving process. This requires actually doing something (a specific behavior) to solve the problem. **Just because a child thinks of a good plan (e.g., "I'll ignore him") doesn't mean she can actually do the plan (e.g., actually ignore him).** Many children need to be taught to do the plan (e.g., taught how to ignore). This can be accomplished by instructing, modeling, and practicing specific behaviors. It may be important to teach your child how to ignore, take turns, share, stay on-task, and so forth. (See Chapter 9 for ideas on how to teach social behavior skills.)

Step 3: Instruct Your Child in Situation Interpretation and Perspective Taking for Social Problem Solving

As mentioned earlier, aggressive children often make mistakes in how they interpret situations, and they do not think of others' perspectives. Situation interpretation and perspective-taking training help children see situations and others' points of view more accurately. These skills require children to think about their own thoughts in order to evaluate how accurate they are and to think of others' perspectives. This requires abstract thinking skills that young children typically do not possess. **Situation interpretation and perspective-taking training are only recommended for children of average intelligence over age 10 years.** A parent can still lead a child to solve social problems without going through this step, but the child may need more parental guidance.

The basic idea in situation interpretation training is to help your child understand how people see things differently. For example, one umpire might call a baseball runner out at home, while another umpire might call the same runner safe. Another example is a child who is bumped by another child while walking down the hall. She might think the person bumped her on purpose. Another child might think the same person bumped her by accident. Discuss other examples of how people might make mistakes in how they see situations. Tell your child of occasions when you have misinterpreted situations. Ask your child to think of times when she made mistakes in interpreting others' behavior.

Explain that people can stop and figure out if they are seeing situations correctly or not. For example, an umpire calls a runner out at home, and the catcher protests the call. The umpire could ask another umpire for another opinion to make sure he sees it correctly. The second umpire might discuss it with the first umpire to determine if the runner was really out or safe. The first umpire might change his mind. Explain that the same can be true of social situations. A person might be bumped in the hallway, think the other person did it on purpose, but then after thinking about the evidence could change his mind to think it was an accident. Ask your child to think of past, real-life social situations where it didn't go too well. For example, your child may recall a time she thought her friend or sibling pushed her, when in reality the other person tripped and fell into her accidently. Ask her to look for the evidence as to who caused this problem. Explain that looking for evidence is the key to seeing "sticky situations" accurately. Tell your child that when something happens, it's important to stop and think of "who or what caused the problem." Parents will need to assist children to figure this out because it is difficult for most children, especially children prone to aggressive problem solving.

The basic idea of perspective-taking training is to help your child put herself "in the other guy's shoes," to understand others' thoughts and feelings. As a starting point, you could page through a magazine, look at pictures, and ask your child to think of each person's thoughts and feelings. Next ask your child to reflect on past, real-life social situations she was involved in where it didn't go too well. For example, your child may recall taking a toy from a friend or sibling yesterday. Again, ask your child to try to explain what she and the other person were thinking and feeling.

Try to incorporate discussions of situation interpretation and perspective taking into ongoing social problem-solving discussions. The Problem Solving chart incorporates these two skills. **Step 2—Who or what caused the problem?—is designed to focus a child to interpret situations accurately.** As you discuss Step 2 with your child, ask her to state her role and the other person's role in creating the problem. **Step 3—What does each person think and feel?—is designed to focus a child to understand others' perspectives.** As you discuss Step 3 with your child, ask her to state the thoughts and feelings of each person who is involved in a particular social problem.

Step 4: Model Problem Solving

You can be a better teacher by modeling problem solving to your child. **To accomplish this, talk out loud more in front of your child in a problem-solving manner.** By doing so, you can demonstrate how to solve problems. At first you could model using problem-solving strategies with neutral or easy situations. For example, you could talk out loud about problems such as what to make for dinner, plans for the evening, where to go out to eat, and so forth. Later, you could model utilizing problem-solving strategies for more difficult and emotional problems, such as how to cope with a boss at work, problems with a friend, and so forth. It is recommended that you **do not discuss adult-only personal problems** (e.g., marital or financial problems, etc.) with your child to demonstrate how to solve problems.

You could model utilizing the problem solving steps in either a formal or an informal manner. A formal way of modeling problem-solving would be to utilize the Problem Solving chart. You could have this chart in hand and go through each step systematically as you solve a problem, while your child observes. Modeling problem solving in an informal way would simply involve thinking through situations and problems out loud for your child to observe. For example, when confronted with a problem, you could say something like, "Hmm, I wonder what the problem is here? What should I do? I think I will try (a strategy/plan). Did it work?" and so forth.

Step 5: Guide Your Child to Use Problem Solving through Directed Discovery Questioning

Try to guide your child to apply problem solving in real-life situations. **"Directed discovery" questioning involves asking your child questions to help her discover how to solve a problem on her own.** This type of questioning requires children to think for themselves, and, therefore, it is necessary for them to have relatively sophisticated thinking abilities. Directed discovery questioning is typically appropriate only for children with average or better intelligence over the age of 8.

Directed discovery questioning can be done using either an open-ended format or a forced-choice format. The open-ended directed discovery format is preferred, but for children who are somewhat younger or who get "stuck" and can't come up with the answers, the forced-choice method could be used.

Examples of open-ended directed-discovery questions include the following:

1. "What can you do?"
2. "I am confused. Explain it to me. How could you solve that problem?"
3. "How are you going to solve that problem?"

4. "What's the first step? Then what do you do? OK, now what's the next step?"

Examples of forced-choice directed discovery questions include the following:

1. "You could try this (option) or that (another option). What do you think would work best?"
2. "It looks like you have two options—this (option) or that (another option). What do you think would work best?"

Don't solve your child's problems for her. Try to guide your child to solve her own problems through directed-discovery questioning. For example, if your child complains that she cannot get along with a friend, prompt your child to use a problem-solving strategy. Essentially, your goal is to respond to your child's ongoing problems and dilemmas by guiding her to solve her own problems.

Step 6a: Implement a Formal Problem-Solving Procedure

The formal method of implementing problem solving involves using the Problem-Solving Worksheet found at the end of this chapter. This worksheet can be used to solve immediate problems or to think retrospectively about how problems could have been solved. **Act as a coach, and guide your child in the problem-solving process by using the worksheet.** First prompt your child to use problem solving. A phrase such as "this might be a good time to use problem solving" would be sufficient. **If you or your child is angry, don't bother prompting her to use problem solving until you both cool off.** (See Chapter 6 for ideas on family anger/conflict management.) Next, guide your child to figure out each step as indicated on the Problem-Solving Worksheet. As you can see from looking at the worksheet, the child and/or parents work together and go through each step of the problem-solving process. After you and your child have worked through a Problem-Solving Worksheet, the last step is to evaluate your child as to how well she used the problem-solving procedure. A 4-point rating scale can be found at the bottom of the worksheet. Its purpose is to give your child some feedback about how well she utilized problem solving.

You or your child could fill out the Problem-Solving Worksheet. It's not so important who actually writes on the worksheet, but that it be used as a vehicle to structure the problem-solving process. You could act as the "secretary" and write down what your child says if that makes your child more willing to use the procedure.

The Tally for Using Problem-Solving Worksheet at the end of this chapter can be used to reinforce a child in a formal way. This chart is used with the Problem-Solving Worksheet. You and/or your child would add up the problem-solving ratings (1, 2, 3, or 4) from any of the worksheets completed for a designated time period. The idea is to add up the 1 and 2 ratings, and the 3 and 4 ratings. If there are more 3 and 4 ratings than 1 and 2 ratings, your child gets to select a reward. (See the "Reinforcement" section in Chapter 5.)

Step 6b: Implement an Informal Problem-Solving Procedure

You may elect not to use the formal worksheet but still provide opportunities to learn and practice problem solving in a less formal manner. This could be accomplished by prompting your child to use problem solving as the need arises. You could ask questions similar to those on the Problem-Solving Worksheet, but you would not actually utilize it. The Problem Solving chart at the end of this chapter can be used to help children to use problem solving informally. You and your child could look at either of these charts as you guide her to solve a particular problem.

Informal reinforcement of problem solving would involve praising. Each time your child or adolescent solves a problem, either via the Problem-Solving Worksheets or more informal problem solving, you would praise your child or adolescent for her work.

USING PROBLEM SOLVING FOR CONFLICT RESOLUTION

Why do people have conflicts? Often it is because people disagree on how to handle a situation or solve a problem. Children prone to behavioral problems seem to have many conflicts with siblings, peers, and others. Problem solving could help children resolve conflicts, but often children do not use the skills because they are too angry or because they don't think of it.

Parents can assist children through a problem-solving conflict resolution process. First, make sure that your child, and other children who may have conflicts with your child, really understand the problem-solving process, by going through all the steps in the preceding "Teaching Children Problem Solving" section. Next, ask your child, and other children who may have conflicts with your child, to agree to sit down with you to solve a problem the next time a conflict comes up. When a conflict does arise, ask the children involved to sit down at a table with you to resolve the conflict. Your job is to lead the children through the problem-solving steps while trying to prevent the children from blaming, name-calling, yelling, and so forth. If tempers flare, separate the children until they are calm, and then try it again. You may want to enlarge the Problem Solving chart into a poster and have it near by to guide the children. An alternative would be to go through a Problem-Solving Worksheet to work through the problem-solving steps. Once the children agree on a solution to the problem, you may need to assist them to make sure they actually do what they agreed on.

FAMILY PROBLEM SOLVING REVISITED

The procedures described above are designed essentially for child-focused problem solving. However, not all problems involve only your child. Furthermore, some children are resistant to child-focused problem solving. **Using child-focused problem solving implies that the child has a problem, and some children are defensive about this implication.** "Collaborative problem solving" involves solving problems together with your child. Here the emphasis is on working with your child to solve your child's problems or problems between you and your child. Family problem solving is utilized to accomplish the goals of collaborative problem solving. **Family problem solving works better in some situations than child-focused problem solving.** Younger children (under age 8 to 10) and some adolescents (who don't like to be singled out) often prefer and benefit more from this approach.

The reader is referred back to Chapter 6 to review the "Family Problem Solving" section. If your child is resistant to child-focused problem solving, then it may be wise to use only family problem-solving procedures. Even if family problem solving procedures are emphasized, your child will still learn problem solving. By utilizing family problem solving to work through ongoing family difficulties, your child learns more about the skill of problem solving.

"THINKING AHEAD" PROBLEM SOLVING

So far we have reviewed problem-solving procedures used to handle immediate problems that occur at a given moment. Another form of problem solving involves thinking ahead to solve a problem or achieve a goal. This type of problem solving is important for a child who routinely responds "I don't know" when an adult asks her how to reach a goal she wants to achieve.

"Thinking ahead" problem solving involves the following steps:

1. What is my goal?
2. What steps do I need to do to reach my goal?
   Step 1.
   Step 2.
   Step 3.
   Step 4.
3. Did I reach my goal?

The Thinking Ahead chart and Thinking Ahead Problem-Solving Worksheet found at the end of this chapter can be used to teach children about thinking ahead skills. Parents should use similar methods as described in the "Teaching Children Problem Solving" section of this chapter to teach a child about thinking ahead problem solving.

SUMMARY POINTS

1. Children who are impulsive and/or don't think before acting are more likely to have behavioral, social, and emotional problems.
2. Children under age 8 years may not benefit from problem-solving training.
3. To solve social problems, children can benefit from learning to interpret

situations accurately and think about others' perspectives, as part of the problem-solving process.

4. You can teach your child problem-solving skills through instructing, modeling, and guiding her in applying the skills.
5. Directed discovery questioning involves asking your child questions that guide her to apply problem solving to real-life difficulties.
6. Problem solving can be used to resolve conflicts between your child and other children or family members. You can assist your child to use problem-solving skills to work out conflict situations.
7. Thinking ahead problem solving involves helping your child articulate the steps necessary to achieve or reach a goal.

Thinking before Acting

Back to Sally and Brenda: Brenda decides that she's going to try to teach Sally to think before she acts through problem-solving training. At first, Brenda emphasizes modeling and instructing as she teaches Sally the problem-solving process. Later she tries to guide Sally to apply the problem-solving procedure by utilizing the Problem-Solving Worksheet. At first, they practice using the worksheets with some contrived problems. Later Sally is encouraged to use the Problem-Solving Worksheet after a problem situation occurred. Sally was still having problems with not thinking, but was willing to fill out the worksheet after the fact. Gradually, Sally began to utilize the problem-solving process on her own. Brenda was startled one day when Sally actually came up to her and said, "Mom, I think I'm going to use a Problem-Solving Worksheet to solve this problem with Michael." Sally has continued to show progress in learning the problem-solving technique. Brenda is utilizing the Tally for Using Problem-Solving Worksheet to reinforce Sally for her efforts formally . Sally is saving up tokens to go to a movie.

CHARTS FOR CHAPTER 10

PROBLEM SOLVING

1. Stop! What is the problem?

2. Who or what caused the problem?

3. What does each person think and feel?

4. What are some plans?

5. What is the best plan?

6. Do the plan.

7. Did the plan work?

Note. Steps 2 and 3 can be skipped if the problem is not a social problem.

From *Skills Training for Children with Behavior Disorders: A Parent and Therapist Guidebook* by Michael L. Bloomquist. © 1996 The Guilford Press.

PROBLEM-SOLVING WORKSHEET

Name: _____

Date: _____

Directions: The parent and/or child can complete this form. Answer each question as it pertains to the problem at hand. You can use the worksheet to solve a problem as it occurs or to figure out how you could have solved a problem after it's over.

1. **Stop! What is the problem?**

2. **Who or what caused the problem?** (optional) Try to figure out your role and other people's roles in causing the problem.

3. **What does each person think and feel?** (optional) Put yourself in the "other guy's shoes" to see how that person thinks and feels.

4. **What are some plans (solutions)?** List as many plans (solutions) as possible that could be used to solve the problem.

5. **What is the best plan?** Think ahead about what would happen if you used the plans in Step 4. Then decide which one will work best.

6. **Do the plan.** How will I do the plan? What will I do to make the plan work?

7. **Did the plan work?**

Problem-Solving Rating (circle one)
1. Didn't use problem solving at all.
2. Tried to use problem solving a little, but it didn't really work.
3. Tried hard, went through problem-solving steps, but didn't really use the best plan.
4. Tried hard, went through problem-solving steps, and used the best plan.

Note. Steps 2 and 3 can be skipped if the problem is not a social problem.

From *Skills Training for Children with Behavior Disorders: A Parent and Therapist Guidebook* by Michael L. Bloomquist. © 1996 The Guilford Press.

EXAMPLE:
PROBLEM-SOLVING WORKSHEET

Name: *Sally*

Date: *Tuesday*

Directions: The parent and/or child can complete this form. Answer each question as it pertains to the problem at hand. You can use the worksheet to solve a problem as it occurs or to figure out how you could have solved a problem after it's over.

1. **Stop! What is the problem?**
   I want to watch a show on TV, but my brother wants to watch a different show.

2. **Who or what caused the problem?** (optional) Try to figure out your role and other people's roles in causing the problem.
   We both have a role in this problem because we want to watch different shows.

3. **What does each person think and feel?** (optional) Put yourself into the "other guy's shoes" to see how that person thinks and feels.
   My brother and I both want to watch our own show and we both feel frustrated.

4. **What are some plans (solutions)?** List as many plans (solutions) as possible that could be used to solve the problem.
   I could watch my show. He could watch his show. I could ask Mom to help. We could try to work out a deal.

5. **What is the best plan?** Think ahead about what would happen if you used the plans in Step 4. Then decide which one will work best.
   I will try to work out a deal with my brother.

6. **Do the plan.** How will I do the plan? What will I do to make the plan work?
   I will ask my brother if we could take turns. I will ask him to watch my show now, and he can watch a show he wants next.

7. **Did the plan work?**
   He said OK. It worked.

Problem-Solving Rating (circle one)

1. Didn't use problem solving at all.
2. Tried to use problem solving a little, but it didn't really work.
3. Tried hard, went through problem-solving steps, but didn't really use the best plan.
4. Tried hard, went through problem-solving steps, and used the best plan.

Note. Steps 2 and 3 can be skipped if the problem is not a social problem.

From *Skills Training for Children with Behavior Disorders: A Parent and Therapist Guidebook* by Michael L. Bloomquist. © 1996 The Guilford Press.

TALLY FOR USING PROBLEM-SOLVING WORKSHEET

Name: _____

Date: _____

Directions: At the end of a designated time period, add up all the ratings from the Problem-Solving Worksheets. Add up all the 1 and 2 ratings and then add up all the 3 and 4 ratings. If there are more 3 and 4 ratings, then the child gets to select a reward.

Total ratings of 1 and 2 _____   **Total ratings of 3 and 4**_____

Reward =

EXAMPLE:
TALLY FOR USING "PROBLEM-SOLVING WORKSHEET

Name: *Sally*

Date: *Wednesday*

Directions: At the end of a designated time period, add up all the ratings from the Problem-Solving Worksheets. Add up all the 1 and 2 ratings and then add up all the 3 and 4 ratings. If there are more 3 and 4 ratings, then the child gets to select a reward.

Total ratings of 1 and 2 _2_   **Total ratings of 3 and 4** _3_

Reward = *Stay up late on Friday and watch a movie.*

THINKING AHEAD

1. **What is my goal?**

2. **What steps do I need to do to reach my goal?**

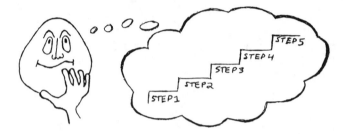

3. **Did I reach my goal?**

THINKING AHEAD
PROBLEM-SOLVING WORKSHEET

Name: _____

Date: _____

Directions: The parent and/or child can complete this form. Answer each question as it pertains to the problem at hand. You can fill this out to solve a problem occurring at the moment or to figure out how you could have solved a problem better.

1. **What's my goal?**

2. **What steps do I need to take to reach my goal?**

   Step 1.

   Step 2.

   Step 3.

   Step 4.

3. **Did I reach my goal?**

Problem-Solving Rating (circle one)

1. Didn't use problem solving at all.
2. Tried to use problem solving a little, but it didn't really work.
3. Tried hard, went through problem-solving steps, but didn't really reach my goal.
4. Tried hard, went through problem-solving steps, and reached my goal.

From *Skills Training for Children with Behavior Disorders: A Parent and Therapist Guidebook* by Michael L. Bloomquist. © 1996 The Guilford Press.

EXAMPLE:
THINKING AHEAD
PROBLEM-SOLVING WORKSHEET

Name: *Sally*

Date: *Thursday*

Directions: The parent and/or child can complete this form. Answer each question as it pertains to the problem at hand. You can fill this out to solve a problem occurring at the moment or to figure out how you could have solved a problem better.

1. **What's my goal?**
   To get a job this summer.

2. **What steps do I need to take to reach my goal?**

   Step 1. *Look for job ads in the newspaper.*

   Step 2. *Fill out job applications.*

   Step 3. *Call up job sites to arrange interviews.*

   Step 4. *Buy a new shirt for my interview outfit.*

3. **Did I reach my goal?**
   Yes.

Problem-Solving Rating (circle one)
1. Didn't use problem solving at all.
2. Tried to use problem solving a little, but it didn't really work.
3. Tried hard, went through problem-solving steps, but didn't really reach my goal.
4. Tried hard, went through problem-solving steps, and reached my goal.

From *Skills Training for Children with Behavior Disorders: A Parent and Therapist Guidebook* by Michael L. Bloomquist. © 1996 The Guilford Press.

11

Enhancing Children's Ability to Cope with Anger

Children with behavior disorders often have difficulty controlling their anger. These children may not know how to control strong emotions. If these children don't learn how to cope with this problem, it can lead to many future personal and social problems. This chapter will provide you with some ideas to help your child learn to control anger.

Blowing a Cork

Miles is a 14-year-old male who, according to his parents, Frank and Beverly, often "blows his cork." It takes very little to get him angry. Whenever things don't go his way or he gets frustrated, he is sure to explode in rage or anger. He seems to have this problem at home, at school, with his parents, and with his friends. It doesn't matter where he is or who he's with; he is prone to getting extremely angry. Recently, because he could not find his jeans, he yelled at his mother. Another time he tried to fix a lawn mower in the garage, became frustrated, and threw a wrench, damaging the garage door. If his parents confront him about his behavior, he often becomes more angry. Although he has never been violent, his parents are concerned that his anger problem is getting serious and might get worse.

WHAT IS AN ANGER PROBLEM?

When a child has habitual anger outbursts that seem out of proportion to the situation at hand, it is a problem that needs to be addressed. There is a real anger problem when a child becomes too angry too often and in many settings such as at home, in school, in the neighborhood, and so forth.

It is important and necessary to consider when and where the child displays his anger problem. **If your child only displays this problem when interacting with parents or family members, it may not be an anger problem. Instead, this may be a problem related to noncompliance, not following the rules, and/or family conflict.** Consult Chapters 6, 7, and 8 for ideas on how to deal with these issues.

HELPING CHILDREN LEARN TO COPE WITH ANGER

All children will experience anger or frustration at various points in their lives. Some children are able to cope with these feelings better than others. The following section describes how you can help your child develop skills important for coping with this very strong and usually negative feeling.

Step 1: Determine If Your Child Is Ready to Learn How to Cope with Anger

Some children will not be able to benefit from many of the procedures discussed in this chapter. Many children are too young to learn the skills necessary to manage their anger. Young children (below the age of 8 to 10 years) may not be able to learn how to cope with anger on their own. Also, some children are too defensive to learn how to cope with anger. They deny that they have problems with their feelings. Sometimes their defenses are so strong that they are not able to benefit from learning to control anger.

If you have determined that your child is too young or too defensive, you may wish to reconsider whether or not he will be able to benefit from instruction on coping with anger. An alternative strategy might be simply to teach your child how to understand and better express his feelings (see Chapter 13). Many children become angry, frustrated, sad, anxious, and so forth because they cannot articulate and express their feelings very well. **A parent may be wise to start with any child who has a problem managing anger by helping him learn to understand and express feelings first.**

Another alternative would be to avoid using anger management with a defensive child. Instead, emphasizing family conflict management (see in Chapter 6) may be more productive. Your child may be less resistant if "everyone" is working on one issue instead of just him. By participating in family conflict management training, your child would still be learning many skills that relate to anger management.

Step 2: Define Anger

You may be surprised to find out that many kids with anger problems aren't very good at defining anger. Ask your child to give a definition of "anger." Help your child understand that **anger is a negative emotion, a feeling of displeasure that occurs in response to a real or perceived situation that doesn't go as one would like it to.** Help your child understand that anger feelings can range from frustrated (mild) to mad (moderate) to rageful (severe). Ask your child to describe times or situations when he felt frustrated, mad, or rageful forms of anger. Be sure to help your child define different levels of anger in later discussions of anger with him.

Step 3: Teach Your Child to Recognize Anger Signals

Learning to recognize when one is angry involves understanding the "signals" that are often indicators that emotions are high. This can be accomplished through a discussion with your child about signals. First explain that everyone feels anger, but it is how one handles it that determines whether or not it is a problem. Explain further that most strong feelings have three parts, including a "body part," a "thought part," and an "action part." Work with your child to develop a list on a piece of paper of all the "body signals," "thought signals," and "action signals" that you and he can generate.

Common body, thought, and action signals for anger are as follows:

Body signals	Thought signals	Action signals
• Breathing rate increased	• "I hate myself"	• Punch/hit
• Heart rate increased	• "I feel like hurting myself"	• Yell
• Sweating increased	• "I hate her"	• Cry
• Red face color	• "I'm going to hit him"	• Threaten
• Tense muscles	• "I hate doing homework"	• Faint
• Body feels "hot"	• "I want to break something."	• Fidget
	• "I am dumb."	• Tremble
	• "I can't do anything right."	• Run
	• "I give up."	• Withdraw

After all of the signals have been listed, take some time to discuss and role play what these signals are all about. Ask your child to think about times when he was very upset and what signals he thinks may have applied during those situations. After some discussion has taken place, role play what the signals might look like. For example, you might model and then have your child role play what tense muscles look like when one is angry. The modeling and role plays can be taken further where the parent might act out being very angry and frustrated. Ask your child to identify the signals that were present during your demonstration. This could be repeated several times. Later you could ask your child to demonstrate anger, and you could identify signals in him.

Step 4: Teach Your Child to Relax

Once your child has learned how to identify when he is experiencing anger, he then can learn to use skills to cope with or reduce the anger. **Learning to reduce body tension through relaxation is an important first step.** This can be accomplished in a number of different ways, depending on your child's age and level of sophistication.

The following is a list of possible methods you could use to instruct your child to relax:

1. **Deep breathing.** Instruct, model, and have your child demonstrate how to do deep breathing exercises. The basic idea is to have him inhale deeply and exhale very slowly.

2. **Visualization.** Have your child visualize a very relaxing scene in his mind. For example, he might visualize himself floating on a raft on a lake. He would

continue to visualize floating on the lake, going up and down gently with the waves, with the sun beating down, and so forth. You can combine deep breathing with visualization. For example, ask your child to visualize a candle in front of him. As he exhales, he makes the candle flicker but not go out. You can help a younger child by discussing the visualization process and helping him construct the visual scene. Older children probably can construct their own visual scenes.

3. **Robot/rag doll technique.** The robot/rag doll technique is a useful muscle tension/release relaxation approach used with younger children (age 10 years and below). At first, ask your child to tense up all muscles in the body and visualize himself as a robot. Have him hold this tense state for approximately 15 seconds. Then ask your child to release all the tension and visualize himself as a rag doll with all muscles very loose. He should hold this relaxed state for 15 seconds. Have him continue to practice the robot/rag doll technique until he appears to know how to relax.

4. **Systematic muscle tension/release relaxation procedure.** The systematic muscle tension/release procedure is better suited for older children and adolescents (age 11 and above). There are professionally constructed audiotapes that are available in many bookstores and other specialty shops that would aid in this regard. The basic idea is to have your child or adolescent tense up small muscle groups one at a time, starting at the lower end of the body and working up. For example, your child would tense up his feet, holding them tense for 5 to 10 seconds and then relaxing them for 5 to 10 seconds. This would be followed by going up to the lower legs, upper legs, abdomen, chest, shoulders, neck, and, finally, the face. During each of these steps while he progressively goes up the body, he practices holding that particular area tense for 5 to 10 seconds, releasing and maintaining a relaxed state for 5 to 10 seconds. Eventually, his entire body will be relaxed. Once a person gets good at this, he can learn to relax all muscle groups simultaneously and quickly.

Try one or two of these methods over several meetings to teach your child to relax. Make sure he knows this skill before proceeding to the next skill.

Step 5: Teach Your Child to Use Coping Self-Talk

The next area of coping with anger involves utilizing "coping self-talk." This involves talking to oneself in a helpful manner. First explain to your child that if he talks to himself in a helpful manner, he will be able to control anger better.

Explain to your child that **self-talk involves saying things to oneself (thoughts) to calm down. Tell him this goal can be met by talking to himself in a manner such as the following:**

- "Take it easy."
- "Stay cool."
- "Chill out."
- "Take some deep breaths."

- "It's OK if I'm not good at this."
- "I'm sad Tanya doesn't want to play with me, but many other kids like to play with me."

- "I'm getting tense. Relax!"
- "Don't let him bug me."
- "I'm gonna be OK."

- "I'll just try my hardest."
- Try not to give up."

After your child seems to understand the purpose of coping self-talk, then you can move on to modeling and role-play exercises. You could model how to use coping self-talk when you are angry. For example, you could demonstrate getting frustrated with trying to fix some plumbing under a kitchen sink. First, you could demonstrate how not to cope with this particular situation (e.g., throwing tools, swearing, yelling, etc.). Next you could model how to cope with this same situation utilizing coping self-talk such as, "I need to relax," "I'm going to cool down," "I won't let this get to me," and so forth. After you have modeled this skill several times, ask your child to do similar role plays.

Step 6: Teach Your Child to Take Effective Action

The final step in learning how to cope effectively with anger is to take action and/or solve the problem that originally made the person angry. **Taking action might involve expressing feelings, asking for a hug, going for a walk, relaxing, being assertive with someone, and so forth.** Problem-solving skills, which were discussed in Chapter 10, can also be used to take action. It is important to tell your child that he still needs to solve the problem that made him feel upset. Review all the procedures with your child so that he understands what taking action and problem solving are all about.

Step 7: Model Coping with Anger

It is extremely important for you to model anger control skills. This can be done on an ongoing basis while you cope with normal situations at home that cause anger and frustration. You should try to cope effectively with your own feelings and to be a good example for your child. This can be done by informing your child that you are going to try to cope with anger, and then model relaxing, using coping self-talk, and taking effective action. Try to fill out an anger coping worksheet (see Step 8, below) occasionally and share it with your child.

Step 8a: Implement a Formal Anger-Coping Procedure

The ultimate goal is to help your child apply the anger management skills in real-life situations. The formal manner of helping your child use the skills involves completing the Coping with Anger Worksheet at the end of this chapter. Ask your child to complete this worksheet when he gets angry. The worksheet instructs your child to go through a step-by-step procedure of coping with anger. The first step involves your child writing down what event or problem made him feel angry. The second step entails your child writing down the body, thought, and action signals that told him he was experiencing anger. The third, fourth, and fifth steps are about describing how he is going to cope with the anger (relaxing, using coping self-talk, taking action, etc.). Finally, he would rate himself on a 4-point rating scale as to whether or not he has effectively coped with his anger. It's tough to learn anger management. So occasionally your child may explode, but could still complete the worksheet afterward.

Your child can fill out this chart either independently or with your guidance, depending on what you think is best for him. It's not that important who actually completes the form, but that it be used to structure the anger-coping process.

It is important to use reinforcement to promote your child's use of anger management skills. The formal method of reinforcement would involve using the Tally for Using Coping with Anger Worksheet chart that is found at the end of this chapter. This chart is used with the Coping with Anger Worksheet. At the end of a specified time period, total up the 1 and 2 ratings, and 3 and 4 ratings, from the Coping with Anger Worksheet, and transfer that information to the tally chart. If there are more 3 and 4 ratings, your child gets a reinforcement. (See the "Reinforcement" section in Chapter 5.)

Step 8b: Implement an Informal Anger-Coping Procedure

The informal method of helping a child incorporate these new skills in everyday situations would be simply to ask him to use the skills when needed. If your child becomes angry or frustrated, you might say something such as, "This might be a good time to try to practice coping with anger." The Cool Down chart, found at the end of this chapter, can be used as a visual cue to guide your child through the steps of anger management. You might want to remind your child to look at this chart as he is trying to cool down. Try to use directed-discovery questions to guide your child to use anger management skills. (See Chapter 10, Step 5, for information on directed discovery questioning.)

Informal reinforcement involves you noticing, commenting on, and praising your child for using the skills. Try to reinforce your child regularly and often enough to promote his use of the skills.

SUMMARY POINTS

1. A child with a significant anger problem is prone to numerous personal and social problems.
2. A child may not have a true anger problem if he displays the anger only while interacting with parents or other family members. This more likely indicates a parent–child or family problem.
3. Young (below age 8–10 years) and/or resistant children may not benefit from learning to cope with anger.

4. Teach your child to recognize the body, thought, and action signals associated with anger.
5. Teach your child relaxation skills to cope with anger.
6. Teach your child to use coping self-talk to cope with anger.
7. Teach your child to take effective action and problem solve to cope with anger.

Capping the Cork

Back to Miles, Frank, and Beverly: Frank and Beverly decide that they are going to try to take some action with young Miles. They sit down with him and explain how he might be able to learn how to control his anger by utilizing some coping with anger skills. At first Miles is resistant, but through a friendly and supportive discussion, they get him to acknowledge that he may benefit from working on anger control skills. They go through all the steps and procedures involving learning to recognize when one is angry, as well as learning how to cope with the feelings of anger through relaxing, using coping self-talk, and taking effective action. Miles and his parents have worked out an agreement so that when he is able to utilize the Coping with Anger Worksheet successfully five times, he will have earned the privilege of going to a concert of his choice. At first Miles stumbles and has difficulty. At one point his mother asked him to use anger management, and that made him even more angry. Gradually, over time, however, Miles begins to incorporate the anger management strategies. At this point he still gets angry occasionally, but his anger outbursts have become less frequent, and he is aware of his anger problem.

CHARTS FOR CHAPTER 11

COPING WITH ANGER WORKSHEET

Name: _____

Date: _____

Directions: A child and/or parent can complete this worksheet. It's best to fill out the worksheet while you are angry, but it's also OK to fill it out after you have coped with anger.

1. **What event or problem is making me feel angry?**

2. **What are the signals that tell me I am angry?**

    a. **Body signals**

    b. **Thought signals**

    c. **Action signals**

3. **What can I do to relax my body?**

4. **What "coping self-talk" can I use to control my thoughts?**

5. **What effective action can I take to deal with the situation or solve the problem?**

Coping with Anger Rating (circle one)

1. Didn't try to cope with anger at all.
2. Sort of tried to cope with anger, but it didn't really work.
3. Tried hard to cope with anger, but it didn't really work.
4. Tried hard to cope with anger, and it worked.

From *Skills Training for Children with Behavior Disorders: A Parent and Therapist Guidebook* by Michael L. Bloomquist. © 1996 The Guilford Press.

EXAMPLE:
COPING WITH ANGER WORKSHEET

Name: *Miles*

Date: *Sunday*

Directions: A child and/or parent can complete this worksheet. It's best to fill out the worksheet while you are angry, but it's also OK to fill it out after you have coped with anger.

1. **What event or problem is making me feel angry?**

   The kid next door keeps bugging me and my friends. He won't leave us alone.

2. **What are the signals that tell me I am angry?**

   a. **Body signals** *My muscles are tense. My heart is pounding.*

   b. **Thought signals** *I wish he would go away. He's gonna steal my friends.*

   c. **Action signals** *I yelled at him.*

3. **What can I do to relax my body?**

   I will take some deep breaths and try to relax my body.

4. **What "coping self-talk" can I use to control my thoughts?**

   "Don't let him bug me." "Keep cool." "Relax."

5. **What effective action can I take to deal with the situation or solve the problem?**

   I'll talk to him. I'll ask him to let me play with my friends alone. If that doesn't work, I'll ask Dad for help.

Coping with Anger Rating (circle one)

1. Didn't try to cope with anger at all.
2. Sort of tried to cope with anger, but it didn't really work.
3. Tried hard to cope with anger, but it didn't really work.
4. Tried hard to cope with anger, and it worked.

From *Skills Training for Children with Behavior Disorders: A Parent and Therapist Guidebook* by Michael L. Bloomquist. © 1996 The Guilford Press.

TALLY FOR USING COPING WITH ANGER WORKSHEET

Name: _____

Date: _____

Directions: At the end of a designated time period, add up all the ratings from the Coping with Anger Worksheets. Add up all the 1 and 2 ratings, and then add up all the 3 and 4 ratings. If there are more 3 and 4 ratings, then your child gets to select a reward.

Total ratings of 1 and 2 _____   **Total ratings of 3 and 4** _____

Reward =

EXAMPLE:
TALLY FOR USING COPING WITH ANGER WORKSHEET

Name: *Miles*

Date: *Monday*

Directions: At the end of a designated time period, add up all the ratings from the Coping with Anger Worksheets. Add up all the 1 and 2 ratings, and then add up all the 3 and 4 ratings. If there are more 3 and 4 ratings, then your child gets to select a reward.

Total ratings of 1 and 2 _3_   **Total ratings of 3 and 4** _5_

Reward = *Have a friend stay overnight on Friday.*

From *Skills Training for Children with Behavior Disorders: A Parent and Therapist Guidebook* by Michael L. Bloomquist. © 1996 The Guilford Press.

COOL DOWN

1. **Am I angry?**

2. **Cool down my body.**

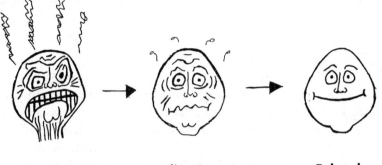

| Tense | Cooling Down | Relaxed |

3. **Use cool-down thoughts.**

4. **Do something to solve the problem.**

From *Skills Training for Children with Behavior Disorders: A Parent and Therapist Guidebook* by Michael L. Bloomquist. © 1996 The Guilford Press.

12

Enhancing Children's Self-Directed Academic Behavior Skills

Success in academics is extremely important for children. The goal is not to make children into academic wizards. Rather, given the amount of time children spend in the academic environment, it is helpful for them to achieve a sense of success and gratification, instead of failure and demoralization, when they confront academic tasks. To be successful academically, children need to acquire certain skills beyond academic knowledge. Children who lack these skills are likely to struggle academically. This chapter focuses on how to help children develop self-directed academic behavior skills.

Not Working Up to Potential

Thirteen-year-old Kyoko is highly intelligent. She does very well on standardized achievement tests, yet receives poor grades at school. Apparently she has the ability, and she is learning, but she can't do the day-to-day work necessary to get good grades. Kyoko's parents, Reiko and Kim, get notes from teachers stating that "Kyoko is frequently off-task," "Kyoko doesn't complete assignments," "Kyoko wastes time," and "Kyoko is not working up to her potential."

WHAT ARE SELF-DIRECTED ACADEMIC BEHAVIOR SKILLS?

Simply going to school is not enough for academic success. In order to do well in school, children must possess certain skills that have nothing to do with actual academic subjects. These skills can be lumped under the category of "self-directed academic behaviors." Children who are unorganized, do not budget their time well, are frequently off-task while at school, and/or have poor study skills are more likely to experience academic difficulties. Children with self-directed academic behavior skills have good organizational capabilities, good study skills, can stay on-task, and so forth. The level of parent involvement at school is also related to a child's academic success and can impact the development of a child's self-directed academic behaviors.

IMPROVING YOUR CHILD'S ORGANIZATIONAL SKILLS

You can use a variety of strategies and techniques to help your child develop organizational skills. Younger children will need more monitoring and help to develop these skills than will older children. The skills you teach need to be adjusted to your child's age.

The following is a list of organizational strategies that may be helpful:

1. **Assignment notebook system.** Teach your child to keep track of her assignments. Obtain a loose-leaf notebook or a commercially produced calendar. Help her develop a system where she writes down assignments and when they are due, and then checks them off as the assignments are completed.

2. **Time budgeting.** Teach your child to plan how to use her time. Help her develop a system where she writes down all of the work that needs to be done, on either a daily or a weekly basis, and estimates how much time it will take to complete each task. Then she plans on her calendar, for either that day or that week, when and how much time she will devote to each assignment. For example, when your child sits down for her daily homework, she could write down all of her assignments for that day and allocate a certain amount of time for each assignment. For longer assignments, the planning should be done for an extended time basis. For example, if your child needs to write a paper or do a special project, she could plan and write down a schedule of different steps to accomplish over several weeks (e.g., when to go to library, when to write, etc.).

3. **Organizational checklists.** Your child can develop organizational checklists with your guidance. Typically, this involves listing all subactivities that comprise a larger activity. Your child then checks off the subactivities as she completes the larger activity. Organizational checklists can be used for getting ready for school in the morning, getting ready to come home from school at the end of the school day, preparing to do homework, doing math problems, and so forth. The Example: Organizational Checklists chart found at the end of this chapter provides some ideas.

IMPROVING HOMEWORK

A child can improve homework skills by developing routines.

Below are some good routines to follow:

1. **Designate a study area in your home.** Set aside a place for your child to study. This place should be free of distraction, have adequate lighting, and be stocked with necessary school-related supplies (e.g., paper, pencils, erasers, etc.). Ideally, your child would also have this particular area decorated with posters, art work, and so forth so as to make it desirable for her to spend time there.

2. **Designate a homework time.** Assign a designated time for homework. For example, you might require your child to study between 5 and 6 P.M. It may also

be more successful to designate a standard amount of time for homework regardless of whether the child has homework or not. This reduces the child's tendency to rush or "forget" homework, because she has to study anyway.

3. **Teach your child to organize homework.** Help your child organize homework each day by seeing what needs to be done, planning how it will be done and how much time to spend on each task, and so forth.

4. **Take breaks.** Help your child to take periodic breaks during homework. It may be unrealistic to expect your child to sit still for 1 hour and study. Some children vary in terms of their ability to stay on-task and pay attention, and this should be taken into account. For children who have particular difficulty in this area, it may be helpful to study for 10 minutes, take a 5-minute break, study for 10 minutes, take a 5-minute break, or some variation of this pattern.

5. **Assist your child.** Be available to assist or check your child's work, without doing her work.

6. **Praise your child.** It is important to praise your child for studying. Most homework experts agree that children should not be paid for studying. Paying them won't promote a desire to learn just for the sake of learning. Praise and encouragement will help inspire a desire to learn in your child. It is wise to **praise your child's effort** as she pursues academic activities. The focus should be on praising your child for putting in a good day's work, completing an assignment, reading a chapter, and so forth. You should focus less on getting good grades. **If your child is reinforced for her effort, good grades will follow.**

HELPING CHILDREN SELF-MONITOR TO STAY ON-TASK

Many children get off-task, their attention wanders, and then they can't get their work done. **Some children actually need to be trained to self-monitor (be aware of themselves) so that they can better stay on-task.** This section will review a self-monitoring procedure that you can initiate at home to help your child learn this important skill and thereby improve on-task behavior. Usually this self-monitoring exercise would be done during homework time, but could also be used for other tasks (e.g., doing chores). Self-monitoring for on-task behavior is most successful for children over the age of 8. Children under the age of 8 probably need more external monitoring by their parents to make sure that they stay on-task.

Step 1: Instruct Your Child about On-Task Behavior

It is necessary for your child to understand clearly what on-task behavior is. Define on-task behavior for her, and model this behavior. For example, with homework, you would explain to your child that on-task behavior means looking at one's work, having the pencil touch the paper, writing, calculating, reading, and so forth. It may be helpful to demonstrate or model these behaviors.

Step 2: Use Self-Monitoring to Improve On-Task Behavior

The Staying On-Task chart found at the end of this chapter can be used to help your child improve on-task behavior. The first step is to designate a task for your child to complete and a time interval during which the task will be completed. Your child is to make an effort to stay on-task while attempting to complete the task. After the time interval has passed, both your child and you rate how well she stayed on task according to the criteria described on the Staying On-Task chart.

At first, it is most helpful to focus on whether or not your child's rating matches your rating. If desired, you could provide a reinforcer to your child if her rating matches your rating (see the "Reinforcement" section in Chapter 5). At this point it is not so important that your child actually improve on-task behavior, but that her ratings match yours. By focusing on matching, your child will become more aware of when she is on- or off-task. Keep up the matching procedure until your child is good at self-observation of on-task behavior.

The next step is to use the Staying On-Task chart to improve on-task behavior. This would be accomplished by the child actually obtaining ratings of 3, 4, or 5 on the chart. You could provide your child a reinforcement if she achieves a good rating on the Staying On-Task chart (see the "Reinforcement" section in Chapter 5).

INCREASING PARENTAL INVOLVEMENT AT SCHOOL

General Tips

You can make use of a variety of common sense procedures to increase your involvement in your child's school-related activities. First, and probably foremost, **communicate to your child that you value academics**. Without lecturing, it is helpful to discuss the value of an education with your child on a routine basis. Perhaps more important, however, is that she sees you actively involved in some sort of a learning process yourself. Your involvement in a learning process could be formal, such as taking classes, or more informal, such as watching educational TV, reading, and so forth. It is best if your child sees you practicing what you preach in terms of promoting the value of education.

Another practical suggestion is to have **ongoing contact with school personnel**. Whenever possible, try to attend school functions. This includes school conferences, day visits, meetings, and activities that your child is involved with during and after the school day. To be truly involved, you should have active and ongoing contact with school personnel, not just when problems arise.

Another helpful strategy is to **assist your child with academic activities**. This means being available to consult with your child regarding homework issues or planning for school-related activities. You would not do these activities for your child, but would simply be there to assist her in making decisions, planning, organizing, and so forth.

Home–School Note System

It can be very helpful to strengthen the ties between school and home by forming a structured collaborative relationship between school personnel and parents. When school and home work together, your child is likely to be more successful with academic endeavors.

A home–school note system often can help you monitor your child's progress at school. To implement this procedure, you and your child's teacher agree on a system of ongoing communication between home and school. Many teachers already have systems developed for this purpose.

The basic idea is to have a note passed between parents and teachers each day with your child acting as the delivery agent. At first this may be hard for your child, but, over time and with reinforcement, she can learn to do the home–school note delivery successfully. In some instances, it is necessary to administer a mild punishment if your child continuously "forgets" the note. Usually a form is developed that targets a specific behavior or behaviors (e.g., stays on-task, completes classroom work, cooperates with teacher, etc.) and how well your child did on that behavior each day (e.g., poor, fair, good, etc.). The teacher signs the form and sends it home. You countersign it and send it back to school the next day. You may choose to administer a reward or negative consequence at home, depending on your child's behavior at school that day.

A sample Home–School Note is found at the end of this chapter. This note can be modified to meet your child's unique needs.

Intensive Home–School Collaboration

In some instances, a child may be having such serious school problems that a structured and vigorous home–school plan is necessary. A series of special school meetings involving parents and school personnel is usually undertaken to bring home and school together to help the child achieve more success at school.

The Parent–School Partnership Planning Worksheet found at the end of this chapter can be used to collaborate effectively with school officials. This worksheet should be completed by parents and school personnel during a face-to-face meeting. It provides some structure for defining the child's school problems, planning for techniques/strategies to use to help the child, designating what each person's responsibilities will be, and planning for periodic reviews. This chart can be modified to meet the unique needs of children and school settings.

SUMMARY POINTS

1. Self-directed academic behaviors are necessary for academic success regardless of a child's ability. These behaviors include organizational skills, study skills, ability to stay on-task, and so forth.

2. Teach your child to improve organizational skills with assignment notebooks, time budgeting, and organizational checklists.

3. Teach your child to improve homework by providing a good place to study, developing predictable routines, organizing tasks related to homework, taking planned breaks, and praising your child for effort on homework.

4. Teach your child to increase on-task behavior through self-monitoring training. This involves training her to observe her own behavior and evaluate performance.

5. Children's academic performance can be improved through increasing parent involvement in academic activities. A home–school note is one formal method to accomplish this.

6. Parent–teacher collaboration can be used to coordinate the parent and teacher to work more effectively on behalf of your child.

Working Up to Potential

Back to Kyoko, Reiko, and Kim: Reiko and Kim decide to help Kyoko develop skills necessary for academic success. At first, they focus on strengthening on-task behavior through self-monitoring training. Kyoko utilizes the self-monitoring procedure for homework. They also meet with the teacher and develop a home–school note system to monitor Kyoko's academic progress more closely. Behaviors targeted in the home–school note include staying on-task, completing assignments, and using time wisely. Her parents have also helped Kyoko develop organizational checklists for homework. Gradually, over time, Kyoko shows success in developing self-directed academic behaviors. Everyone is pleased when Kyoko's report card shows improved grades.

CHARTS FOR CHAPTER 12

EXAMPLE:
ORGANIZATIONAL CHECKLISTS

For Getting Ready for School in the Morning

___ Get up at 6:30 A.M.
___ Take a shower
___ Get dressed
___ Eat breakfast
___ Get backpack
___ Go catch bus

For Preparing to Come Home from School

___ Get backpack
___ Pack all needed books
___ Pack homework calendar
___ Ask teacher to sign home–school note
___ Pack home–school note
___ Go catch bus

For Homework

___ Get out all books
___ Sharpen pencil
___ Write down all tasks that need to be done
___ Do homework
___ Check my work
___ Ask for help if needed

For Math Worksheet

___ Get out worksheet
___ Look at the "sign" for each math problem
___ Do math problem
___ Ask for help if needed

STAYING ON-TASK

Name: _____

Date: _____

Directions: Indicate below what task you will be doing (e.g., school work, cleaning up your room, a special project, etc.) and the time period you will be working on the task. After you have completed the task, or after the time period is over, rate yourself as to how well you stayed on-task. Next a parent should rate how well you stayed on-task.

Task to be Completed and Time Period

1. **I will work on this task during this time:**

Child Evaluation

2. **How well did I stay on-task?** (circle one)

1	2	3	4	5
Not at all	A little	OK	Pretty good	Great

Parent Evaluation

3. **How well did child stay on-task?** (circle one)

1	2	3	4	5
Not at all	A little	OK	Pretty good	Great

Reward

4. **If my rating matches my parent rating, I get this reward:**

OR

5. **If my parent rates me as a 3, 4, 5, I get this reward:**

EXAMPLE: STAYING ON-TASK

Name: _Kyoko_

Date: _Monday_

Directions: Indicate below what task you will be doing (e.g., school work, cleaning up your room, a special project, etc.) and the time period you will be working on the task. After you have completed the task, or after the time period is over, rate yourself as to how well you stayed on-task. Next a parent should rate how well you stayed on-task.

Task to be Completed and Time Period

1. **I will work on this task during this time:**

   Homework from 5 p.m.–6 p.m.

Child Evaluation

2. **How well did I stay on-task?** (circle one)

1	2	3	(4)	5
Not at all	A little	OK	Pretty good	Great

Parent Evaluation

3. **How well did child stay on-task?** (circle one)

1	2	3	(4)	5
Not at all	A little	OK	Pretty good	Great

Reward

4. **If my rating matches my parent rating, I get this reward:**

   Stay up late Friday night

OR

5. **If my parent rates me as a 3, 4, 5, I get this reward:**

   Stay up late Friday night

From *Skills Training for Children with Behavior Disorders: A Parent and Therapist Guidebook* by Michael L. Bloomquist. © 1996 The Guilford Press.

HOME–SCHOOL NOTE

Name: _____   Date: _____

Morning

	Circle One		
Obeyed teacher and classroom rules	Poor	Fair	Good
Stayed on-task	Poor	Fair	Good
Interacted with peers positively	Poor	Fair	Good

Comments: _____

Teacher signature: _____

Afternoon

	Circle One		
Obeyed teacher and classroom rules	Poor	Fair	Good
Stayed on-task	Poor	Fair	Good
Interacted with peers positively	Poor	Fair	Good

Comments: _____

Teacher signature: _____

Today's homework assignments are:

_____

_____

_____

_____

_____

Reviewed by Parent/Guardian

Parent/Guardian signature: _____

From *Skills Training for Children with Behavior Disorders: A Parent and Therapist Guidebook* by Michael L. Bloomquist. © 1996 The Guilford Press.

PARENT–SCHOOL PARTNERSHIP PLANNING WORKSHEET

Name: _____

Date: _____

Directions: Parents and school personnel can use this worksheet to plan and collaborate to work with children exhibiting attentional and behavioral problems at school. This form should be completed during a face-to-face meeting between parents, teachers, and school personnel. This procedure would not take the place of standard school planning processes.

1. **Define all potential concerns.** Check off all that apply to the child:

   _____ Frequently off-task   _____ Poor organizational skills

   _____ Problems completing classwork   _____ Problems completing homework

   _____ Argues with adults   _____ Blurts out and/or bugs other kids

   _____ Problems following school rules   _____ High anger/low frustration tolerance

   _____ Poor social skills/poor relationships   _____ Impulsive/doesn't think before acting

   _____ Sad or nervous   _____ Doesn't express feelings

   _____ Thinks unhelpful thoughts   _____ Other

2. **Rank the top two concerns from #1 above.**

   Most important concern: _____

   Second most important concern: _____

3. **Define all possible methods to work with the child at school and to build parent–school partnership.** Check all that could apply and be used:

   _____ Train child in self-monitoring to increase on-task behavior.

   _____ Train child to use homework notebook.

   _____ Train child to use organizational checklist.

   _____ School-based behavioral management system for these behaviors:

   _____

   _____ Train child in problem solving.

   _____ Train child in social skills/social problem solving.

   _____ Train child in anger/frustration management.

   _____ Use home–school note communication for these behaviors:

   _____ Train child to express feelings.

   _____ Train child to think more helpful thoughts.

   _____ Other _____

(cont.)

4. **Rank the top two preferred methods to use from #3 above.**

   Most preferred method: _____

   Second most preferred methods: _____

5. **Determine and define roles/responsibilities of parents and school personnel:**

   a. What are parents' roles/responsibilities? _____

   _____

   b. What are teachers' roles/responsibilities? _____

   _____

   c. What are other school personnel's roles/responsibilities? _____

   _____

6. **Periodic review/update:**

   a. How should reviews be conducted (e.g., phone calls, conferences, etc.)? _____

   _____

   b. How often should reviews be conducted (e.g., weekly, monthly, etc.)? _____

   c. Who will be involved in review? _____

   _____

Signatures of Agreement

_____   _____   _____

_____   _____   _____

EXAMPLE:
PARENT–SCHOOL PARTNERSHIP PLANNING WORKSHEET

Name: _Kyoko_

Date: _Wednesday_

Directions: Parents and school personnel can use this worksheet to plan and collaborate to work with children exhibiting attentional and behavioral problems at school. This form should be completed during a face-to-face meeting between parents, teachers, and school personnel. This procedure would not take the place of standard school planning processes.

1. **Define all potential concerns.** Check off all that apply to the child:

   __x__ Frequently off-task   __x__ Poor organizational skills

   _____ Problems completing classwork   __x__ Problems completing homework

   __x__ Argues with adults   _____ Blurts out and/or bugs other kids

   __x__ Problems following school rules   _____ High anger/low frustration tolerance

   _____ Poor social skills/poor relationships   _____ Impulsive/doesn't think before acting

   _____ Sad or nervous   _____ Doesn't express feelings

   _____ Thinks unhelpful thoughts   _____ Other

2. **Rank the top two concerns from #1 above.**

   Most important concern: _Argues with adults_

   Second most important concern: _Problems completing homework_

3. **Define all possible methods to work with the child at school and to build parent–school partnership.** Check all that could apply and be used:

   _____ Train child in self-monitoring to increase on-task behavior.

   __x__ Train child to use homework notebook.

   __x__ Train child to use organizational checklist.

   __x__ School-based behavioral management system for these behaviors:

   Arguing, problems following rules

   _____ Train child in problem solving.

   _____ Train child in social skills/social problem solving.

   _____ Train child in anger/frustration management.

   __x__ Use home–school note communication for these behaviors:

   Arguing, problems following rules and completing homework

   _____ Train child to express feelings.

   _____ Train child to think more helpful thoughts.

   _____ Other

(cont.)

183

4. **Rank the top two preferred methods to use from #3 above.**

   Most preferred method: _School-based behavioral management_

   Second most preferred methods: _Home-school note_

5. **Determine and define roles/responsibilities of parents and school personnel:**

   a. What are parent's roles/responsibilities? _Review home-school note on a daily basis. Give rewards at home for good school behavior._

   b. **What are teachers' roles/responsibilities:** _Complete home-school note with the child, and send it home with the child._

   c. **What are other school personnel's roles/responsibilities?** _School psychologist will help set up school-based behavior management program._

6. **Periodic review/update:**

   a. How should reviews be conducted (e.g., phone calls, conferences, etc.)? _Phone calls_

   b. How often should reviews be conducted (e.g., weekly, monthly, etc.)? _Weekly_

   c. Who will be involved in review? _Parents and teachers_

Signatures of Agreement

Kyoko N.   _Reiko N._   _Kim N._

Ms. Jackson   _Mr. Washington_

From *Skills Training for Children with Behavior Disorders: A Parent and Therapist Guidebook* by Michael L. Bloomquist. © 1996 The Guilford Press.

13

Enhancing Children's Ability to Understand and Express Feelings

Children with behavior problems often find it difficult to understand and express their feelings. These children often bottle up their feelings or "blow up" instead of expressing their feelings directly. This chapter will present some ideas to help children learn to express their feelings better.

What's Going On in There?

Eleven-year-old Dominique has always been more defiant and aggressive than most kids. His parents, Keisha and Willie, often have to deal with angry outbursts and tantrums. Lately Dominique appears to be more sad and withdrawn. He rarely discusses his problems or feelings. Sometimes Keisha is concerned and asks Dominique, "What's going on in there?"

HOW FEELINGS ARE RELATED TO BEHAVIOR PROBLEMS IN CHILDREN

Difficulties dealing with feelings can be either a result or a cause of behavior problems. Some children experience a lot of negative feedback from others and are less successful in everyday life because of behavior problems. Over time they learn to "stuff" their feelings because they find it too painful to face them. These children can develop emotional problems. Other children become angry, frustrated, sad, and so forth, and because they don't know how to put their feelings into words, they act out through defiance, aggression, or other emotional outbursts. Helping children with their feelings can both help them feel better and reduce behavior problems.

HELPING CHILDREN UNDERSTAND AND EXPRESS EMOTIONS

The foundation of emotional well-being is the ability to understand and express one's own feelings. **Learning to understand and express feelings doesn't solve**

problems; however, it can help children cope and feel better. Parents can help their children learn how to express their feelings better.

Step 1: Increase Your Child's "Feelings Vocabulary"

If your child does not have a feeling word in his vocabulary, he cannot express that particular emotion very well. For example, if your child does not understand and use the word "enraged," he may not be able to express himself adequately when he is extremely angry and upset. He may "act out" his feelings instead.

The first step in helping your child increase his feelings vocabulary is to instruct him about different feelings. The Feelings Vocabulary Chart at the end of this chapter can be used for this purpose. This chart lists a variety of feeling words, with accompanying facial expressions. Give a copy of this chart to your child to look at. Ask your child if he understands all of the words on the chart. Ask him if he has experienced any of the feelings shown on the chart. Review and explain the feelings listed on this chart. If you are unsure how to explain the feelings, you may want to ask someone else or look up the word in the dictionary. It's important to explain the words clearly so that your child understands each feeling shown on the chart. With younger children, you may want to circle 10 feelings to focus on instead of the whole list.

It might be helpful to discuss and role play different situations that might create certain feelings. For example, someone resting in bed at night who hears a loud noise might experience the feeling of being "frightened." Try to get your child actively involved in discussing situations that might bring about different feelings.

Step 2: Model the Expression of Feelings

An extremely powerful way children learn how to express feelings is by observing their parents. If a parent keeps his or her feelings inside, the child may deal with emotions in a similar way. If the child observes his parent expressing feelings regularly, the child will be more likely to do so as well. Don't underestimate the power you have in modeling expression of feelings.

Try to be aware of times when you are experiencing feelings and to express them. When the time seems right, practice expressing these feelings when your child is present and can observe your demonstration. This can be done in a formal or informal manner. Expressing feelings in a formal manner would involve experiencing an emotion, getting out the Feelings Vocabulary Chart, pointing to various facial expressions, and using the terms on the chart to express your feelings at that time. For example, if you burn some food on the stove, you could get out the chart and point to the feelings of disappointed and frustrated. Expressing feelings in an informal way can be accomplished by simply talking out loud while you are experiencing emotions. For example, if you burn something on the stove, you would simply state out loud that you are disappointed and frustrated.

Step 3: Practice Being Aware of and Expressing Emotions

A very powerful method of practicing how to be aware of and to express feelings involves routinely discussing feelings as events occur each day. Ask your child to express himself when you see him experiencing an emotion. For example, when your child is frustrated because he cannot understand the directions of how to put a toy together, you might ask him to express his feelings. Prompting can take the form of asking open-ended questions such as, "What are you feeling right now?" or of a closed question such as, "Are you frustrated?" Sometimes you need to be persistent and supportive when trying to get your child to express feelings. Keep asking questions and offer support until the child expresses the feeling. **If your child becomes too frustrated with your questions, drop it, and try again another time.**

A final way you can help your child understand his emotions is to label feelings for him. This can be especially helpful for a younger child or when a child is either defensive or unwilling to participate in a discussion of his feelings. For example, you might notice your child becoming frustrated while trying to put together a toy and simply state, "You look frustrated." This labeling technique can be applied to a variety of emotional experiences and situations for the child.

Step 4a: Implement a Formal Procedure to Help Your Child Express Feelings

One formal method to help your child practice being aware of and expressing feelings involves using the Feelings Diary at the end of this chapter. Utilizing the Feelings Diary requires your child to write down positive and negative events that occur in his daily experience and also to write down the feelings that accompany those experiences.

The child should have the option of sharing the diary, or keeping it private. Many children also benefit when a parent fills out a Feelings Diary and shares it with the child. This helps the child feel less alone in the process and gives the child the added benefit of learning by observing the parent. If you decide to keep a Feelings Diary too, be sure to write about neutral and not-too-personal events. It would be helpful to write about how you felt in a traffic jam, but not how you felt while arguing with your child's other parent.

A formal way to reinforce the child for expressing his feelings is to give him a tangible reward for filling out the Feelings Diary. For example, you and your child might agree that if he fills out four of seven diaries for a week, he can earn a certain reward. (See the "Reinforcement" section in Chapter 5.)

Step 4b: Implement an Informal Procedure to Help Your Child Express Feelings

An informal method would involve using the discussion and labeling techniques discussed in Step 3 above, on an ongoing basis. Look for opportunities to discuss and label your child's feelings as events unfold.

Reinforcing your child in an informal way simply involves praising him when he expresses feelings. When your child does express his feelings, you might state, "I'm proud of you for expressing your feelings," "I'm glad you expressed your feelings to me," "You did a good job of expressing your feelings," and so forth.

SUMMARY POINTS

1. Over time, children with chronic behavior problems can develop emotional difficulties.
2. You can teach your child to understand and express emotions better by increasing his feelings vocabulary and by discussing feelings related to daily events.

Let's Talk About It

Back to Dominique, Keisha, and Willie: One day Dominique comes home from school and goes straight to his room and closes the door. Willie follows Dominique and knocks on his door. Dominique lets his father in his room. Dominique looks sad, but he won't say what is going on. Because Willie is persistent, Dominique gradually talks about being teased by some kids at school and how sad he feels. Later Willie proposes that he and Dominique try to work on expressing their feelings. They review the Feelings Vocabulary Chart and discuss different feelings. Willie shows Dominique the Feelings Diary. He suggests that he and Dominique tell Keisha about this and that all three of them use it to work on understanding and expressing feelings. Dominique agrees to this plan. All three family members now work together on expressing with feelings.

CHARTS FOR CHAPTER 13

FEELINGS VOCABULARY CHART

AGGRESSIVE   ANGRY   ARROGANT   BASHFUL   BORED   CAUTIOUS

CONFIDENT   CONFUSED   CURIOUS   DISAPPOINTED   DISAPPROVING   DISBELIEVING

DISGUSTED   ECSTATIC   ENRAGED   ENVIOUS   EXASPERATED   FRUSTRATED

GRIEVING   GUILTY   HAPPY   HORRIFIED   HURT   JEALOUS

JOYFUL   LONELY   MISERABLE   NEGATIVE   NERVOUS   OPTIMISTIC

REGRETFUL   SAD   SATISFIED   SCARED   SHOCKED   STUBBORN

SURPRISED   SUSPICIOUS   SYMPATHETIC   UNDECIDED   WITHDRAWN

From *Skills Training for Children with Behavior Disorders: A Parent and Therapist Guidebook* by Michael L. Bloomquist. © 1996 The Guilford Press.

FEELINGS DIARY

Name: _____

Date: _____

Directions: Write down positive and negative evants that happened to you. Then write down how you felt in response to those events. Use the Feelings Vocabulary Chart to help you label your feelings. You can fill the diary out when an event occurs or afterward. You can share this feelings diary with others or keep it private.

Positive Events   **My Feelings**

1.   1.

2.   2.

3.   3.

4.   4.

Negative Events   **My Feelings**

1.   1.

2.   2.

3.   3.

4.   4.

From *Skills Training for Children with Behavior Disorders: A Parent and Therapist Guidebook* by Michael L. Bloomquist. © 1996 The Guilford Press.

EXAMPLE:
FEELINGS DIARY

Name: *Dominique*

Date: *Friday*

Directions: Write down positive and negative evants that happened to you. Then write down how you felt in response to those events. Use the Feelings Vocabulary Chart to help you label your feelings. You can fill the diary out when an event occurs or afterward. You can share this feelings diary with others or keep it private.

Positive Events

1. *I got a star on my math worksheet.*

2. *My mom hugged me.*

3.

4.

My Feelings

1. *Happy*

2. *Happy, joyful*

3.

4.

Negative Events

1. *Joe pushed me.*

2. *Some kids called me names.*

3.

4.

My Feelings

1. *Mad, sad, lonely, enraged*

2. *Sad, lonely, scared*

3.

4.

From *Skills Training for Children with Behavior Disorders: A Parent and Therapist Guidebook* by Michael L. Bloomquist. © 1996 The Guilford Press.

14

Enhancing Children's Ability to Think Helpful Thoughts

Children with disruptive behavior problems often receive more negative feedback than positive feedback from parents, siblings, peers, teachers, neighbors, and others. Over time this can negatively affect how these children think. They may worry, think negative thoughts about themselves and their world, and/or may think others (e.g., adults, peers, etc.) don't like them. This chapter will highlight some ideas to help children think more helpful thoughts.

I'm No Good

Thirteen-year-old Jonathan has had a tough year. It seems he gets in trouble about two or three times a week at school because of his behavior. Although he has several friends around the neighborhood, he gets teased by other kids at school. At home, he and his single father, Jeff, argue a lot. Jeff thinks they have more negative interactions than positive interactions. Over the year, Jonathan has become more irritable and moody. Sometimes he comes home from school, slams the door, and stamps his feet. When Jeff asks, "What's wrong?", Jonathan responds loudly and abruptly, "Nothing!" Jonathan has also been watching more TV. He just doesn't seem very happy. Last night Jeff asked why Jonathan hadn't yet completed his homework. Jonathan replied, "Because I'm no good!"

HOW UNHELPFUL THOUGHTS ARE RELATED TO BEHAVIOR PROBLEMS

Unfortunately, many children with behavior problems become negative thinkers over time because of the many negative experiences they have on a day-to-day basis. This negative thinking can lead to increased behavior problems and emotional difficulties if left unchecked. For example, if a child believes no one likes her, she may be more likely to withdraw, bug other children, or be even more aggressive toward others. Another example is a child who believes she's no good, which could lead to feeling depressed and/or to self-destructive behavior. It is very important for parents to help their children change negative thinking.

HELPING CHILDREN CHANGE UNHELPFUL THINKING

This section is designed to give parents ideas on how to help older children (age 10 and up) change negative thinking patterns. **The following three general steps are involved: (1) helping your child learn to identify her own negative thoughts, (2) helping your child understand how these negative thoughts negatively influence her emotions, and (3) helping your child learn strategies to change the negative thoughts so she can experience more positive emotions.**

Step 1: Determine If Your Child Is Ready to Learn to Change Negative Thinking

The procedures discussed in this chapter are fairly complex. Children under the age of 10 may not yet possess the mental abilities to benefit from this approach. Also, children who have not yet acquired the ability to understand and express feelings, regardless of their age, may not be able to accomplish the skills outlined in this section. If your child is too young or has not mastered the skills of understanding and expressing feelings, you should not try the methods described here. It may be more useful, in these instances, to focus on helping a child learn to express feelings (see Chapter 13).

You will need to conduct a discussion or series of discussions with your child to work on changing negative thoughts. Be sure that your child is a willing participant in these discussions. Do not coerce or force your child to do this. **If your child is resistant, then perhaps some of the skills discussed earlier in the book should be emphasized instead of this approach.**

Step 2: Explain Unhelpful and Helpful Thinking

This step involves explaining the difference between unhelpful and helpful thinking. Explain that **unhelpful thinking involves thinking thoughts that are untrue, blown out of proportion, magnified, awful, and negative.** Explain that negative thoughts can have a bad influence on one's behavior and emotions. For example, if your child attempts to give a piano recital and thinks, "I'm going to do awful," "I'm too nervous," and so forth, then she will be more to likely perform poorly and feel nervous. However, if she is giving a piano recital and thinks, "I'll do the best I can," "If I try, I'll do fine," she will be more likely to well and feel confident. Discuss other examples until your child sees a relationship between thoughts and feelings.

Next ask your child to do some self-evaluation by completing the Unhelpful Thoughts for Children chart found at the end of this chapter. Guide your child to accurately complete the ratings. If it's helpful, you could also complete the same ratings in terms of how you believe your child thinks (i.e., the parent rates the child on a separate rating form). At the end of the Unhelpful Thoughts for Children chart are several questions. Ask the child to answer those questions for the thoughts rated as a 3, 4, or 5. Continue to discuss how negative thinking is often unhelpful using this chart as a springboard.

The next task is to **help your child learn to counter unhelpful thinking with more helpful thinking.** To accomplish this, you can use the Helpful "Counter" Thoughts for Children chart found at the end of this chapter in conjunction with the Unhelpful Thoughts for Children chart. Thought #1 on the Unhelpful chart can be countered (or replaced) with Thought #1 on the Helpful chart and so on. There are more questions at the end of the Helpful chart to ask for each thought. Guide your child to answer these questions about her own helpful thoughts. Ideally your child will see the benefit of these helpful thoughts.

Step 3: Model Helpful Thinking

One powerful method to help your child learn how to think in a more helpful way is to model this type of thinking for her. As discussed elsewhere in this book, children learn a lot by observing their parents. **They may learn a "good way" or a "bad way" to think based on their observations of you.**

The formal way of modeling helpful thinking is to talk out loud when you are confronted with a particular event and to utilize a Changing Unhelpful Thoughts Worksheet (discussed in next section) in front of your child. You might say that you are going to use the worksheet and then encourage your child to watch.

An informal way to model this type of thinking is simply to talk out loud when you notice that you are thinking some unhelpful thoughts. For example, you may try to patch up some cement work in the basement and not do a very good job. You might make some disparaging comments such as, "This looks terrible! I can't do anything around the house. I must be all thumbs." Then you might say something such as, "This isn't very helpful thinking. I'm going to try to change my thoughts. Just because I can't do cement work doesn't mean the world is going to end or that I'm a terrible person. It would be more helpful to realize that I can't do everything perfectly, and, even if I did mess up, it's not the end of the world."

Step 4a: Implement a Formal Procedure to Help Your Child Use Helpful Thinking

The Changing Unhelpful Thoughts Worksheet found at the end of this chapter can be used to help your child apply these skills in real life. This chart takes her through the process in a step-by-step manner. You may want to assist your child in completing the chart. It can be completed either on the spot or after a problem has already occurred.

Prompting a child to use helpful thinking skills can be done by noticing when the child may be thinking in an unhelpful manner (i.e., as evidenced by what the child says) and asking her to change those thoughts. Questions such as, "Are you sure that thought is helpful?", "Remember what we discussed before?", "Are you thinking in a helpful way?" would suffice.

The Tally for Using Helpful Thoughts Worksheet at the end of this chapter can be used as a formal way to reinforce a child for using the helpful thinking skills. This chart is used with the Changing Unhelpful Thoughts Worksheet. At the end of each of the worksheets, there is a 4–point evaluation rating scale. The idea is to add up all the 1 and 2 ratings, and all the 3 and 4 ratings, accumulated on the worksheets, and to transfer that information to the tally chart. If your child has more 3 and 4 ratings than 1 and 2 ratings, she would be able to select a reinforcer. (See the "Reinforcement" section in Chapter 5.)

Step 4b: Implement an Informal Procedure to Help Your Child Use Helpful Thinking

Less formal ways can also be used to help a child use helpful thinking skills. These methods would involve prompting your child to use the skills. When you notice your child doing some unhelpful thinking, you could ask her to use helpful thinking and then praise her if she does so. The Helpful Thinking chart at the end of this chapter can be used as a visual aid for changing thoughts. You might want to remind your child to look at this chart as she is trying to change her thoughts. Try to use directed discovery questions to guide your child to use helpful thinking skills. (See Chapter 10, Step 5, for more information on directed discovery questioning.) Informal reinforcement involves noticing, commenting, and praising your child for using the skills. Try to reinforce her often enough to help her really learn this skill.

SUMMARY POINTS

1. Children with behavior problems often learn to think negatively about themselves and their world.
2. Help your child change unhelpful thinking by teaching her to identify her own negative thoughts, understand the unhelpful nature of these thoughts, and implement strategies to change these thoughts to more helpful ones.

I Guess I'm OK

Back to Jonathan and Jeff: Jeff's concern about Jonathan culminated in him deciding to try to help Jonathan think more positively. He realizes that both he and Jonathan are negative thinkers. Jeff introduces the notion of trying to change unhelpful thinking to Jonathan. They have several discussions about unhelpful thinking. Jeff makes a point to model helpful thinking and to discuss informally what's happening when Jonathan displays unhelpful thinking. Jonathan and Jeff both fill out Changing Unhelpful Thoughts Worksheets for several weeks. Once Jeff observed Jonathan talking about changing his thoughts without any prompting. Jonathan seems happier since they have been working on increasing helpful thinking.

CHARTS FOR CHAPTER 14

UNHELPFUL THOUGHTS FOR CHILDREN

Listed below are a variety of thoughts children may have about themselves. Read each thought and indicate how frequently that thought (or a similar thought) typically occurs for you over an average week. There are no right or wrong answers to these questions. Ask for help if you don't understand something on this form. Use the 5-point rating scale to answer how often you have these thoughts:

1	2	3	4	5
Not at all	A little	OK	Pretty good	Great

Thoughts about Self

1.____ I'm no good.

2.____ I can't do anything right; I'm a failure.

3.____ I'm a brat.

4.____ I **must** do well in school, sports, and so forth.

Thoughts about Peers

5.____ Most peers don't like me.

6.____ Most peers think I'm stupid.

7.____ Most peers think I'm a pest.

8.____ I don't fit in with the crowd.

Thoughts about Parents/Family

9.____ Our family is all messed up.

10.____ It's my fault the family is having problems.

11.____ My parent is to blame for my problems at home.

12.____ My brother or sister is to blame for my problems.

13.____ My parent just wants to run my life.

14.____My parent is unfair.

Thoughts about Teacher/School

15.____ My teacher is to blame for my problems at school.

16.____ My teacher is unfair.

17.____ I give up as far as school is concerned.

Thoughts about the Future

18.____ My future doesn't look too good. I see trouble ahead.

19.____ I give up. I've tried everything. There's nothing more I can do.

Thoughts about the World/Life

20.____ I've been given a raw deal in life. Life is unfair to me.

21.____ I'm not responsible for my own behavior.

22.____ I can't help it. I've got a problem.

(cont.)

Thoughts about Who Needs to Change

23.___ My parent or family needs to change more than I do because it's their fault.

24.___ My teacher needs to change more than I do because it's the teacher's fault.

25.___ My friend needs to change more than I do because it's his/her fault.

26.___ I need to change more than anyone else because it's my fault.

For each thought you rated a 3, 4, or 5, ask yourself the following questions:

1. What is unhelpful about this thought?
2. How does this thought make me feel?
3. Is it helpful to keep thinking this thought?

HELPFUL "COUNTER" THOUGHTS FOR CHILDREN

Listed below are helpful "counter" thoughts that children can use instead of unhelpful thoughts. Unhelpful Thought #1 corresponds to Helpful Thought #1 and so on. Compare the unhelpful thoughts to the helpful thoughts.

Thoughts about Self

1. I'm too hard on myself. I'm OK.
2. I make mistakes, but I also do a lot of things OK.
3. I can behave positively too.
4. All I can do is try. I have to accept myself for who I am. I'll concentrate on what I do well.

Thoughts about Peers

5. It's impossible for everyone to like me. Some peers do like me.
6. I'm blowing it out of proportion. Some peers think I'm OK.
7. I'm blowing it out of proportion. Some peers think I'm OK.
8. I fit in with some people. I do have friends.

Thoughts about Parents/Family

9. It doesn't help to think about the family being all messed up. Instead we need to take action.
10. It's not all my fault. Other people also play a role in the problems.
11. It doesn't help to blame my parent. I should focus on solutions to the problems.
12. It doesn't help to blame my brother or sister for the problems. I should focus on solutions to the problems.
13. My parent is trying to help. If I would take more responsibility, my parent would probably let up on me.
14. My parent seems unfair at times, but if I really look at it, I know that my parent treats me OK.

Thoughts about Teacher/School

15. It doesn't help to blame my teacher. I need to think about solutions.
16. My teacher is trying to help. If I would take more responsibility, my teacher would probably let up on me.
17. It doesn't help to give up. I need to keep trying.

Thoughts about the Future

18. I'm being irrational. I have no proof that I will have problems in the future. I need to wait until the future.
19. I can't give up. I have to keep trying.

Thoughts about the World/Life

20. I can't use this as an excuse. I need to take control of my own life.
21. I can't use this as an excuse. I need to take control of my own life.
22. I can't use this as an excuse. I need to take control of my own life.

Thoughts about Who Needs to Change

23. It's unhelpful to think my parent is the only one who needs to change. We all need to change.
24. It's unhelpful to think my teacher is the only one who needs to change. We all need to change.
25. It's unhelpful to think my friend is the only one who needs to change. We all need to change.
26. It's unhelpful to think I am the only one who needs to change. We all need to change.

For each thought you rated a 3, 4, or 5, ask yourself the following questions:

1. What is helpful about this thought?
2. How does this thought make me feel?
3. Is it helpful to keep thinking this thought?

From *Skills Training for Children with Behavior Disorders: A Parent and Therapist Guidebook* by Michael L. Bloomquist. © 1996 The Guilford Press.

CHANGING UNHELPFUL THOUGHTS WORKSHEET

Name: _____

Date: _____

Directions: A child and/or parent can complete this worksheet. Answer each question as it pertains to changing unhelpful thoughts. Fill out the worksheet during or after you have experienced an unhelpful thought.

1. **Am I thinking unhelpful thoughts?**

2. **What is the unhelpful thought I am thinking?**

3. **How do my unhelpful thoughts make me feel?**

4. **Is it helpful to keep thinking this thought?** Why or why not?

5. **What is a different or more helpful way I can think?**

6. **How does the new helpful thought make me feel?**

7. **Is it helpful to keep thinking the new thought?** Why or why not?

Changing Unhelpful Thoughts Rating (circle one)
1. Didn't change my thoughts to be more helpful at all.
2. Tried a little to change my thoughts to be more helpful, but it didn't really work.
3. Tried hard, went through the steps, but it didn't help to change my thoughts.
4. Tried hard, went through the steps, and changed my thoughts to be more helpful.

From *Skills Training for Children with Behavior Disorders: A Parent and Therapist Guidebook* by Michael L. Bloomquist. © 1996 The Guilford Press.

EXAMPLE:
CHANGING UNHELPFUL THOUGHTS WORKSHEET

Name: *Jonathan*

Date: *Tuesday*

Directions: A child and/or parent can complete this worksheet. Answer each question as it pertains to changing unhelpful thoughts. Fill out the worksheet during or after you have experienced an unhelpful thought.

1. **Am I thinking unhelpful thoughts?**
   Yes.

2. **What is the unhelpful thought I am thinking?**
   Sarah doesn't like me.

3. **How do my unhelpful thoughts make me feel?**
   Awful, sad, lonely.

4. **Is it helpful to keep thinking this thought?** Why or why not?
   No. It makes me feel bad.

5. **What is a different or more helpful way I can think?**
   Sarah probably does like me. I might be imagining that she doesn't. We usually play together. It doesn't help me to think this thought.

6. **How does the new helpful thought make me feel?**
   Better. I feel OK.

7. **Is it helpful to keep thinking the new thought?** Why or why not?
   Yes. I feel better.

Changing Unhelpful Thoughts Rating (circle one)

1. Didn't change my thoughts to be more helpful at all.
2. Tried a little to change my thoughts to be more helpful, but it didn't really work.
3. Tried hard, went through the steps, but it didn't help to change my thoughts.
4. Tried hard, went through the steps, and changed my thoughts to be more helpful.

From *Skills Training for Children with Behavior Disorders: A Parent and Therapist Guidebook* by Michael L. Bloomquist. © 1996 The Guilford Press.

TALLY FOR USING CHANGING UNHELPFUL THOUGHTS WORKSHEET

Name: _____

Date: _____

Directions: At the end of a designated time period, add up all the ratings from the Changing Unhelpful Thoughts Worksheets. Add up all the 1 and 2 ratings, and then add up all the 3 and 4 ratings. If there are more 3 and 4 ratings, then the child gets to select a reward.

Total ratings of 1 and 2 _____   **Total ratings of 3 and 4 _____**

Reward =

EXAMPLE:
TALLY FOR USING CHANGING UNHELPFUL THOUGHTS WORKSHEET

Name: *Jonathan*

Date: *Wednesday*

Directions: At the end of a designated time period, add up all the ratings from the Changing Unhelpful Thoughts Worksheets. Add up all the 1 and 2 ratings, and then add up all the 3 and 4 ratings. If there are more 3 and 4 ratings, then the child gets to select a reward.

Total ratings of 1 and 2 *1*   **Total ratings of 3 and 4** *5*

Reward = *Select from reinforcement menu*

HELPFUL THINKING

1. **Am I thinking unhelpful thoughts?**

2. **Are these thoughts going to help me?**

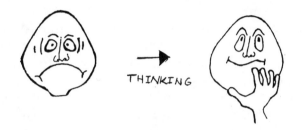

3. **What is a different or more helpful way I can think?**

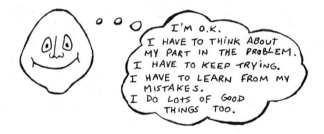

15

Enhancing Children's Self-Esteem

It's probably true that most children are not born with either low or high self-esteem. Self-esteem seems to develop gradually as a child experiences life. If a child experiences more positive input than negative input, he is more likely to develop a higher sense of self-esteem. Unfortunately, many children with behavior problems receive more negative feedback from their world than positive feedback and over time can develop a low sense of self-esteem. This chapter will discuss some common sense approaches to promote high self-esteem in children.

What's Wrong with You?

Eight-year-old Toni lives with her parents, Sharon and David, and her 6-year-old sister, Stacy. Toni has a long history of behavior problems including being defiant with her parents and being aggressive with her sister and some of the neighborhood children. For many years, she has caused much trouble in the family. A lot of arguing goes on in the family. Many other parents complain about Toni, which increases the tension between Toni and her parents. Sharon and David try to be as positive as they can with Toni, but often find themselves saying very negative things to her when they are angry and upset with her. Even Toni's sister Stacy says many negative things to her. A typical example of this occurred the other day when Toni grabbed some of Stacy's toys from her and ran to her room with them. Stacy became very upset and ran after Toni and a big argument developed in Toni's room. David came into the room to find his two children screaming at each other. He had heard what had gone on prior to this, and he knew that Toni was in the wrong. He was so steamed up and angry that he shouted at Toni, "What's wrong with you?"

HOW IS SELF-ESTEEM RELATED TO CHILDREN'S BEHAVIOR PROBLEMS?

Self-esteem is how one evaluates oneself. Many children evaluate themselves in a very negative way, and they engage in behaviors that confirm the way they see themselves. In other words, when children think poorly of themselves, they often

210

behave poorly. Children with low self-esteem think other people think of them negatively, and so they behave negatively with these people. The implication is that if a parent addresses a child's low self-esteem, the child's behavior problems might also improve.

Parents have a vital role in promoting children's self-esteem. Although heredity plays a large role in who we are, the role of parents is obviously extremely important as well. To a great extent, children are what their parents make them. This is especially true with children's self-esteem. Parents can have a profound influence on children's development of positive self-esteem.

COMMON SENSE IDEAS PARENTS CAN USE TO PROMOTE SELF-ESTEEM

Teach Children Skills

Most of this book is geared toward promoting skills development in children. Throughout the book, the role of the parents has been emphasized in achieving this goal. **Parents can teach children life skills to help them become more successful.** If they are successful, they will receive more positive feedback from others and will feel good about themselves, thus leading to a better sense of self. Try to work on helping your child develop the skills described in this book, because they could enhance his self-esteem.

Give Positive Feedback

What parents say, and how they say it, has a great deal to do with their child's internal sense of self and self-esteem. During childhood, children receive feedback from others—the most important feedback coming from parents. If the negative feedback outweighs the positive feedback, the child will develop a negative view of self. **If the positive feedback outweighs the negative feedback, over time the child will develop a positive view of self.** Providing more positive feedback than negative feedback is quite challenging for parents of children with behavior disorders. These children often do not display enough positive behavior to warrant positive feedback. So look at the small good things your child does, and praise him for these successes.

Be Involved in Your Child's Life

For children to feel really good about themselves, they have to know that their parents care about them and are involved with them. Some of the ideas described in Chapter 5 help increase this involvement. **Try to improve the quality of your relationship with your child by becoming more involved and emphasizing positive reinforcement.**

Maintain Healthy Family Interactions

Ongoing family interactions can have a strong effect on a child. If the family is having problems, everyone suffers. Pay attention to and emphasize the skills discussed in Chapter 6 regarding family interactions. In particular, **try to avoid certain kinds of communication such as negative questions, blaming, put-downs, and sarcasm** (see Chapter 6 for more details). These types of communication have a negative effect on a child's self-esteem because they suggest the child is "bad." If a child repeatedly hears negative statements about himself he may end up viewing himself as bad. **Good communication and problem solving within the family will promote your child's self-esteem.**

Really Listen to Your Child

It's very tempting to correct your child or give him advice when he tells you about his troubles or difficulties. This can turn your child off. He may avoid talking to you. **Really listening to your child can help him feel better about you and himself.**

There are several methods you can use to improve listening. One method is paraphrasing. This involves restating what your child says, so that he knows you really understand him. Another method is to accept your child's feelings (even if you disagree with your child's behavior). Tell the child what you think he feels like or restate the feeling he expresses.

Accept Your Child

Many of your child's problems are chronic and very difficult to change. It may not be useful to keep focusing on the same problems over and over. **Try to determine which behaviors you can realistically change and which behaviors you need to accept.**

Help Your Child Handle Mistakes and Failures

Children with disruptive behavior problems make a lot of mistakes and have a lot of setbacks. They struggle at school, have fewer friends, get in trouble, make impulsive decisions, and so forth. When a problem arises, don't "shame" your child by dwelling on it, or asking, "Why did you do that?" Instead give your child a consequence, if needed, and **ask what he can learn from this mistake.** Also, try to down play your child's "failure" (e.g., a low grade on a test). Assure him it's OK. Tell him that the main thing is to keep trying. Then help him focus on effort (trying) rather than outcome (success or failure).

Help Your Child Accept Successes

Many children with low self-esteem don't like to admit they did something good. Doing something good doesn't fit with their view of themselves. Keep reminding your child he is a good person. Emphasize the things he does well and has succeeded in. **Help your child see that he is responsible for his successes.**

Promote Your Child's Talents

Every child has some talent in such areas as art, sports, music, dance, working with animals, volunteer work, and so forth. **Make extra effort to help your child develop whatever talents he has.** Your child will be able to receive more positive feedback, thus helping his self-esteem.

Don't Attribute Your Child's Good Behavior to Medications

Many children who have ADHD display improved behavior when on psychostimulant or other medications. **If your child is taking medications and is one of those who show a positive response, make sure you don't put too much emphasis on the effects of the medication when your child is behaving well.** Sometimes parents will make the mistake of asking the child if he "took the pill" when he misbehaves. This implies that the child does not behave well unless he is on medication. Sometimes parents will describe their child's positive behavior as resulting from taking the medication. Over time this can have a negative effect on a child's self-esteem. He may begin to think that he is not a good person unless he is on medication. Even if the medication is having a strong positive effect on your child, be sure and help him see that he is the one responsible for his positive behavior.

SUMMARY POINTS

1. Promote your child's self-esteem by teaching life skills, giving ongoing positive feedback and approval, getting involved in your child's life, maintaining healthy family interactions, really listening to your child, accepting your child's limitations, helping your child handle mistakes and failures, helping your child accept successes, and not attributing all of your child's positive behavior to medications.

I Like What I See

Back to Toni, David, Sharon, and Stacy: David and Sharon are concerned about Toni's self-esteem. They think that the way they have been talking to Toni and dealing with some of her behaviors has not been very positive and may be contributing to her low self-esteem. They decide that they will to try to "accentuate the positive." They decide to teach Toni some skills and focus initially on helping her learn how to understand, identify, and express her feelings. They resolve to give her much more positive feedback and to try to accept her more for who she is. At the end of several weeks they notice that they are also being much more positive, not only to Toni, but to Stacy and to each other. They hope that, if they continue to emphasize the positive, Toni's self-esteem will improve.

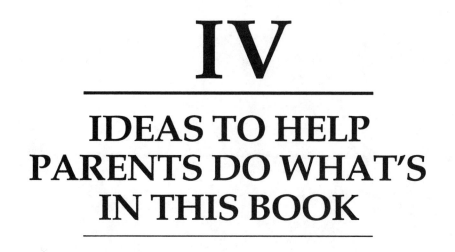

IV

IDEAS TO HELP PARENTS DO WHAT'S IN THIS BOOK

16

Keeping It Going: Maintaining Improvements for Your Family and Child

Starting something and then keeping it going are two very difficult tasks. How often have you made a New Year's resolution? How often have you carried out that New Year's resolution to its completion? Have you ever decided you were going to embark on a diet/exercise program? How successful were you in actually carrying out your health program? It's very difficult to keep it going.

By the time you get to this chapter, you very likely have decided to work on one or two parent/family or child skills areas. Perhaps you have even tried to develop some of these skills. Maybe it worked very well, maybe not. Getting started is a difficult first step, but keeping it going is equally challenging.

Keeping it going is a very tough job. Research suggests that **many patients do not follow health care regimens** prescribed by their physicians. Many patients also fail to follow the treatment plans of mental health providers. Even physicians and mental health providers themselves do not always follow the suggestions and guidelines that they give their clients. Indeed, I don't always do what I have written on these pages with my own family!

The information contained in this book is designed to help you and your child learn skills. The underlying assumption is that, by learning these skills, your child's development will be enhanced. Even under the best of circumstances, development unfolds over a long period of time, so **you can expect it will take a long time for you and your child to learn the skills described in this book.**

There is a high risk that you may start out with good intentions but not carry things through because skills are difficult to learn and the disruptive behavior problems of your child are chronic in nature. Therefore, **it is very important to think about how to keep it going and maintain improvements once you get started.** You need to take some concrete action and plan on how to maintain improvements successfully.

What follow are some practical, common sense suggestions on how you can maintain improvements for you and your child.

Pick the Right Skills to Work On

Make sure that you have identified the correct skill area for your family or child. Think it through very carefully, and select a specific skill area to work on. Try it for a while. Evaluate the effects of the skills training. **If you decide it's not a good match, maybe you should try something else.** For example, if you elect to help your child learn how to do problem-solving, but she is extremely resistant, then perhaps you need to focus on a different skill, possibly one related to parent/family functioning.

Realistic Thoughts

Modern society seems to be obsessed with quick fixes and cures. We want things to happen overnight. This is exactly the wrong attitude to have when it comes to trying to learn new skills. These things take time. If you have a realistic attitude at the outset, you're much more likely to be successful. **Sometimes it can take weeks, months, or even years before you see significant changes in your family or child.**

Enlist the Help of Others

We know that when people work together they tend to have more success with whatever task they undertake. People who work together are more likely to stick with exercise routines, quitting smoking, and so forth as compared with individuals who attempt the same programs by themselves. The same is true when you try to learn new skills. If you have a spouse/partner available, it may be wise to enlist that person's help in the change process. Try to enlist school personnel to work with your child at the school. Perhaps extended family members could also be of assistance. **Inform these people of the skills that you are working on and try to get them to help you.**

Enlisting help seems to have two effects on people. First, people are more likely to stick with the program they started because they have support. Secondly, one person has some accountability to the other. If one person tells someone else that he is going to do something, he is more likely to do so than if he hasn't told anybody.

Goal Setting and Self-Reinforcement

It's a very good idea to set a goal and then **break the goal down into small, realistic steps.** For example, you may set a goal that you are going to try to teach your child some problem-solving skills. A realistic small step toward that goal would be to state that you are going to use problem-solving worksheets with your child for 2 weeks. At the end of 2 weeks, evaluate your progress, and determine whether you should continue or try something else.

We know that when people are rewarded they tend to perform better. The same can be true in this case. **Self-reinforcement involves administering a reinforcement to yourself after you've reached your goal.** For example, if you were able to use problem-solving worksheets with your child for 2 weeks, you might reward yourself with a movie.

Practice Self-Awareness

Sometimes when we set out to change a behavior, we continue the same old behavior anyway, without even realizing it. For example, a dieter reaches for a cookie, eats it, and then realizes what she did. Another example would be the parent who sets out to teach her child problem-solving skills. One day her two sons start a fight about which TV program to watch. This very same mother jumps in and tells her children to take turns watching different shows. Later she realizes that she solved a problem for her children that she could have better used as an opportunity to teach them how to solve their own problems.

There are several strategies one can use to increase self-awareness. There are numerous charts throughout the book. **Make copies of charts from this book and put them up in strategic locations in your house.** For example, hang up charts on the refrigerator or on a door. You might also try hanging up a sign somewhere to cue yourself on specific behaviors that you'd like to do. For example, you might put a sign that says "reinforcement" above the clock in your kitchen. Every time you look at the clock, this will remind you to reinforce your child for some good behavior. You could ask other family members to prompt you when they notice an opportunity for you to engage in the new behavior. For example, a father might remind a mother to not give in to a child's noncompliant behavior and to use time-out instead. There are other exercises related to self-monitoring that parents could use (see Chapter 5).

Conduct Periodic Reviews

It may be very helpful if you set out to review your progress periodically . During these reviews, the goal is to take stock, **evaluate how it's going, and make modifications if needed.** For example, you and your spouse/partner might agree to meet every Sunday evening to review the progress on a specific skill area that you are trying to train your child on. It may help to write down these periodic review sessions on a calendar.

Plan Relapse Prevention

We know that there is a high risk that you and your family will lapse back to the "old ways." People who are trying to change various addictions, develop new health habits, and so forth, frequently have relapses. It is even more likely that lapses will occur when one is dealing with a child who has a chronic disruptive behavior problem. How you respond to these relapses is what determines failure or success. The failure response is to think, "It's no use," and to give up. The success response is to gear up and keep trying.

Because relapses are bound to occur, it makes sense to plan ahead for how you will respond to them. The first step is to recognize the signals of relapse. For example, if you notice that your child's behavior problem is getting worse, that you're getting calls regarding your child's behavior at school, that you feel under more stress, and so forth, you may be receiving signals that a relapse is occurring. Once you recognize the signals, have a plan of action already in place. Remember that relapses are inevitable, so don't get discouraged. At the point of relapse, you need to gear up and reapply some of the skills that perhaps you have let fall by the wayside. This might entail getting out the charts that you tried several months ago and reusing them.

Don't Give Up

We know that these skills are very difficult to learn and to keep using over time. **If you are consistent and persistent, you will see results.** These skills training procedures fail most often because a parent applies them inconsistently or gives up. Keep trying!

V

INFORMATION
AND SUGGESTIONS
FOR THERAPISTS

17

Skills Training for Children with Behavior Disorders: Theory and Research Overview

This chapter will provide a rationale, and a review of supporting evidence, for conducting skills training with parents and children with behavior disorders. Therapists will gain an appreciation of the developmental foundation of skills training and understand why it is imperative to focus interventions on parents. Therapists will also be better informed of available research evaluating skills training interventions, which should ultimately lead to more effective interventions for children with behavior disorders.

DEVELOPMENTAL COMPETENCE ENHANCEMENT MODEL OF SKILLS TRAINING

The goal of skills training interventions is to help children achieve "competence" in mastering developmental tasks (August, Anderson, & Bloomquist, 1992). A developmentally competent child is one who is able to make use of environmental and personal resources to achieve a good developmental outcome (Waters & Sroufe, 1983). Children progress through stages of development in which they master successive developmental tasks and eventually achieve a high degree of competency in different developmental domains. **If a child doesn't successfully negotiate an earlier stage, he or she will be less able to negotiate later stages, and will ultimately be less competent in later life** (Arend, Gove, & Sroufe, 1979; Sroufe, 1983; Masten et al., 1995). Table 5 describes normal child development in self-control, social, academic, and affective domains. These developmental stages came from my review of several introductory child psychology textbooks. At each age, different developmental tasks are listed. A child can successfully move on to the next stage when he or she is competent (i.e., has mastered tasks) in the preceding stage. The "academic" developmental domain is not typically written

TABLE 5. Developmental Tasks in Four Areas of Child Development and Parental Facilitative Behavior

Age	Child tasks				Parent facilitative behavior
	Self-control development	Social development	Academic development	Affective development	
Infancy (0–1 yr)	Explores environment using caregiver as a secure base	Attaches with primary caretaker Displays social smile and cry	Explores environment using caregiver as a secure base	Displays basic emotions	Instructing—providing external control and explicit behavior training for younger or developmentally delayed children to facilitate early competence
Toddler (1–3 yr)	Responds to external control of adults Complies with adults' requests	Separates from caregiver to interact with others Plays with others in a parallel fashion	Is curious about world	Displays more complex emotions Expresses emotions through behavior and play	
Preschool (3–6 yr)	Follows rules Talks out loud when playing or as a means to control own behavior	Plays with others in an interactive fashion Cooperates with others Shares with others Helps others Competes with others	Adjusts to being away from parents Develops an attitude of excitement about learning	Expresses emotions verbally Sympathizes with others	

Stage					
Elementary School (6–12 yr)	Uses thoughts to direct own behavior Develops beginning problem-solving skills Manages impulses Develops awareness of own behavior	Understands others' perspectives Conforms to peer group norms and standards Solves social problems Plays fair Has primarily same gender friends	Concentrates and stays on task Organizes school materials and tasks Begins to develop special skills and interests	Overcomes fears Regulates strong emotions such as anger, frustration, anxiety, sadness	Guiding—providing guidance for older or developmentally advanced children to facilitate internal self-regulation and later competence.
Adolescence (12–20 yr)	Develops more sophisticated problem-solving skills and is more aware of own behavior	Interacts primarily in cliques Has same gender and opposite gender friends "Launches" from family	Consolidates special skills and interests Engages in career planning and preparation	Understands relationship between thoughts, behavior, and emotions Thinks accurately and rationally about self and world	

Note. It is assumed that early developmental tasks are mastered and remain operational throughout later development. These are "typical" stages of development. Not all children, however, meet all of these tasks at the same age. Parent facilitative behavior will vary according to a child's level of competence.

about. It makes sense to think of children's academic development, however, given its importance as an area of focus for children, and because it is often an area of difficulty for children that prompts referrals for interventions.

Parents influence children's development through ongoing parent–child interactions (Vygotsky, 1962, 1978). It is hypothesized that parents need to do certain **"facilitative behaviors"** to assist children in their negotiation of developmental tasks. Table 5 describes parent facilitative behaviors which correspond to different stages of developmental competence in children. **With a younger or developmentally delayed child, it is facilitative if a parent "instructs" the child to negotiate developmental tasks. Instructing** involves a parent providing external control to a child and telling him or her how to behave. For example, when a preschool child is attempting to solve a problem, it is facilitative if a parent provides instructions to a child as to how to solve the problem (Roghoff, Ellis, & Gardner, 1984; Saxe, Guberman, & Gearhart, 1987). **With an older or developmentally advanced child, it is facilitative if a parent "guides" the child to negotiate developmental tasks. Guiding** involves a parent assisting a child to develop internal self-regulation abilities so the child can direct his or her own behavior. For example, when an elementary school age child is solving a problem, it is facilitative if a parent guides the child to think of good ways to solve the problem (Roghoff et al., 1984; Saxe et al., 1987). Effective parents are able to adjust their facilitative behavior to match their child's age and level of competence so as to assist the child with developmentally relevant tasks (Vygotsky, 1962, 1978; Wood, 1980).

Whether or not a child emerges as competent depends on the "risk" and "protective" factors the child is exposed to throughout his or her development (Luther & Zigler, 1991; Masten & Garmezy, 1986; Rae-Grant, Thomas, Offord, & Boyle, 1989). **Risk factors** include biological and genetic predispositions to psychological problems (e.g., biologically based psychiatric disorder) as well as environmental stressors (e.g., ineffective parenting, low socioeconomic status, high frequency of stressful life events, etc.). **Protective factors** include personal resources (e.g., persistence, talents, intelligence, problem-solving abilities, social skills, etc.), as well as environmental resources (effective parenting, good schools, supportive community programs, etc.), that serve to buffer the effects of exposure to the aforementioned risk factors. **It is hypothesized that when the ratio and weight of protective factors is greater than the ratio and weight of risk factors, the child is more likely to emerge as developmentally competent.**

Table 6 summarizes parent/family risk factors associated with the development of disruptive behavior disorders in children. Parents of behavior problem children often have more stress/personal problems such as depression, substance abuse; marital/relationship difficulties; and/or social isolation (Dumas & Serketich, 1994; Webster-Stratton, 1989). The parents of children with behavior problems often attribute the child's misbehavior to negative internal child traits, think they have little control over their child's behavior, expect the child to assume developmentally inappropriate levels of responsibility and are prone to have negative or irrational beliefs about the child (Campis, Lyman, & Prentice-Dunns, 1986;

TABLE 6. Parent/Family Risk Factors Associated with Disruptive Behavior Disorders, Hypothesized Affected Developmental Process, Skills Training Interventions to Promote Hypothesized Protective Factors, and Anticipated Parent/Family Outcomes

Parent/family risk factors	Hypothesized affected developmental process	Skills training interventions to promote hypothesized protective factors	Anticipated parent/family outcomes
• Parental stress/personal problems	• Insufficient parental facilitation of child development	• Parent stress management (Chapter 3)	• Enhanced parent personal functioning
• Inaccurate parental attributions, expectations, and beliefs	• Insufficient parental facilitation of child development	• Changing parent thoughts (Chapter 4)	• Enhanced accurate parental thinking
• Low parent–child cohesion, low rates of positive reinforcement	• Insufficient parental facilitation of child development	• Increasing parental involvement/ positive reinforcement (Chapter 5)	• Enhanced parent–child relationship cohesion
• Inconsistent, ineffective, and harsh discipline	• Insufficient parental facilitation of child development (also related to child social development)	• Helping children learn to comply (Chapter 7) and follow rules (Chapter 8)	• Enhanced parental discipline (also enhanced child social relationships)
• Ineffective facilitation of child skills development	• Insufficient parental facilitation of child development	• Training parents to guide child skill development (Chapters 7–15)	• Enhanced parental facilitation of child development
• Family interaction difficulties	• Insufficient parental facilitation of child development (also related to child social development)	• Family interaction training (Chapter 6)	• Enhanced family interactions (also enhanced child social relationships)

Sobol, Ashbourne, Earn, & Cunningham, 1989; Vincent Roehling & Robin, 1986). The parent–child relationship, where behavior problem children are involved, is often characterized by low levels of cohesion and by parents not reinforcing positive child behavior (DuPaul & Barkley, 1992; Ramsey & Walker, 1988). Further, parents of behavior problem children are often inconsistent and ineffective in discipline because they give in more to child noncompliance (negative reinforcement), do not supervise/monitor adequately, and/or use harsh discipline techniques (Anderson, Hinshaw, & Simmel, 1994; DuPaul & Barkley, 1992; Haapasalo & Tremblay, 1994; Patterson, 1982; Ramsey & Walker, 1988; Ramsey, Walker, Shinn, O'Neill, & Stieber, 1989; Strassberg, Dodge, Pettit, & Bates, 1994; Weiss, Dodge, Bates, & Pettit, 1992). These same parents are less able to facilitate (i.e., instruct/guide) their child in the development of self-regulation skills (Bloomquist, August, Anderson, Skare, & Brombach, in press; DuPaul & Barkley, 1992; Olson, Bates, & Bayles, 1990). Finally, the families of behavior problem children have more interactional problems characterized by poor problem solving/communication and high conflict (Dadds, Sanders, Morrison, & Rebgetz, 1992; Ramsay & Walker, 1988; Sanders, Dadds, Johnston, & Cash, 1992). **It is hypothesized that, when these parent/family risk factors are present, it adversely affects the parent's ability to facilitate a child's development in the self-control, social, academic, and affective domains.**

Table 7 summarizes child risk factors associated in the development of disruptive behavior disorders in children. Behavior problem children are more likely to be noncompliant/defiant with adults (DuPaul & Barkley, 1992; Gard & Berry, 1986; Sattersfield, Swanson, Schell, & Lee, 1994) and to violate rules at home, at school, or in the community (Kazdin, 1995; Masten et al., 1995; Patterson, 1982) as compared with children without behavior problems. Impulsive cognitive tempo (e.g., not thinking in a planful manner), and, especially, hyperactive–impulsive behavior (e.g., impatience, demanding, butting in line, talking out of turn, and other forms of behavioral disinhibition), have been strongly linked to behavior disordered children (Hamlett, Pellegrini, & Connors, 1987; Iaboni, Douglas, & Baker, 1995; Tant & Douglas, 1982; White et al., 1994). Children with behavior difficulties often lack social behavior skills (e.g., sharing, expressing feelings, cooperating, playing by the rules, etc.) resulting in the child being more aggressive with, or rejected by, peers (Carlson, Lahey, Frame, Walker, & Hynd, 1987; Newcomb, Bukowski, & Pattee, 1993). Much research exists showing that aggressive children are deficient in social problem solving, in that they often focus on aggressive cues of others, misinterpret others' benign behavior as being hostile in intent, generate fewer and more aggressive solutions to problems, and value aggressive solutions over prosocial solutions (Dodge, 1993; Lochman & Dodge, 1994; Weiss et al., 1992). Aggressive and socially deficient disruptive children are also often poor at perspective taking (i.e., understanding others' thoughts and feelings), which interferes with effective social problem solving (Chandler, 1973; Gurucharri, Phelps, & Selman, 1984). Disruptive and/or aggressive children are prone to be easily frustrated and to show anger outbursts (Barkley, 1990; Lochman, Nelson, & Sims, 1981). Many ADHD and/or academically delayed disruptive children have limited sustained attention and poor organizational skills, and are more likely to be off-task with

TABLE 7. Child Risk Factors Associated with Disruptive Behavior Disorders, Hypothesized Affected Developmental Domain, Skills Training Interventions to Promote Hypothesized Protective Factors, and Anticipated Child Outcomes

Child risk factors	Hypothesized affected developmental domain	Skills training interventions to promote hypothesized protective factors	Anticipated child outcomes
• Noncompliance	• Delayed self-control development (also related to parent–child problems)	• Compliance training (Chapter 7)	• Enhanced compliance (also enhanced parent–child relationship)
• Rule-violating behavior	• Delayed self-control development (also related to parent–child problems)	• Rule-following training (Chapter 8)	• Enhanced rule-following behavior (also enhanced parent–child relationship)
• Impulsive cognitive tempo, hyper-activity–impulsivity	• Delayed self-control development (also related to parent–child problems)	• General and thinking ahead problem-solving training (Chapter 10)	• Enhanced reflectivce thinking ability (also enhanced parent–child relationship)
• Social behavior skills deficits	• Delayed social development	• Social behavior skills training (Chapter 9)	• Enhanced social relationships
• Social problem-solving deficits	• Delayed social development	• Social problem-solving training (Chapter 10)	• Enhanced social relationships
• Low frustration tolerance/anger outbursts	• Delayed affective development	• Anger management training (Chapter 11), affective education (Chapter 13)	• Enhanced strong emotion regulation ability
• Limited sustained attention, off-task behavior, poor organization	• Delayed academic development	• Self-directed academic behavior skills training (Chapter 12)	• Enhanced academic productivity and effort
• Low self-esteem, emotional problems	• Delayed affective development	• Affective education (Chapter 13), helpful thinking training (Chapter 14)	• Enhanced self-esteem and emotional well-being

tasks requiring effort (Douglas, 1983; Hooks, Milich, & Lorch, 1994). Finally, many behavior problem children have low self-esteem and/or depressive symptoms (Jensen, Burke, & Garfinkel, 1988; McConaughy & Skiba, 1993), which can result in these children making cognitive errors and maladaptive attributional processes for success and failure (Curry & Craighead, 1990; Hoza, Pelham, Milich, Pillow, & McBride, 1993). **It is hypothesized that, when these child risk factors are present, they adversely affect the child's development in self-control, social, academic, and affective domains.**

The risk factors discussed in Tables 6 and 7 need to be put into perspective. These risk factors are "proximal" in that they are readily observable and easier to modify in skills training interventions. There are other more "distal" risk factors such as IQ, gender, family size, medical, socioeconomic, school, and community factors that also relate to development and maintenance of behavior disorders in children (see Kazdin, 1995, for a thorough discussion). Although important, these distal risk factors are not as readily observable or modifiable, and are not the direct focus of skills training interventions. It is important to note that not all parents/families/children are exposed to all of these risk factors. It is the case, however, that the more risk factors evident, the more likely the child will have behavioral problems (Loeber, 1990). However, the issue of causation is not always clear. For example, it may be that ineffective parenting leads to increased child noncompliance or that a high level of child noncompliance leads to ineffective parenting. It is probably true that parent/family factors and child factors affect each other in a circular manner, which intensifies the problems.

When many of the risk factors described in Tables 6 and 7 are present, the child is more likely to go down a negative developmental pathway. He or she will not successfully negotiate normal developmental tasks and will manifest developmental deviations such as behavioral and psychological problems. Child risk factors such as early onset hyperactivity–impulsivity, aggression, and noncompliance predict social rejection and academic delays in children during the elementary school years, which in turn predict serious CD, delinquency, and substance abuse for these same individuals in adolescence and adulthood (Loeber, 1990; Moffit, 1993; Patterson, DeBarshe, & Ramsey, 1989). The parent/family risk factors described earlier activate, accelerate, and stabilize the behavior disorder trajectory of development in children (Frick, 1994; Loeber & Stouthamer-Loeber, 1986).

Developmental competence enhancement interventions attempt to promote protective factors through skills training interventions. When protective factors are enhanced, they buffer the child against the effects of risk factors, potentially enabling the child to go down a positive developmental pathway. He or she will be more likely to negotiate developmental tasks successfully and to exhibit developmental competence in important developmental domains. Tables 6 and 7 summarize interventions hypothesized to promote protective factors in parents/families and children. The interventions listed in Tables 6 and 7 are described in detail in Chapters 3–15 of this book.

Figure 3 provides a visual representation of the hypothesized instrumental relationship between risk/protective factors, developmental competence enhancement interventions, and eventual developmental outcomes in children. Naturally occurring risk/protective factors are what a child is born with and is exposed to in his or her natural environment. It is hypothesized that protective factors are increased when children are exposed to developmental competence enhancement interventions, thereby increasing the likelihood of a good developmental outcome.

The skills training interventions used to promote developmental competence in this book are derived and adapted from cognitive-behavioral therapy (CBT) approaches (e.g., Barkley, 1987, 1990; Bernard & Joyce, 1984; Blechman, 1985; Braswell & Bloomquist, 1991; Finch, Nelson, & Ott, 1993; Forehand & McMahon, 1981; Kendall, 1991; Kendall & Braswell, 1993; Robin & Foster, 1989; Spence, 1994; Stark, 1990). CBT is defined here broadly as a collection of goal-oriented, short-term skills training interventions, that incorporate both behavioral and cognitive therapeutic interventions. The "Ecological–Developmental Model of CBT" (Braswell & Bloomquist, 1991) applies here as to how interventions are delivered. The ecological part of this model involves intervening with the child and other individuals in the child's environment. The developmental part of this model focuses on providing different types of skills training interventions that match the child developmentally. The basic idea is to teach a child and his or her parents to think and behave in a different manner, with the goal of ultimately promoting the child's development. Throughout this book, parents are given ideas on how to incorporate the skills training into the child's environment and how to use the

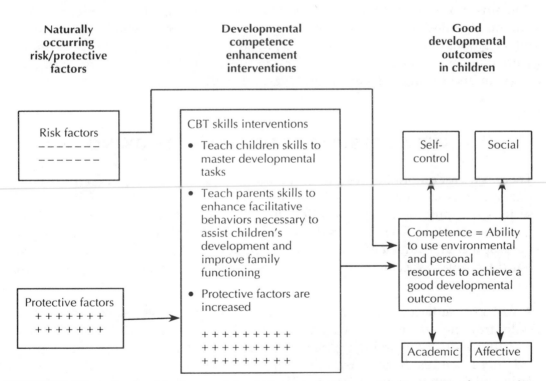

FIGURE 3. Hypothesized instrumental relationship between risk/protective factors, developmental competence enhancement interventions, and developmental outcomes in children.

best methods to account for developmental differences. Therapists can also assist the parents to use skills training procedures that take ecological and developmental factors into account.

One might ask how CBT methods assist children in making developmental gains. To illustrate this, it is helpful to think of "implicit" and "explicit" developmental learning in children. For example, most children learn how to speak by observing others and gradually accumulating the ability during "critical periods" of development. Learning to speak is a good example of implicit developmental learning. When a child is delayed and/or exhibits developmental problems, then he or she needs to be trained **explicitly** in developmentally related skills. If a child is delayed in the area of speaking, then he or she would most likely receive explicit instruction through speech and language therapy to assist him or her in developing the skills necessary to speak functionally. It is argued here that when a child is developmentally delayed in self-control, social, academic, and/or affective developmental domains, then explicit skills training and developmental learning is necessary. CBT therapeutic methods are explicit instructional skills building procedures that closely relate to developmental skills. **Explicit skills training for children in the self-control, social, academic, and affective domains, and for parents to improve facilitating through instructing and guiding, enhances the child's developmental status. The goal is not necessarily to "cure" the child but to "get the child going" down a positive developmental trajectory.**

It was noted above that not all children are delayed in all the developmental domains, nor are all the risk factors described in Tables 6 and 7 present in all parents/families/children. Therefore, no one parent/family/child requires all the interventions described in Tables 6 and 7. The therapist can assist by collaborating with the parents and child to determine which skills training areas are most relevant and to conduct skills training accordingly.

RESEARCH SUPPORT FOR SKILLS TRAINING

There is a vast amount of research evaluating the effects of various skills training interventions with children exhibiting behavior disorders and their families. This section will provide a brief overview of the main conclusions drawn from this research literature. The findings discussed do not directly evaluate the theoretical developmental competence enhancement model of intervention described above, but do evaluate specific training interventions that are part of this intervention model.

A word of caution needs to be stated about applying these research findings to skills training efforts employing this book. The research discussed below was usually conducted with highly trained therapists under ideal and highly controlled circumstances. In contrast, this book can be used either as a self-help guide or in collaboration with a therapist. This method is not as rigorous as the procedures typically utilized in research studies. There is no available research specifically evaluating use of this book in a self-help format or with the assistance of a therapist. Although the research results discussed below provide support for what the book offers, one should not necessarily expect the same results when using this book.

Parent Training Targeting Noncompliant, Rule-Violating, Aggressive Child Behavior and Parent–Child Interactions

The studies discussed in this section typically involved parents being trained by therapists to modify child behavior and parent–child interactions. Usually parents were trained in behavior management techniques to reduce disruptive child behavior and to increase positive child behavior. Parents were also trained to engage in child-directed play/relationship building activities. The studies targeted children from preschool through adolescent years, with most of the studies focused on elementary school age children.

There are numerous reports of quasi-experimental and experimental studies evaluating the effects of parent training on disruptive child behavior (see Hinshaw & Erhardt, 1990; McMahon, 1994; Webster-Stratton, 1993). Parent training has been found to be effective in reducing noncompliant, rule-violating, and aggressive behavior in children, and to improve parent–child interactions. Researchers have found that the effects of treatment generalize to the home environment. Intervention effects have been maintained even up to 4.5 years after the intervention had been completed. The research results were typically stronger when preschool and elementary school age children were targeted as opposed to adolescents. A recent study also found that training parents in child behavior management before parent–child relationship building resulted in children who achieved more improved behavior and parents who were more satisfied, as compared with training parents in parent–child relationship building before child behavior management (Eisenstadt, Eyberg, McNeil, Newcomb, & Funderburk, 1993). Parent training also has been found to have a positive effect on parents through reduced stress and improved parenting self-esteem (Anastopoulos, Shelton, DuPaul, & Guevremont, 1993).

Family Training Targeting Noncompliant, Rule-Violating, Aggressive Child Behavior and Family Interaction Skills

In these studies, family members were trained together by a therapist. The primary focus was typically on improving family interaction skills related to problem solving, communication, negotiation, and conflict resolution. Some emphasis was also placed on changing maladaptive thoughts that parents and/or children/teenagers held about each other. Parents often also received child behavior management instruction to improve the child's noncompliant and rule-violating behavior. Usually children who were late elementary school or adolescent age were the subjects in these studies.

A series of studies employing family interaction skills training with adolescents has been conducted utilizing the family skills intervention training techniques described by Robin and Foster (1989). Researchers employing this type of training have found reductions in family conflict and improvement in family interaction skills (Foster, 1979, as discussed in Robin & Foster, 1989; Robin, Kent, O'Leary, Foster, & Prinz, 1977). One study also found that a combination of family interaction skills training and parents' child behavior management training reduced disruptive child behavior and maintained effects better than family skills training alone (Phiffner, Jouriles, Brown, Etscheidt, & Kelly, 1990).

Several research groups have also focused on family interaction skills training with children exhibiting severe CD and delinquency. Functional Family Therapy, as developed by Alexander and Parsons (1982), has been evaluated in several studies. Functional Family Therapy emphasizes family interaction skills training but also places a premium on training parents in child behavior management skills and a variety of other practical skills. Functional Family Therapy treatment has been found to be superior to comparison interventions and control conditions in reducing child disruptive behavior, delinquency, referrals to the court, as well as improving family interaction skills, along with maintenance of treatment effects up to 2.5 years after intervention (Alexander & Parsons, 1973; Klein, Alexander, & Parsons, 1977; Parsons & Alexander, 1973). Henggeler and colleagues have developed a therapeutic model known as Multi-Systemic Family Therapy (Henggeler & Borduin, 1990). Multi-Systemic Family Therapy is similar to Functional Family Therapy, but in addition it emphasizes CBT with a child, and often involves in-home family therapy and community/school interventions. Multi-Systemic Family Therapy has been found to be superior to alternative treatment groups in reducing adolescent delinquent behavior and improving parent–child relationships, with effects being maintained for 1–4 years (Borduin, Henggeler, Blaske, & Stein, 1990; Bourduin et al., 1995; Henggeler, Melton, & Smith, 1992; Henggeler et al., 1986).

Child Training Targeting Child Social Behavior Skills

In these research studies, children have been trained to increase specific social behavior skills through training with a therapist in individual sessions or in groups. Typically the focus was on improving prosocial behavior skills such as expressing feelings, sharing, cooperating, initiating conversations, assertiveness, and so forth. Aggressive and/or rejected children were usually targeted. Oftentimes behavior management techniques were employed in group training.

Research has supported the efficacy of social behavior skills training. Pelham and Bender (1982) found that social behavior skills training with children, combined with behavior management to reduce disruptive behavior, was superior to social behavior skills training alone. Bierman and colleagues treated aggressive and rejected children and found social behavior skills training was effective in improving their prosocial behavior skills and in reducing their aggression (Bierman

& Furman, 1984; Bierman, Miller, & Stabb, 1987). A recent study by Prinz, Blechman, and Dumas (1994) focused on teaching children communication/exchange of information skills and combined that with behavior management. These researchers found that children who received this type of treatment were able to exchange more information with each other and showed reduced aggressive behavior.

Child Training Targeting Child Hyperactive–Impulsive Behavior

There are numerous studies evaluating the effects of helping children to "think before they act" via self-instructional and problem-solving training to reduce hyperactive–impulsive behavior. Through this type of training, children were trained to utilize self-statements to mediate behavioral responding. Hyperactive–impulsive children were trained either individually or in groups. In research evaluating this type of training, the children were usually elementary school age.

Kendall and Braswell (1993) summarized early research using subjects who were selected either on the basis of performance of cognitive measures of impulsivity or teachers' referral as exhibiting impulsive behavior in the classroom. Many of these subjects exhibited subclinical levels of disruptive behavior problems. Across most of these early studies, self-instruction/problem-solving training was found to reduce impulsive responding as measured on tests assessing cognitive impulsivity, and to improve teacher and parent ratings of disruptive behavior for these children.

Kendall and colleagues (Kendall, 1981, 1982; Kendall & Braswell, 1982; Kendall & Finch, 1978; Kendall & Wilcox, 1980; Kendall & Zupan, 1981) conducted a series of studies evaluating self-instruction/problem-solving training with "non-self-controlled" (hyperactive–impulsive) children as referred by teachers. Children who received self-instruction/problem-solving training were found to benefit more than children who participated in a variety of control or comparison groups. The researchers found that general, broad-based self-instruction/problem-solving statements were better than task-specific statements in facilitating generalization of children's performance across training tasks. Group delivery of skills training to children was found to be equally as effective as individual delivery. Self-instruction/problem-solving training with children that combined behavioral contingencies during training was found to be superior to self-instruction/problem-solving training alone. Long-term and follow-up effects were evaluated in several of the studies. Children who received treatment were found to maintain treatment effects, but were not different than children in control and comparison groups, possibly suggesting a maturation effect.

Numerous studies have evaluated the effects of self-instruction/problem-solving training with children meeting clinical criteria for ADHD (hyperactive–impulsive). The children who participated in these studies had a more severe level of clinical impairment than children who participated in some of the studies that were reviewed above. In general, self-instruction/problem-solving training has not been found to be effective in working with clinically diagnosed ADHD children (see Abikoff, 1987; Braswell & Bloomquist, 1991; Kendall & Braswell, 1993). Brown and colleagues (Brown, Borden, Wynne, Schleser, & Clingerman, 1986; Brown, Wynne, & Medenis, 1985) evaluated the effects of combining self-instruction/problem-solving training with and without methylphenidate medication for treatment of ADHD children. In these studies, Brown and colleagues found that methylphenidate was equal to methylphenidate plus self-instruction/problem-solving training and both of the treatments involving methylphenidate were superior to a self-instruction/problem-solving training alone intervention. Notably, when either the self-instruction/problem-solving training or the methylphenidate were discontinued, the treatment ceased to be effective.

Bloomquist, August, and Ostrander (1991) examined a school-based intervention for ADHD (hyperactive–impulsive) elementary school age children that combined child group training in problem-solving/social skills with parent and teacher education/consultation. Children who received this combination training improved more than children in alternative or control groups on observations of in-class, disruptive, off-task behavior. The results of the study were interpreted negatively, however, because children who received the combined treatment did not improve on teachers' ratings or self-report measures.

Child Training Targeting Child Aggressive Behavior/Anger Problems

In these studies, therapists trained aggressive or aggressive/conduct disordered children to employ cognitive strategies related to social problem solving, perspective taking, situation interpretation, and anger management, along with social behavior skills. Often behavioral contingencies were employed during the sessions to facilitate acquisition of the skills. Typically children in the elementary school or early adolescent years were the subjects.

Lochman and colleagues (Lochman, 1992; Lochman, Burch, Curry, & Lampron, 1984; Lochman & Curry, 1986; Lochman, Lampron, Gemmer, Harris, & Wyckoff, 1989; Lochman & Lenhart, 1993) have developed and evaluated an Anger Coping Program. Children participating in the Anger Coping Program made more improvements than children in control and alternative treatment conditions in terms of reduced in-class observations of aggressive behavior and parent and teacher ratings of aggressive behavior. Additionally, children who participated in the Anger Coping Program have been found to have higher levels of self-esteem and more proficiency at problem-solving skills after the intervention. The researchers found that children who had the poorest problem-solving skills prior to onset of the treatment benefited the most from the intervention. Lochman also found that children who received the Anger Coping Program continued to show improvements in self-esteem and were using less drugs 3 years after treatment, as compared with children who received alternative treatments. Unfortunately, however, children who received the Anger Coping Program did not show any difference compared with children in the alternative conditions in terms of aggressive/delinquent behavior after 3 years.

Kazdin and colleagues (Kazdin, Bass, Siegel, & Thomas, 1989; Kazdin, Esveldt-Dawson, French, & Unis, 1987a, 1987b; Kazdin, Siegel, & Bass, 1992) conducted a series of treatment studies with aggressive-conduct disordered children. Compared with children in control or comparison groups, children who received a social problem-solving intervention exhibited more reductions in teacher and parent ratings of disruptive and aggressive behavior at posttest and at 1-year follow-up. In one study, Kazdin and colleagues found that the combination of child training, along with parent training in child behavior management, reduced child disruptive/aggressive behavior better than child-only training.

Child Training Targeting Child Inattentiveness/Off-Task Behavior

In these studies, therapists or teachers in classrooms trained children to self-monitor their on-task behavior. Self-monitoring training involved children learning how to monitor specific behaviors, record the occurrence of these behaviors, evaluate their performance in terms of improvements, and to administer self-reinforcement if their behavior improved. Usually children of elementary school age participated in these studies.

Evans and Sullivan (1993) summarized the literature evaluating self-monitoring training to improve on-task behavior. Self-monitoring training has been found to improve children's on-task behavior, as well as academic productivity in the classroom. The effects of the self-monitoring training were increased in children when behavioral reinforcement was utilized to reinforce the same behavior that was being self-monitored.

Child Training Targeting Child Low Self-Esteem/Internalizing Problems

As discussed previously, many children with behavior disorders also have problems with depression/anxiety and/or low self-esteem. Studies have been conducted that targeted children with internalizing problems alone or in combination with disruptive behavior problems. Usually cognitive restructuring techniques, along with problem solving, affective education, and relaxation skills training were utilized in these studies. Children typically were trained in groups, but have been also trained in individual therapy sessions. Typically elementary school age children were the subjects for these studies.

Ollendick and King (1994) summarized the research literature regarding cognitive-behavioral treatments for internalizing problems. With children who were defined as depressed, CBT was found to equal relaxation training, with both of these interventions being superior to control or comparison conditions. Relaxation training has been found to be particularly helpful with children who are suffering from anxiety symptoms.

Intensive Summer Training Targeting Child Disruptive Social and Academic Behavior

Pelham and colleagues (Pelham & Gnagy, 1995; Pelham & Hoza, in press) have developed and evaluated an intensive Summer Treatment Program for children with ADHD and associated behavior problems. Children received a full-time 8-week intervention during the summer months, totaling 360 hours. Children were involved in classroom and recreational activities. During the activities, children worked with counselors/teachers on social, classroom, and problem-solving skills. There was a behavioral management strategy in place at all times. Parents received weekly training in child behavior management. Many children were on psychostimulant medication. There was also follow-up training available after the summer program including Saturday training sessions for children, parent sessions, and school consultation.

Pelham and Gnagy (1995) reported data on 258 children who completed the Summer Treatment Program. Significant improvements were found for children on measures ranging from consumer satisfaction to parent/teacher/counselor ratings of child behavior to child self-report. Parents also rated themselves as feeling better about parenting their children.

Preventive Intervention Targeting High-Risk Aggressive Children

Vitaro and Tremblay (1994) developed a preventive program that targeted elementary school age aggressive children, in an effort to improve these children's short- and long-term developmental outcome. Aggressive children in this study received an intensive 2-year intervention consisting of behavioral parent training and child social skills/problem-solving training. The effects of the program were studied yearly for 3 years following the intervention.

Vitaro and Tremblay (1994) found that aggressive children who received the intervention showed greater improvements, as compared with aggressive children in a control condition, on teacher ratings of disruptive/aggressive behavior, with the effects more pronounced over time each year the children were assessed. Peer nomination measures also revealed that the treated children made gains in forming friendships with more prosocial peers over the 3 years. Vitaro and Tremblay hypothesized that the children in the treatment condition were able to make better friends over time, which led them on a more positive developmental trajectory, and this was related to less aggressive/disruptive behavior in the treated children over time.

Tremblay, Pagani-Kurtz, Masse, Vitaro, and Pihl (1995) reported on the extended long-term effects of the original preventive intervention (e.g., Vitaro & Tremblay,

1994). They found the intervention effects were attenuated on measures of delinquency at age 15. Tremblay et al. argue that booster sessions may be needed to maintain initial effects of preventive interventions over the long-term.

CONCLUSIONS REGARDING SKILLS TRAINING WITH PARENTS/FAMILIES AND CHILDREN

McMahon (1994) offered suggestions to maximize intervention effectiveness for therapists using skills training procedures with children exhibiting behavior disorders and with their parents. McMahon stated that it's important to target risk factors or processes that have significant implications for long-term adjustment in these children. The most important areas to target in this regard are parenting practices along with reducing noncompliant, aggressive, and impulsive behavior in children. McMahon suggested that interventionists use procedures that have the strongest empirical support. The parent/family training procedures aimed at reducing disruptive behavior and improving parent–child/family interactions are proven interventions. Additionally, child-focused social problem-solving/anger management training should also be utilized with aggressive children because this has proven to be efficacious. With ADHD children, McMahon recommended that skills training be utilized along with medication treatment. When working with children and/or families, McMahon argued it is probably the best idea to target external child management with the adults in the child's environment first, and then to concentrate on helping the child to learn internal self-regulation skills. Finally, McMahon suggested that children who are showing early signs of disruptive behavior be targeted for intervention rather than waiting for them to become older with more entrenched problems.

The intensity of treatment also needs to be considered by therapists working with behavior problem children and their parents. Intensive treatments (i.e., lengthy, multimodal treatments) are needed to effect changes in these children. To illustrate this point, it is instructive to contrast the studies by Bloomquist et al. (1991) and Pelham and Gnagy (1995). In both studies, ADHD children with associated behavioral problems were targeted and children received training in problem solving/social skills in academic settings. The Bloomquist et al. (1991) intervention was about 20 hours long with education/consultation for parents and teachers. The improvements in the Bloomquist et al. study were minimal. In contrast, the Pelham and Gnagy (1995) intervention totaled 360 hours with extensive parent training and many children being simultaneously treated on psychostimulant medications. The Pelham and Gnagy study yielded significant improvements for the children involved and their parents.

Treatment for children with behavior disorders and their families must be ongoing and episodic (Kazdin, 1995). Although most of the treatment studies reviewed above found statistically significant changes for children, very few of these efforts "cured" the children. Most children continued to show problems necessitating follow-up treatment. Behavior disorders in children should be thought of as "chronic" problems, which suggests the need for ongoing treatment (Kazdin, 1995).

Preventive skills training interventions have potential for improving the developmental outcomes of high-risk children. Preliminary evidence exists demonstrating that comprehensive, intensive skills training interventions may be able to reduce disruptive behavior in at-risk children over 3 years (Vitaro & Tremblay, 1994). It probably is necessary to provide ongoing interventions to maintain initial gains when conducting preventive interventions (Tremblay et al., 1995). More research is needed to evaluate the short- and long-term effects of preventive programs.

18

Procedures for Therapists to Help Parents and Children in Skills Training

The aim of this chapter is to provide descriptions of procedures to assist therapists in skills training with parents and children. Practical suggestions about how to incorporate this book in intervention efforts will also be presented.

This chapter will not review how to conduct a diagnostic evaluation for a child who may or may not have a disruptive behavior disorder (see Barkley, 1990; Braswell & Bloomquist, and 1991; and Hinshaw, 1994, for information on conducting diagnostic evaluations). It is assumed an evaluation has already been conducted and the therapist is now embarking on a skills training intervention.

SELECTING PARENTS AND FAMILIES FOR INTERVENTION

Most children with a disruptive behavior disorder diagnosis will benefit from a skills training intervention to some degree. **There are several exclusionary criteria a therapist should consider that might indicate that skills training by itself would be either insufficient or perhaps inappropriate.** These exclusionary criteria include severe levels of a disruptive child behavior disorder (e.g., repeated violent behavior), low intellectual functioning/organic difficulties with the child, severe marital and/or family problems, severe parental psychopathology, or a history of significant abuse/neglect of the child. If all or some of these exclusionary criteria exist in a particular case, then the skills training approach might only serve as one facet of an overall comprehensive intervention.

Once the therapist has determined that a child, parent, or family is appropriate for this intervention, he or she needs to determine what mode or method of delivery should be utilized. **Parent skills training group therapy is often a very powerful and effective intervention for children and families with mild to moderate levels of problems. Family interventions are more appropriate when a child or family is exhibiting higher levels of difficulty.**

PREPARATION FOR CHANGE

Preparation for change is absolutely critical and should be conducted before skills training (Braswell & Bloomquist, 1991). As the phrase implies, **the goal is to prepare the child, parents, or family to be able to profit from skills training.**

Collaboration

One way to facilitate preparation for change is to **collaborate actively with the child, parents, or family**. A first step in collaboration is to explain the disruptive behavior disorder diagnosis and all the implications of that particular problem (see Chapter 1). The next thing to collaborate on concerns treatment options. The therapist should fully explain the skills training approach, but should also discuss alternative interventions including medications, school-based services, community-based services, and so forth. After all this has been accomplished, the therapist and child, parents, or family should collaborate to determine which skills to focus on in the intervention. The therapist may have an idea of what he or she thinks would be appropriate, but without the client's input, preparation for change may not be successfully accomplished. Chapter 2 provides parents with an opportunity to rate themselves, the family, and the child in the ten areas of focus. This may serve as a springboard for discussion to determine what areas should be focused on with that particular client.

Dealing with Resistance

Resistance is inevitable in every change process and is often related to not being prepared for change. Therefore, it makes sense to deal with resistance a priori. **Resistance to skills training usually takes the form of unhelpful beliefs/cognitions held by parents and for children, lack of compliance with homework, and/or the parents having too many personal/family problems to benefit from this approach** (Braswell & Bloomquist, 1991).

Resistance stemming from beliefs/cognitions occurs when the parents and/or child have unhelpful beliefs about the intervention. If the parents and/or child seem to blame each other for the problems, then a skills training approach will not work. The therapist should spend some time before attempting any skills training to make sure that all family members at least hold a shared sense of responsibility for many of the problems and, more importantly, for the solutions to the problems. If the parents expect the child to do all the changing, or vice versa, then change will not be able to take place effectively using skills training. Everyone has to commit to the change process before change can really occur.

Cognitive reframing techniques can be used to help individuals see their role in the problem. For example, a common statement therapists hear from parents is something like, "He's a brat." This statement implies the child is "at fault" and therefore the child should be the focus of the intervention. Most therapists realize they will not get too far treating a noncompliant child individually because it is important to involve the parent. Yet if the parent sees the child as the problem, the therapist won't get far working with the parent. The therapist could begin cognitive reframing by asking the parent to describe an example of when the child is behaving like a "brat." The parent may say, "I tell him to do something and he refuses." The therapist could then reframe the problem by stating something like, "So, there really are two issues here as you describe them. One is you tell him to do something and the other is he refuses. Let's discuss the way you tell him to do things as the first issue, and then let's discuss how he refuses. We may need to change your behavior and his behavior. What do you think of this plan?" This statement has reframed the problem as being "caused" by both the parent and child. Ideally this will help the parent be more receptive to subsequent discussions of compliance training. Other reframing techniques can be used to help prepare individuals for change.

Therapists can also assist family members in accepting shared responsibility for problems by processing in-session client behavior. For example, parents and teens often blame each other for family disputes and conflicts. As the therapist sits with the family, inevitably a dispute or conflict will occur in the session. The therapist could then reframe the problem by pointing out how each of their behavioral responses to each other fueled the conflict. The therapist could use this example to help family members see that they all have a role in the problem. The family members may then be more receptive to subsequent discussions about family interaction skills training.

It is also important that children and parents have appropriate expectations for the skills training approach to intervention. Make sure your clients fully understand that these interventions take a long time and a lot of effort. It may help to frame the intervention in developmental terms (e.g., it takes time to facilitate development). Explain the four areas of childhood development (see Chapter 17, Table 5) and that the goal of the intervention is to get the child "back on track" developmentally.

Behavioral resistance is also an important factor to consider. This usually takes the form of noncompliance with homework activities. Throughout this book, attempts have been made to make all homework assignments very easy to understand and implement (e.g., charts at the end of each chapter). This should reduce some of the behavioral resistance to implementing homework assignments. It still will be necessary for the therapist actively to monitor the client's progress in terms of homework and to make adjustments when necessary to facilitate the homework process.

Children, in particular, often resist homework assignments. Ideally the child will be intrinsically motivated, but it doesn't always work that way. Therapists can try to reframe it so the child sees the benefit of doing homework. If that doesn't work, perhaps the parent could extrinsically motivate the child through tangible reinforcement to get things going. Explicit instructions about how to reinforce children are discussed throughout this book. It may be helpful to assist the parent in coming up with a reinforcement plan for unmotivated children. Work it out so the external reinforcement is gradually faded.

When behavioral resistance occurs, it can be useful to recollaborate and/or discuss obstacles interfering with homework completion. The therapist could inquire as to whether the skill targeted in the homework exercise was really the best area to focus on. For example, a parent decides to use a daily behavior contract (Chapter 8) with her child, but doesn't. The therapist could inquire as to whether the area of improving children's rule-following behavior via behavioral contracts was the best area to focus on. If the parent says "No," perhaps the therapist and parent should review potential target areas and methods again in a collaborative way. If the parent says "Yes," perhaps a discussion of "obstacles" interfering with the parent's ability to do the daily behavioral contract would be useful. Obstacles could range from a parent "forgetting" to feeling "too depressed lately." The therapist and parent could then discuss strategies to deal with these obstacles (see Chapter 16 to get ideas on how to deal with obstacles).

Another commonly seen source of resistance is the parents' own personal problems which interfere with their ability to employ the parent training procedures consistently. Parent personal problems can range from a parent "reliving" their own childhood by dealing with their own child (e.g., a parent feels depressed when their child is teased by peers because the parent was also teased by peers as a child) to mental health or social problems. In these cases, it may be necessary to refer a parent to mental health or chemical health services for him- or herself, or to refer the family for various social services. Often these other problems are more pressing than skills training. If these problems are not addressed, there will be little success in skills training.

Preparation for change should be thought of as a fluid, somewhat elusive part of an intervention. A therapist may need to alternate between skills training and preparation for change over the course of working with a family.

SELECTING AN AREA OF FOCUS

Although it is important to collaborate with the clients, **the therapist should lead the clients down the right path so they can choose skills training approaches that can be most realistically accomplished.** You might have clients who rate many or all of the ten areas of focus as significant problems. When this happens, the therapist needs to lead the clients in the right direction. A rule of thumb is to **focus on salient parent and family variables before focusing on the child.** When it comes to working with the child, it is essential first to **make sure the child is compliant and following rules before working with the child to develop other specific developmental competencies.** A child's developmental level should also be considered in selecting an area of focus. The focus areas relating to problem-solving, anger management, and helpful thinking require abstract thinking skills. These areas should not be focused on with younger children.

There are some unique features that are involved when utilizing the parent group training format. It is hard to individualize the content of the area of focus to each family participating in the group program. A "cafeteria" procedure works best, which involves presenting an overview of all the information contained in this book, and then helping individual families within the group choose the area of focus that fits them the best. A later section in this book describes methods to conduct parent groups.

The task of individualizing the skills training approach is easier when working with families. The therapist would simply collaborate with the family to help them select the areas of focus utilizing the rating scales of the ten areas of focus in Chapter 2.

TRAINING METHODS TO BE USED BY THE THERAPIST

This book describes many different skills training procedures that could be followed by parents. The therapist can help the parents learn these skills by utilizing behavioral training techniques. These behavioral techniques would include all or some of the following methods:

1. **Didactic explanation:** Explain the skills training methods to the parents and/or child.
2. **Modeling/demonstration:** "Act out" a skill and allow the parents and/or child to observe you implementing the skill.
3. **Role playing:** Instruct the parents and/or child to act out and demonstrate how they might implement the skill.
4. **Application in real-life environment:** Instruct the parents and/or child to use the new skills in real life.
5. **Homework:** Give the parents and/or child specific homework assignments utilizing the many forms and charts that are found in this book.
6. **Periodic review:** Over the course of intervention, whether it be in parent groups or family sessions, review and evaluate the progress of the parents and/or child.
7. **Processing therapeutic events:** As therapy naturally unfolds, many problems come up in the sessions. After certain skills have been introduced, look for opportunities to prompt the parents and/or child to use the skills in session.
8. **Having parents and/or child "teach" each other:** One of the best ways to learn is to teach. Ask the parents and/or child to teach each other about specific skills they have learned.
9. **Socratic questioning:** Do not tell the parents and/or child what to do, but guide them using Socratic questioning to focus on areas the parents and/or child think are important.
10. **Follow-up:** Continue to monitor the progress of the parents and/or child over time to ensure maintenance and to guard against relapses.

The therapist would use many of these methods to help parents and family members learn skills.

PROCEDURES FOR CONDUCTING PARENT GROUP THERAPY

It is important to do a good job selecting parents for the group. Do not select parents with high levels of personal problems. Make sure preparation for change has been done with all parents individually before enrolling them in parent groups.

The number of participants and therapists for a group depends on the setting. In a smaller setting, it is recommended that the therapist limit the size of the group to the parents of about six to eight children. Two therapists are ideal to conduct this type of group, but one therapist could work with a group of parents if person-power was limited. In a larger setting (e.g., school, community center), large numbers of parents could receive training. In this context, the training would have more of a lecture format, allowing time at the end for small break-out group discussions. One therapist could conduct the presentation, but there would need to be at least one therapist in each small group as well.

The format the therapist uses to conduct the parent session is important. A good format to follow is about 15 minutes for introduction/check-in, about 30–45 minutes for didactic instruction/modeling/role playing, and about 30–45 minutes for parents to discuss and practice the skills presented in that session. It is recommended that some time for small break-out group discussions be set aside if a therapist is working with a large number of parents.

The notion of providing parental support cannot be overemphasized. Although most of the training is focused on skill acquisition, be sure to leave enough time for the parents to discuss their own individual concerns and problems. Many parents comment that the support part of the group therapy experience is very important and helpful to them.

The exact number of parent group sessions may vary depending on the therapist's goals. Ten 2-hour group therapy sessions is a format that provides the minimum length of time necessary to cover all the material in this book. Of course, the therapist could elect to cover less material in any length of time desired. Usually, it takes about a session to cover one content area. It's always good to review previous material in subsequent sessions.

The amount and type of content covered in a parent group may vary depending on the goals of the intervention. The therapist could decide not to cover certain chapters, so as to have more time to spend on other chapters. The therapist could focus on Chapters 1–8 exclusively, for example, if the group consists of parents of early elementary school age children. If the group consists of parents of older elementary school age children or teens, then information from the other chapters could be selected.

The following is a proposed list that indicates session number, topic to be discussed/presented, and readings that the parents could have prepared before the group session if the therapist is covering all of the material in ten sessions:

Session	Topic	Chapter from parents' guide
1	Introduction, overview of disruptive behavior disorders, self-evaluation in the ten areas of focus	Chapters 1 and 2
2	Parent stress management, parent thoughts.	Chapters 3 and 4
3	Parent involvement, positive reinforcement, family interactions.	Chapters 5 and 6
4	Discipline related to compliance and rule following.	Chapters 7 and 8
5	Social behavior skills in children.	Chapter 9
6	Social and general problem-solving skills in children.	Chapter 10
7	Anger management in children.	Chapter 11
8	Self-directed academic skills in children.	Chapter 12
9	Emotional well-being and self-esteem in children.	Chapters 13, 14, and 15
10	Maintenance of intervention effects and planning for the future.	Chapter 16

It is also possible to conduct parent group training concurrently while children are being trained in child skills training groups. It is beyond the scope of this chapter to discuss details of conducting child skills training groups. Suffice it to say, however, that one effective way to deliver skills training is for different therapists to be working with children and parents in a coordinated fashion. For example, a child skills training group could be focused on social behavior skills training, while a parent skills training group could be focused on facilitating children's social behavior skills development at home. Most of the child and parent training could be conducted separately, with some time during each session devoted to joint training/socializing activities. Braswell and Bloomquist (1991) offer detailed descriptions of how to conduct child skills training groups, and how to coordinate such groups with parent skills training groups.

PROCEDURES FOR CONDUCTING FAMILY THERAPY

Several things need to be considered when conducting family sessions. The first consideration is who should be invited to attend the sessions. Obviously, the parents and the child should be there, but it may also be helpful to have siblings or other extended family members attend the sessions. Generally speaking, siblings who are affected by or affect the child in a significant manner, and are over the age of about 5 or 6 years, can benefit from the family sessions. The sibling could learn similar skills, and the parents could guide the child and the sibling together in their application. There may be situations also in which a child spends a lot of time with extended family members (e.g., grandparents). It may be helpful to involve extended family members in the therapy sessions so that they can better understand the child and be able to instruct and guide the child in skill development.

In most instances, it is recommended that the therapist initially contract with the family for about ten sessions. Usually, it's best to conduct five or six sessions once a week and then spread out the remaining sessions over an extended period of time to give the clients enough time to practice the skills. Even after the ten sessions, it is common to continue to monitor the child and family's progress for an extended period of time.

One way to deliver skills training with families is to train parents to train the child. The goal with this delivery method is to enable the parents to train and facilitate the child in skill development. The therapist would first meet with the parents to instruct, model, role play, plan, and so forth. Once the therapist has trained the parents, the child would be invited into the session. Then the parents would instruct, model, role play, plan, and so forth with the child to train him or her in the skill.

Another way to deliver skills training with families is first to train the child and then to train the parents. The goal of this delivery method is to help the parents learn how to facilitate skill development at home after the therapist has trained the child. The therapist would first meet with the child to instruct, model, role play, plan, and so forth regarding a certain skill training area. The therapist could use the instructions from the book as a basis for training the child. For example, if the therapist is training the child in anger management skills, the instructions in Chapter 11 could be used by the therapist. After the child has been preliminarily trained, the parents would be invited into the session. If the child is able, it can be useful to have the child give a preliminary explanation of the skill training procedures to the parent. The therapist would also instruct, model, role play, plan, and so forth with the parents as to how they can instruct and guide the child in using the skills at home with the child.

A final way to deliver skills training with families is to work with all family members simultaneously. The goal of this delivery method is to train family members together in skills development and to train the parents to facilitate skill development at home. This method may be preferred when the focus is on family interaction skills (e.g., Chapter 6). The therapist would meet with the family members to instruct, model, role play, plan, and so forth regarding a certain skill and as to how parents can facilitate skill use at home.

WORKING WITH MULTIPROBLEM FAMILIES

Many families presenting for mental health services have numerous problems. These problems might include financial problems, child abuse/neglect, domestic abuse, parents with personal problems and/or limited education, no transportation, or a high frequency of stressful life events (e.g., deaths in family, changing residence frequently, divorce/separation, etc.). It will be more challenging to do skills training with families facing these circumstances and problems.

Preparation for change is very important with multiproblem families. To ensure success with skills training, it is essential to reduce the problems listed above. This may involve referring the family to mental health, chemical health and/or social services agencies before skills training commences.

It is important to provide access to the skills training intervention. It may be necessary to deliver skills training in a school or community center or provide transportation. Child care may need to be provided. To motivate families who have all sorts of pressures, it may be wise to provide food, fun social activities, and so forth.

The timing of skills training should also be considered in skills training with multiproblem families. It may be wise to conduct traditional individual therapy (Tuma, 1989) or family systems therapy (Minuchin, 1979) or to refer for medications before conducting skills training.

Multiproblem families can benefit from skills training as long as it is combined with other practical and therapeutic strategies.

SENSITIVITY TO MULTICULTURAL ISSUES

Efforts should be made to make interventions multiculturally sensitive. Individuals from varying cultural backgrounds differ in terms of language, structure of the family, structure of community, views on child development, views on parenting, views on seeking help from mental health/educational institutions, and so forth (Ho, 1987). A therapist should take these factors into account and adjust delivery of skills training accordingly. It is beyond the scope of this book to review all concepts and procedures involved in delivery of multiculturally sensitive mental health services (interested readers are referred to Canino & Spurlock, 1994, and Ho, 1987, for more on this topic), but I offer several suggestions based on my experience in delivering skills training to children and families of different cultural backgrounds.

One procedure that helps to ensure multicultural sensitivity is to **emphasize collaboration.** This involves spending much time and effort in actively listening to the clients, presenting intervention options, and seeking as much input from the family members as possible to be able to focus on issues and use procedures that are meaningful to and comfortable for the clients.

Framing the skills training intervention in developmental terms may also assist clients from different cultures in acceptance of the intervention. The basic idea is to describe skills training as methods to help children enhance their level of development. Although there are culturally influenced differences in child development, **there are also many "universal" stages of child development that seem to cut across most cultures**. For example, most children learn basic social skills in their preschool years, although there may be subtle differences in exactly what social skills are learned for a particular cultural group. The parent should be led to apply broad ideas/methods to themselves and their child, which **the parent can modify as needed to fit their beliefs, values, and goals as shaped by their cultural background.**

I have attempted to make this book sensitive to multicultural issues. Many of the illustrations are either "acultural" (e.g., stick figures, circle faces, etc.) or depict individuals of different cultural backgrounds. The text has stories that are intended to apply to people from different cultures. Much of the text emphasizes enhancement of development. I have found these strategies to be accepted by clients of varying cultural backgrounds who have used earlier drafts of this book.

PROCEDURES FOR USING THIS BOOK IN SKILLS TRAINING INTERVENTIONS

This book can be used in a number of different ways depending on the clients' needs and the goals for the intervention. The therapist could provide the entire book, or the opportunity to purchase the book, to clients. Parents could be asked to read chapters before a session to prepare ahead of time and/or after a session to rehearse afterwards. Alternatively, because the author and publisher grant permission to reproduce any chart in Chapters 3–16 of the text for therapeutic purposes, the therapist could provide copies of selected charts to the clients.

This book is written in a fairly sophisticated manner that may be difficult for some parents. I elected to write in a comprehensive fashion to enhance the parents' understanding of, and ability to do, the skills discussed. Unfortunately not all parents can benefit from this due to limited reading ability. **In cases where parents have limited reading ability, the therapist could utilize oral instructions and modeling instructions as a way of explaining procedures.** The therapist could still use the charts from the book with these parents. The charts are, for the most part, fairly easy to comprehend, and could be used with less educated parents. In particular, the visually oriented charts may be of greatest utility for these clients.

SUGGESTED INSTRUCTIONAL METHODS AND GOALS FOR EACH TOPIC AREA

What follows is a list of potential goals and methods that therapists could use when trying to promote skills in specific areas. These goals and methods can be used in parent group or family sessions.

Topic and chapter in parents' guidebook	Methods and goals
Disruptive behavior disorders (Chapter 1)	• Review major characteristics and prognosis.
	• Emphasize the significant role of noncompliance, aggression, and coercive parent–child relationships in long-term outcome.
	• Review common assessment and treatment methods.
Selecting an area of focus (Chapter 2)	• Assist parents with self-evaluation in the ten areas of focus.
	• Inform parents that skills training may not be sufficient and that other interventions may also be necessary to help the family/child.
Parent stress management (Chapter 3)	• Help the parents understand one cannot provide what a child needs unless the parent is coping and functioning.
	• Instruct parents to discuss and brainstorm different kinds of methods that they can utilize to manage their own stress better.
	• Discuss the option of a mental health or chemical health referral for parents with significant personal problems.
Parent thoughts (Chapter 4)	• Ask the parents to self-evaluate and identify which thoughts found in the unhelpful thoughts list in Chapter 4 are typical of themselves.
	• Ask the parents to ask themselves the questions found in Chapter 4 that relate to whether or not these thoughts are helpful.
	• Review the countering helpful thought list in Chapter 4. Ask the parents to ask themselves the same kinds of questions with the helpful thoughts as they did with the unhelpful thoughts.
	• Have parents self-disclose new ways in which they are going to try to think about their child, themselves, or related areas.
	• Help parents think of their child in developmental terms.

	• Help parents identify where they think their child is functioning developmentally using the developmental norms in Chapter 4.
Parent involvement and positive reinforcement with children (Chapter 5)	• Ask parents to self-disclose whether or not they feel they are involved with and/or providing enough reinforcement to their children.
	• Ask parents to answer the question of how much time they spend with their child that is positive versus negative using a percentile estimation (e.g., 50% positive, 50% negative; 60% positive, 40% negative, etc.).
	• Make sure parents understand the relationship between low levels of positive reinforcement and high levels of behavior problems in children.
	• Review positive activity scheduling and special time activities with children.
	• Review parental self-monitoring.
	• Review all procedures regarding reinforcement.
Family interactions (Chapter 6)	• Explain what family communication, family problem solving, and family conflict management skills are about.
	• Ask parents and family members to self-evaluate on the DON'Ts of the Family Communication skills chart found in Chapter 6.
	• Ask parents or family members to give each other feedback about DON'Ts that they observe in each other.
	• Make sure that the parents or family members understand the link between the DON'Ts and DOs of communication as explained in the Family Communication Skills chart in Chapter 6.
	• Ask parents or family members to commit to increasing the DOs of communication as described in Chapter 6.
	• Model family problem solving using one parent as a participant.
	• Ask parents or family members to problem solve regarding superficial kinds of problem-solving situations (e.g., how would the group

spend $10,000 just won in a mythical lottery) for practice.

- Model what conflict management skills training would look like using one parent as a participant.

- Engage the parents or family members in role-play exercises related to family interaction skills.

- Plan with the parents or family members how they will use family interaction skills at home in real life.

- Give parents or family members an assignment to audio- or videotape the family using new family interaction skills at home and bring the recordings to a session to review.

Helping children learn to comply (Chapter 7)

- Define noncompliance in children, including the parent and child roles in the noncompliance problem.

- Ask parents to do self-evaluation regarding how they issue commands to their children.

- Ask parents to do self-evaluation regarding how they give warnings to their children.

- Ask parents to self-evaluate regarding how they do time-out and removal of privileges with their children.

- Explain the procedures involved in time-out and removal of privileges.

- Model with a parent acting as a child the proper way to conduct time-out or removal of privileges.

- Engage the parents in role-play exercises where they practice doing time-out and removal of privileges.

Helping children learn to follow rules (Chapter 8)

- Explain what rule-following problems are in children.

- Ask parents to self-evaluate how well they have defined and enforced rules with their child.

- Explain daily behavior contracting.

- Engage the parents in a discussion and fill out a hypothetical contract.

- Help parents to complete a daily behavior contract.
- Have parents work together and brainstorm ideas regarding which behaviors to target, which reinforcement procedures to use, and which privileges to remove.

Social behavioral skills in children (Chapter 9)

- Explain the importance of social skills in predicting future outcome for children.
- Help parents learn to identify both positive social behaviors and negative social behaviors in their children.
- Review procedures to modify social behaviors through reinforcement.
- Review procedures to practice new social behavior skills.
- Review procedures to assist children in peer refusal skills.

Social and general problem solving in children (Chapter 10)

- Define impulsivity and problem-solving deficits in children.
- Explain that problem-solving training may not be appropriate for children under age 8.
- Review all steps in training children in problem solving.
- Discuss directed-discovery methods for facilitating problem solving in their children.
- Review procedures involved in a parent mediating child–peer or child–sibling conflicts using social problem solving
- Review the problem-solving procedures and related worksheets.
- Model engaging a child in problem solving using one parent as a participant.
- Engage parents in role-play exercises in which they practice guiding their child to use one of the problem-solving methods using the worksheets.

Anger management in children (Chapter 11)

- Explain the differences between child anger problems, noncompliance, and family conflict difficulties.

	• Explain that anger management training may not be appropriate for children under age 10.
	• Review procedures to help children identify signals for recognizing anger.
	• Review procedures for relaxation training.
	• Review procedures for coping self-talk training.
	• Review procedures for taking action (e.g., problem solving).
	• Review procedures for prompting the child early before anger gets too far out of control.
	• Model and demonstrate how to work with a child to control anger using one parent as a participant.
	• Engage the parents in role-play exercises whereby they act out trying to guide their child to utilize anger management skills using the worksheet.
Self-directed academic behaviors in children (Chapter 12)	• Explain that the focus is on children's academic-related behavior and not their academic skills.
	◦ Review general tips to improve parental involvement in their child's school activities.
	• Review homework tips.
	• Review home–school note and parent–school collaboration procedures.
	• Review procedures to help children with organization, time management, and so forth.
	• Review procedures related to training children in on-task behavior.
Children's emotional well-being and self-esteem (Chapters 13, 14, and 15)	• Review how children with disruptive behavior disorders are at risk for developing emotional problems and low self-esteem.
	• Review procedures related to affective education (i.e., helping children express feelings and problems).
	• Model and demonstrate how a parent could "dialogue" with a child to help a child express feelings and problems.
	• Role play having the parents "dialogue" with the therapist or each other about how they

might help a child express feelings and problems.

- Explain that helpful thinking training may not
be appropriate for children under age 10.
- Review all the procedures involved in helping
the child change unhelpful thoughts.
- Model how to work with a child to change
unhelpful thoughts using one parent as a participant.
- Have the parents role play working with a
child to help the child counter the unhelpful
thoughts with more helpful thoughts.
- Review common sense ideas that parents can
use to improve a child's self-esteem.

**Maintenance of intervention
effects
(Chapter 16)**

- Ask the parents if they have ever set a New
Year's resolution, started a diet/exercise
program, tried to quit smoking, and so forth,
and determine the amount of success they had
with these efforts.
- Explain that it is necessary and helpful to plan
actively how to maintain treatment intervention effects.
- Review all procedures discussed in Chapter
16 related to enhancing maintenance of intervention effects.

FOLLOW-UP WITH FAMILIES

It is not uncommon when using a skills training approach to follow families for
months, or even years, by conducting periodic booster sessions now and then. The
follow-up is a critical component in working with families. **The therapist should
assume that development of skills takes a long time and that there is significant
risk of relapse.** By having these periodic reviews and follow-up sessions, the
therapist can monitor the client's progress, refocus the family if necessary, or
review previously learned skills. Extended follow-up can be accomplished by
intermittently meeting with the family (e.g., several sessions per year, once a
month, etc.) or by asking the family to recontact the therapist should future problems arise.

Appendix: List of Parent Support Organizations

National Learning Disabilities Association
4156 Library Road
Pittsburgh, PA 15234
(412) 341-1515

Children and Adults with Attention Deficit Disorders (CH.A.D.D.)
Suite 109
499 Northwest 70th Avenue
Plantation, FL 33317
(305) 587-3700

National Information Center for Handicapped Children and Youth
P.O. Box 1492
Washington, DC 20013
(703) 893-6061

Federation for Children with Special Needs
Suite 104
95 Bekely Street
Boston, MA 02116
(617) 482-2915

Office of Civil Rights
National Office
Department of Education
Room 5000, Switzer Building
400 Maryland Avenue S.W.
Washington, DC 20202

Federation of Families for Children's Mental Health
1021 Prince Street
Alexandra, VA 22314
(703) 684-7710

References
and Suggested Readings

Note. The factual information discussed in Chapters 1, 17, and 18, as well as many practical ideas described in Chapters 2–16, were derived from these sources.

Abikoff, H. (1987). An evaluation of cognitive behavior therapy for hyperactive children. In B. B. Lahey & A. E. Kazdin (Eds.), *Advances in clinical child psychology* (Vol. 10, pp. 171–216). New York: Plenum Press.

Alexander, J. F., & Parsons, B. (1973). Short-term behavioral intervention with delinquent families: Impact on family process and recidivism. *Journal of Abnormal Psychology, 81,* 219–225.

Alexander, J. F., & Parsons, B. (1982). *Functional family therapy.* Monterey, CA: Brooks/Cole.

American Psychiatric Association. (1994). *Diagnostic and statistical manual of mental disorders* (4th ed.). Washington, DC: Author.

Anastopoulos, A. D., Shelton, T. L., DuPaul, G. J., & Guevremont, D. C. (1993). Parent training for ADHD: Its impact on parent functioning. *Journal of Abnormal Child Psychology, 21,* 581–596.

Anderson, C. A., Hinshaw, S. P., & Simmel, C. (1994). Mother–child interactions in ADHD and comparison boys: Relationships with overt and covert externalizing behavior. *Journal of Abnormal Child Psychology, 22,* 247–265.

Arend, R., Gove, F., & Sroufe, L. A. (1979). Continuity of individual adaptation from infancy to kindergarten: A predictive study of ego-resiliency and curiosity in preschoolers. *Child Development, 50,* 950–959.

August, G. J., Anderson, D., & Bloomquist, M. L. (1992). Competence enhancement training for children: An integrated child, parent and school approach. In S. Christenson & J. Conoley (Eds.), *Home–school collaboration: Enhancing children's academic and social competence* (pp. 175–213). Silver Springs, MD: National Association of School Psychologists.

Barkley, R. A. (1987). *Defiant children: A clinician's manual for parent training.* New York: Guilford Press.

Barkley, R. A. (1990). *Attention-deficit hyperactivity disorder: A handbook for diagnosis and treatment.* New York: Guilford Press.

Bernard, M. E., & Joyce, M. R. (1984). *Rational-emotive therapy with children and adolescents: Theory, treatment strategies, preventative methods.* New York: Wiley.

Bierman, K. L., & Furman, W. (1984). The effects of social skills training and peer involvement on the social adjustment of preadolescents. *Child Development, 55,* 151–162.

Bierman, K. L., Miller, C. L., & Stabb, S. O. (1987). Improving the social behavior and peer acceptance of rejected boys: Effects of social skill training with instructions and prohibitions. *Journal of Consulting and Clinical Psychology, 55,* 194–200.

Blechman, E. A. (1985). *Solving child behavior problems at home and school.* Champaign, IL: Research Press.

Bloomquist, M. L., August, G. J., Anderson, D. L., Skare, S. S., & Brombach, A. M. (in press). Maternal facilitation of children's problem-solving: Relationship to disruptive child behaviors and maternal characteristics. *Journal of Clinical Child Psychology.*

Bloomquist, M. L., August, G. J., & Ostrander, R. (1991). Effects of a school–based cognitive–behavioral training intervention for ADHD children. *Journal of Abnormal Child Psychology, 19,* 591–605.

Borduin, C. M., Henggeler, S. W., Blaske, D. M., & Stein, R. (1990). Multisystemic treatment of adolescent sexual offenders. *International Journal of Offender Therapy and Comparative Criminology, 34,* 105–113.

Braswell, L., & Bloomquist, M. L. (1991). *Cognitive-behavioral therapy with ADHD children: Child, family, and school interventions.* New York: Guilford Press.

Braswell, L., Bloomquist, M. L., & Pederson, S. (1991). *A guide to understanding and helping children with attention deficit hyperactivity disorder in school settings.* Minneapolis: Department of Professional Development, University of Minnesota.

Breen, M. J., & Altepeter, T. S. (1990). *Disruptive behavior disorders in children: Treatment focused assessment.* New York: Guilford Press.

Brown, R. T., Borden, K. A., Wynne, M. E., Schleser, R., & Clingerman, S. R. (1986). Methylphenidate and cognitive therapy with ADD children: A methodological reconsideration. *Journal of Abnormal Child Psychology, 14,* 481–497.

Brown, R. T., Wynne, M. E., & Medenis, R. (1985). Methylphenidate and cognitive therapy: A comparison of treatment approaches with hyperactive boys. *Journal of Abnormal Child Psychology, 13,* 69–88.

Campis, L. K., Lyman, R. D., & Prentice-Dunn, S. (1986). The parental locus of control scale: Development and validation. *Journal of Clinical Child Psychology, 15,* 260–267.

Canino, I. A., & Spurlock, J. (1994). *Culturally diverse children and adolescents: Assessment, diagnosis, and treatment.* New York: Guilford Press.

Cantwell, D. P. (1989a). Conduct disorder. In H. I. Kaplan & B. I. Sadock (Eds.), *Comprehensive textbook of psychiatry* (5th ed., pp. 1821–1827). Baltimore: Williams & Wilkins.

Cantwell, D. P. (1989b). Oppositional defiant disorder. In H. I. Kaplan & B. I. Sadock (Eds.), *Comprehensive textbook of psychiatry* (5th ed., pp. 1842–1845). Baltimore: Williams & Wilkins.

Carlson, C. L., Lahey, B. B., Frame, C., Walker, J., & Hynd, G. (1987). Sociometric status of clinic-referred children with attention deficit disorder with and without hyperactivity. *Journal of Abnormal Child Psychology, 15,* 537–547.

Chandler, M. J. (1973). Egocentrism and antisocial behavior: The assessment and training of social perspective-taking skills. *Developmental Psychology, 9,* 326–332.

Curry, J. F., & Craighead, W. E. (1990). Attributional style and self-reported depression among adolescent inpatients. *Child and Family Behavior Therapy, 12,* 89–93.

Dadds, M. R., Sanders, M. R., Morrison, M., & Rebgetz, M. (1992). Childhood depression and conduct disorder: II. An analysis of family interaction patterns in the home. *Journal of Abnormal Psychology, 101,* 505–513.

Dodge, K. A. (1993). Social-cognitive mechanisms in the development of conduct disorder and depression. *Annual Review of Psychology, 44,* 559–584.

Douglas, V. I. (1983). Attentional and cognitive problems. In M. Rutter (Ed.), *Developmental neuropsychiatry* (pp. 280–328). New York: Guilford Press.

Dumas, J. E., & Serketich, W. J. (1994). Maternal depressive symptomatology and child maladjustment: A comparison of three process models. *Behavior Therapy, 25,* 161–181.

DuPaul, G. J., & Barkley, R. A. (1992). Social interactions of children with ADHD: Effects of methylphenidate. In J. McCord & R.E. Tremblay (Eds.), *Preventing antisocial behavior: Interventions from birth through adolescence* (pp. 162–190). New York: Guilford Press.

Eisenstadt, T. H., Eyberg, S., McNeil, C. B., Newcomb, K., & Funderburk, B. (1993). Parent–child interaction therapy with behavior problem children: Relative effectiveness of two stages and overall treatment outcome. *Journal of Clinical Child Psychology, 22,* 42–51.

Evans, H. L., & Sullivan, M. A. (1993). Children and the use of self-monitoring, self-evaluation, and self-reinforcement. In A. J. Finch, W. M. Nelson III, & E. S. Ott (Eds.), *Cognitive-behavioral procedures with children and adolescents: A practical guide.* Boston: Allyn & Bacon.

Finch, A. J., Nelson, W. M., III, & Ott, E. S. (Eds.). (1993). *Cognitive-behavioral procedures with children and adolescents: A practical guide.* Boston: Allyn & Bacon.

Forehand, R. L., & McMahon, R.J. (1981). *Helping the noncompliant child: A clinician's guide to parent training.* New York: Guilford Press.

Frick, P. J. (1993). Oppositional defiant disorder: A meta-analytic review of factor analyses and cross-validation in a clinic sample. *Clinical Psychology Review, 13,* 319–340.

Frick, P. J. (1994). Family dysfunction and the disruptive disorders: A review of recent empirical findings. In T. H. Ollendick & R. J. Prinz (Eds.), *Advances in clinical child psychology* (Vol. 16, pp. 203–226). New York: Plenum Press.

Gard, G. E., & Berry, K. K. (1986). Oppositional children: Training tyrants. *Journal of Clinical Child Psychology, 15,* 148–158.

Garfinkel, B. D., & Wender, P. H. (1989). Attention-deficit hyperactivity disorder. In H. I. Kaplan & B. I. Sadock (Eds.), *Comprehensive textbook of psychiatry* (5th ed., pp. 1828–1836). Baltimore: Williams & Wilkins.

Gurucharri, C., Phelps, E., & Selman, R. (1984). Development of interpersonal understanding: A longitudinal and comparative study of normal and disturbed youths. *Journal of Consulting and Clinical Psychology, 52,* 26–36.

Haapasalo, J., & Tremblay, R. E. (1994). Physically aggressive boys from ages 6 to 12: Family background, parenting behavior, and prediction of delinquency. *Journal of Consulting and Clinical Psychology, 62,* 1044–1052.

Hamlett, K. W., Pellegrini, D. S., & Connors, C. K. (1987). An investigation of executive processes in the problem-solving of attention deficit–hyperactive children. *Journal of Pediatric Psychology, 12,* 227–240.

Henggeler, S. W., & Borduin, C. M. (1990). *Family therapy and beyond: A multisystemic approach to treating the behavior problems of children and adolescents.* Pacific Grove, CA: Brooks/Cole.

Henggeler, S. W., Melton, G. B., & Smith, L. A. (1992). Multisystemic treatment of serious juvenile offenders: An effective alternative to incarceration. *Journal of Consulting and Clinical Psychology, 60,* 453–61.

Henggeler, S. W., Rodick, J. D., Borduin, C. M., Hanson, C. L., Watson, S. M., & Urey, J. R. (1986). Multisystemic treatment of juvenile offenders: Effects on adolescent behavior and family interaction. *Developmental Psychology, 22,* 132–141.

Hinshaw, S. P. (1994). *Attention deficits and hyperactivity in children.* Thousand Oaks, CA: Sage.

Hinshaw, S. P., & Erhardt, D. (1990). Behavioral treatment. In V. B. Van Hasselt & M. Hersen (Eds.), *Handbook of behavior therapy and pharmacotherapy for children: A comparative analysis.* Boston: Allyn & Bacon.

Ho, M. K. (1987). *Family therapy with ethnic minorities*. Newbury Park, CA: Sage.

Hocutt, A. M., McKinney, J. D., & Montague, M. (1993). Issues in the education of students with attention deficit disorder: Introduction to the special issue. *Exceptional Children, 60*, 103–106.

Hooks, K., Milich, R., & Lorch, E. P. (1994). Sustained and selective attention in boys with attention deficit hyperactivity disorder. *Journal of Clinical Child Psychology, 23*, 69–77.

Hoza, B., Pelham, W. E., Milich, R., Pillow, D., & McBride, K. (1993). The self-perceptions and attributions of attention deficit hyperactivity disordered and nonreferred boys. *Journal of Abnormal Child Psychology, 21*, 271–287.

Iaboni, F., Douglas, V. I., & Baker, A. G. (1995). Effects of reward and response costs on inhibition in ADHD children. *Journal of Abnormal Psychology, 104*, 232–240.

Jensen, J. B., Burke, N., & Garfinkel, B. D. (1988). Depression and symptoms of attention deficit disorder with hyperactivity. *Journal of the American Academy of Child and Adolescent Psychiatry, 27*, 742–747.

Kazdin, A. E. (1993). Treatment of conduct disorder. *Development and Psychopathology, 5*, 277–310.

Kazdin, A. E. (1995). *Conduct disorders in childhood and adolescence* (2nd ed.). Thousand Oaks, CA: Sage.

Kazdin, A. E., Bass, D., Siegel, T., & Thomas, C. (1989). Cognitive-behavioral therapy and relationship therapy in the treatment of children referred for antisocial behavior. *Journal of Consulting and Clinical Psychology, 57*, 522–535.

Kazdin, A. E., Esveldt-Dawson, K., French, N. H., & Unis, A. (1987a). Problem-solving skills training and relationship therapy in the treatment of antisocial child behavior. *Journal of Consulting and Clinical Psychology, 55*, 76–85.

Kazdin, A. E., Esveldt-Dawson, K., French, N. H., & Unis, A. (1987b). Effects of parent management training and problem-solving skills training combined in the treatment of antisocial child behavior. *Journal of the American Academy of Child and Adolescent Psychiatry, 26*, 416–424.

Kazdin, A. E., Siegel, T. C., & Bass, D. (1992). Cognitive problem-solving skills training and parent management training in the treatment of antisocial behavior in children. *Journal of Consulting and Clinical Psychology, 60*, 733–747.

Kendall, P. C. (1981). One-year follow-up of concrete versus conceptual cognitive-behavioral self-control training. *Journal of Consulting and Clinical Psychology, 49*, 748–749.

Kendall, P. C. (1982). Individual versus group cognitive-behavioral self-control training: One-year follow-up. *Behavior Therapy, 13*, 241–247.

Kendall, P. C. (Ed.). (1991). *Child and adolescent therapy: Cognitive-behavioral procedures*. New York: Guilford Press.

Kendall, P. C., & Braswell, L. (1982). Cognitive-behavioral self-control therapy for children: A components analysis. *Journal of Consulting and Clinical Psychology, 50*, 672–689.

Kendall, P. C., & Braswell, L. (1993). *Cognitive-behavioral therapy for impulsive children* (2nd ed.). New York: Guilford Press.

Kendall, P. C., & Finch, A. J. (1978). A cognitive-behavioral treatment for impulsivity: A group comparison study. *Journal of Consulting and Clinical Psychology, 46*, 110–118.

Kendall, P. C., & Wilcox, L. E. (1980). A cognitive-behavioral treatment for impulsivity: Concrete versus conceptual training in non-self-controlled problem children. *Journal of Consulting and Clinical Psychology, 48*, 80–91.

Kendall, P. C., & Zupan, B. A. (1981). Individual versus group application of cognitive-behavioral strategies for developing self-control in children. *Behavior Therapy, 12*, 344–359.

Klein, N. C., Alexander, J. F., & Parsons, B. V. (1977). Impact of family systems intervention on recidivism and sibling delinquency: A model of primary prevention and program evaluation. *Journal of Consulting and Clinical Psychology, 45,* 469–474.

Lochman, J. E. (1992). Cognitive-behavioral intervention with aggressive boys: Three-year follow-up and preventive effects. *Journal of Consulting and Clinical Psychology, 60,* 426–432.

Lochman, J. E., Burch, P. R., Curry, J. F., & Lampron, L. B. (1984). Treatment and generalization effects of cognitive-behavioral and goal-setting interventions with aggressive boys. *Journal of Consulting and Clinical Psychology, 52,* 915–916.

Lochman, J. E., & Curry, J. F. (1986). Effects of social problem-solving training and self-instruction training with aggressive boys. *Journal of Clinical Child Psychology, 15,* 159–164.

Lochman, J. E., & Dodge, K. A. (1994). Social-cognitive processes of severely violent, moderately aggressive, and nonaggressive boys. *Journal of Consulting and Clinical Psychology, 62,* 366–374.

Lochman, J. E., Lampron, L. B., Gemmer, T. V., Harris, R., & Wyckoff, G. M. (1989). Teacher consultation and cognitive-behavioral interventions with aggressive boys. *Psychology in the Schools, 26,* 179–188.

Lochman, J. E., & Lenhart, L. A. (1993). Anger coping intervention for aggressive children: Conceptual models and outcome effects. *Clinical Psychology Review, 13,* 785–805.

Lochman, J. E., Nelson, W. M., III, & Sims, J. P. (1981). A cognitive behavioral program for use with aggressive children. *Journal of Clinical Child Psychology, 10,* 146–148.

Loeber, R. (1990). Development and risk factors of juvenile antisocial behavior and delinquency. *Clinical Psychology Review, 10,* 1–41.

Loeber, R., & Stouthamer-Loeber, M. (1986). Family factors as correlates and predictors of juvenile conduct problems and delinquency. *Journal of Research in Crime and Delinquency, 21,* 7–31.

Luther S. S., & Zigler, E. Z. (1991). Vulnerability and competence: A review of research on residence in childhood. *American Journal of Orthopsychiatry, 61,* 6–22.

Masten, A. S., Coatsworth, D. J., Neeman, J., Gest, S. D., Tellegen, A., & Garmezy, N. (1995). The structure and coherence of competence from childhood through adolescence. *Child Development, 66,* 1635–1659.

Masten, A. S., & Garmezy, N. (1986). Risk, vulnerability and protective factors in developmental psychopathology. In B. B. Lahey & A. E. Kazdin (Eds.), *Advances in clinical child psychology* (Vol. 9, pp. 1–52). New York: Plenum Press.

McBurnett, K., Lahey, B. B., & Phiffner, L. J. (1993). Diagnosis of attention deficit disorders in DSM-IV: Scientific basis and implications for education. *Exceptional Children, 60,* 108–117.

McConaughy, S. H., & Skiba, R. J. (1993). Comorbidity of externalizing and internalizing problems. *School Psychology Review, 22,* 421–436.

McMahon, R. J. (1994). Diagnosis, assessment, and treatment of externalizing problems in children: The role of longitudinal data. *Journal of Consulting and Clinical Psychology, 62,* 901–917.

McMahon, R. J., & Wells, K. C. (1989). Conduct disorders. In E. J. Mash & R. A. Barkley (Eds.), *Treatment of childhood disorders* (pp. 73–132). New York: Guilford Press.

Meichenbaum, D., & Turk, D. (1987). *Facilitating treatment adherence: A practitioners guidebook.* New York: Plenum Press.

Minuchin, S. (1979). *Families and family therapy.* Cambridge, MA: Harvard University Press.

Moffitt, T. E. (1993). Adolescent-limited and life-course persistent antisocial behavior: A developmental taxonomy. *Psychological Review, 100,* 674–701.

Mulvey, E. P., Arthur, M. W., & Reppucci, N. D. (1993). The prevention and treatment of juvenile delinquency. *Clinical Psychology Review, 13,* 133–168.

Newcomb, A. F., Bukowski, W. M., & Pattee, L. (1993). Children's peer relations. A meta-analytic review of popular, rejected, neglected, controversial, and average sociometric status. *Psychological Bulletin, 113,* 99–128.

Ollendick, T. H., & King, N. J. (1994). Diagnosis, assessment, and treatment of internalizing problems in children: The role of longitudinal data. *Journal of Consulting and Clinical Psychology, 62,* 918–927.

Olson, S. L., Bates, J. E., & Bayles, K. (1990). Early antecedents of childhood impulsivity: The role of parent–child interaction, cognitive competence, and temperament. *Journal of Abnormal Child Psychology, 18,* 317–334.

Parsons, B. V., & Alexander, J. F. (1973). Short-term family intervention: A therapy outcome study. *Journal of Consulting and Clinical Psychology, 41,* 195–201.

Patterson, G.R. (1982). *Coercive family process.* Eugene, OR: Castalia Press.

Patterson, G. R., Capaldi, D., & Bank, L. (1991). An early starter model of predicting delinquency. In D.J. Pepler & K.H. Rubin (Eds.), *The development and treatment of childhood aggression* (pp. 139–168). New York: Erlbaum.

Patterson, G. R., DeBaryshe, B. D., & Ramsey, E. (1989). A developmental perspective of antisocial behavior. *American Psychologist, 44,* 329–333.

Pelham, W. E., & Bender, M. E. (1982). Peer relationships in hyperactive children: Description and treatment. In K. Gadow & I. Bialer (Eds.), *Advances in learning and behavioral disabilities* (Vol. 1, pp. 365–435). Greenwich, CT: JAI Press.

Pelham, W. E., & Gnagy, E. M. (1995). A summer treatment program for children with ADHD. *ADHD Report, 3,* 6–8.

Pelham, W., & Hoza, B. (in press). Intensive treatment: Summer treatment program for children with ADHD. In E. D. Hibbs & P. S. Jenson (Eds.), *Psychosocial treatments for child and adolescent disorders* (pp. 311–340). Washington, DC: American Psychological Association.

Pettit, G. S., Bates, J. E., & Dodge, K. A. (1993). Family interaction patterns and children's conduct problems at home and school: A longitudinal perspective. *School Psychology Review, 22,* 403–420.

Phiffner, L. J., Jouriles, E. N., Brown, M. M., Etscheidt, M. A., & Kelly, J. A. (1990). Effects of problem-solving therapy on outcomes of parent training for single-parent families. *Child and Family Behavior Therapy, 12,* 1–11.

Prinz, R. J., Blechman, E. A., & Dumas, J. E. (1994). An evaluation of peer coping-skills training for childhood aggression. *Journal of Clinical Child Psychology, 23,* 193–203.

Rae-Grant, N., Thomas, H. B., Offord, D. R., & Boyle, M. H. (1989). Risk, protective factors, and the prevalence of behavioral and emotional disorders in children and adolescents. *Journal of the American Academy of Child and Adolescent Psychiatry, 28,* 262–268.

Ramsey, E., & Walker, H. M. (1988). Family management correlates of antisocial behavior among middle school boys. *Behavioral Disorders, 13,* 187–201

Ramsey, E., Walker, H. M., Shinn, M., O'Neill, R. E., & Stieber, S. (1989). Parent management practices and school adjustment. *School Psychology Review, 18,* 513–525.

Riccio, C. A., Hynd, G. W., Cohen, M. J., & Gonzalez, J. J. (1993). Neurological basis of attention deficit hyperactivity disorder. *Exceptional Children, 60,* 188–124.

Robin, A. L., & Foster, S. L. (1989). *Negotiating parent–adolescent conflict: A behavioral-family systems approach.* New York: Guilford Press.

Robin, A. L., Kent, R., O'Leary, K. D., Foster, S., & Prinz, R. (1977). An approach to teaching parents and adolescents problem-solving communication skills: A preliminary report. *Behavior Therapy, 8,* 639–643.

Roghoff, B., Ellis, S., & Gardner, W. (1984). Adjustment of adult–child instruction according to child's age and task. *Developmental Psychology, 26*, 193–199.

Sanders, M. R., Dadds, M. R., Johnston, B. M., & Cash, R. (1992). Childhood depression and conduct disorder: I. Behavioral, affective, and cognitive aspects of family problem-solving interactions. *Journal of Abnormal Psychology, 101*, 495–504.

Sattersfield, J., Swanson, J., Schell, A., & Lee, F. (1994). Prediction of antisocial behavior in attention-deficit hyperactivity disorder boys from aggression/defiance scores. *Journal of the American Academy of Child and Adolescent Psychiatry, 33*, 185–190.

Saxe, G., Guberman, S., & Gearhart, M. (1987). Social progresses in early number development. *Monographs of the Society for Research in Child Development, 52*(2, Serial No. 216).

Shapiro, S. K., & Hynd, G. W. (1993). Psychobiological basis of conduct disorder. *School Psychology Review, 22*, 386–402.

Sobol, M. P., Ashbourne, D. R., Earn, B. M., & Cunningham, C. E. (1989). Parent's attributions for achieving compliance from attention-deficit disordered children. *Journal of Abnormal Child Psychology, 17,* 359–369.

Spence, S. (1994). Practitioner review: Cognitive therapy with children and adolescents. *Journal of Child Psychology and Psychiatry, 35*, 1191–1228.

Sroufe, L. A., & Rutter, M. (1984). The domain of developmental psychopathology. *Child Development, 55*, 17–29.

Stark, K. (1990). *Childhood depression: School-based intervention.* New York: Guilford Press.

Strassberg, Z., Dodge, K. A., Pettit, G. S., & Bates, J. E. (1994). Spanking in the home and children's subsequent aggression toward kindergarten peers. *Development and Psychopathology, 6*, 445–461.

Tant, J. L., & Douglas, V. I. (1982). Problem-solving in hyperactive, normal and reading-disabled boys. *Journal of Abnormal Child Psychology, 10*, 285–306.

Tremblay, R. E., Pagani-Kurtz, L., Masse, L. C., Vitaro, F., & Pihl, R. O. (1995). A bimodal preventive intervention for disruptive kindergarten boys: Its impact through mid-adolescence. *Journal of Consulting and Clinical Psychology, 63*, 560–568.

Tuma, J. M. (1989). Traditional therapies with children. In T. H. Ollendick & M. Hersen (Eds.), *Handbook of child psychology* (2nd ed., pp. 419–438). New York: Plenum Press.

Vincent Roehling, P., & Robin, A. L. (1986). Development and validation of the Family Beliefs Inventory: A measure of unrealistic beliefs among parents and adolescents. *Journal of Consulting and Clinical Psychology, 54*, 693–697.

Vitaro, F., & Tremblay, R. E. (1994). Impact of a prevention program on aggressive children's friendships and social adjustment. *Journal of Abnormal Child Psychology, 22,* 457–475.

Vygotsky, L. S. (1962). *Thought and language.* New York: Wiley.

Vygotsky, L. S. (1978). *Mind in society.* Cambridge, MA: MIT Press.

Waters, E., & Sroufe, L. A. (1983). Social competence as a developmental construct. *Developmental Review, 3*, 79–97.

Webster-Stratton, C. (1989). The relationship of marital support, conflict, and divorce to parent perceptions, behaviors, and childhood conduct problems. *Journal of Marriage and the Family, 51*, 417–430.

Webster-Stratton, C. (1993). What really happens in parent training? *Behavior Modification, 17*, 407–456.

Weiss, B., Dodge, K., Bates, J. E., & Pettit, G. S. (1992). Some consequences of early harsh discipline: Child aggression and maladaptive social information processing style. *Child Development, 16*, 1321–1335.

White, J. L., Moffitt, T. E., Caspi, A., Bartusch, J. B., Needles, D. J., & Stouthamer-Loeber,

M. (1994). Measuring impulsivity and examining its relationship to delinquency. *Journal of Abnormal Psychology, 103*, 192–205.

Wood, D. (1980). Teaching the young child: Some relationships between social interaction, language, and thought. In D. Olson (Ed.), *The social foundations of language and thought* (pp. 280–296). New York: Norton.

Index

Quantity Discounts and
a Special Service for Recommending
Skills Training for Children with Behavior Disorders

To the Health Care Professional:

If you wish to order multiple copies of this book, or to recommend it to your clients, we are pleased to offer two convenient methods:

❶ QUANTITY DISCOUNTS

For multiple copies of *Skills Training for Children with Behavior Disorders,* calculate the following discount rates against the list price to get the unit discount price. Then simply multiply the discount price times the quantity you are ordering. Add 5% of your total order for shipping.

QUANTITY	LIST PRICE	DISCOUNT	PRICE PER BOOK
1 book	$29.95	—	$29.95
2–12 books		20% off list price	$23.95
13–24 books		30% off list price	$20.95
25+		33% off list price	$20.05

To order, please call toll-free 1-800-365-7006

❷ PRIORITY ORDER FORMS

Or, when recommending the book, you may have individuals order directly from Guilford—simply photocopy the Priority Order Form on the next page. Priority Order Forms are given immediate attention.

We also assure confidentiality. Customers who use these order forms will be excluded from the Guilford mailing list and will receive no further correspondence.

We suggest that you also photocopy the order form for future use.

PRIORITY ORDER FORM

Send to: **Guilford Publications, Inc., Dept. IV**
72 Spring Street, New York, NY 10012

 CALL TOLL-FREE 1-800-365-7006 Mon.–Fri. , 9am–5pm EST
Or **FAX 212-966-6708**

(Be sure to tell the representative you are ordering from our Priority Order Form.)

NAME

ADDRESS

CITY   STATE   ZIP

DAYTIME PHONE NO.

Method of Payment

☐ Check or money order enclosed.
Please bill my   ☐ VISA   ☐ MasterCard   ☐ AmEx
ACCT. #

☐☐☐☐   ☐☐☐☐   ☐☐☐☐   ☐☐☐☐

Expiration Date:

MONTH ☐☐   YEAR ☐☐   _____
SIGNATURE *(required for all credit card orders)*

Name of recommending professional:

Please Ship:

Qty.		Cat. #	Amount
1	*Skills Training for Children with Behavior Disorders*	0080	$29.95
	*Shipping Priority Mail— 1 to 2 week delivery	Shipping*	$3.50
		NY and PA add sales tax	
		TOTAL	

PRIORITY ORDER
For office use only
**Note: Operator—set up as account type IT—
Mail No—Rush Order SHIP VIA FC**